T0185114

Lecture Notes in Artificial Intelligence 12158

Subseries of Lecture Notes in Computer Science

Series Editors

Randy Goebel
University of Alberta, Edmonton, Canada
Yuzuru Tanaka
Hokkaido University, Sapporo, Japan
Wolfgang Wahlster
DFKI and Saarland University, Saarbrücken, Germany

Founding Editor

Jörg Siekmann
DFKI and Saarland University, Saarbrücken, Germany

More information about this series at http://www.springer.com/series/1244

Amal El Fallah Seghrouchni ·
David Sarne (Eds.)

Artificial Intelligence

IJCAI 2019 International Workshops

Macao, China, August 10–12, 2019
Revised Selected Best Papers

 Springer

Editors
Amal El Fallah Seghrouchni
Sorbonne University – Sciences
Paris, France

David Sarne
Bar-Ilan University
Ramat Gan, Israel

ISSN 0302-9743   ISSN 1611-3349   (electronic)
Lecture Notes in Artificial Intelligence
ISBN 978-3-030-56149-9   ISBN 978-3-030-56150-5   (eBook)
https://doi.org/10.1007/978-3-030-56150-5

LNCS Sublibrary: SL7 – Artificial Intelligence

This Springer imprint is published by the registered company Springer Nature Switzerland AG
The registered company address is: Gewerbestrasse 11, 6330 Cham, Switzerland

Preface

As one of the primary AI conferences, the 28th International Joint Conference on Artificial Intelligence (IJCAI 2019) was accompanied by a rich workshops program aiming to provide a structured setting for the discussion of specialized technical topics between researchers from academia and industry. The program which included 38 workshops, was held during August 10–12, 2019, and preceded the main conference in the convention center of the Venetian Macao Hotel Resort. The different workshops, in which 437 carefully selected papers that went through a rigorous review process were presented, attracted 2,271 participants overall. Most workshops were a full-day event, although some were planned for half a day or over two days.

Many of the workshops focusing on a particular research area were recurring ones, continuing long-lasting gatherings of well-established communities. For example, the workshop on Artificial Intelligence for Knowledge Management and Innovation (held for the 7th time), the International Workshop on Neural-Symbolic Learning and Reasoning (held for the 14th time), the International Workshop on Qualitative Reasoning (held for the 32nd time), the workshop on FCA (Formal Concept Analysis) for Artificial Intelligence (held for the 7th time), the International Workshop on Agent-based Complex Automated Negotiations (held for the 12th time), the International Workshop on Natural Language Processing for Social Media (held for the 7th time), and the workshop on Strategic Reasoning (held for the 10th time). Others, held for the first time, were focused on emerging topics and applications, or on open research questions and challenges. For example the workshop on Financial Technology and Natural Language Processing, the workshop on Education in Artificial Intelligence K-12, the workshop on AI and the SDGs (Sustainable Development Goals), the workshop on Human Brain and Artificial Intelligence, the workshop on Deep Learning for Human Activity Recognition, the workshop on AI for Social Good, the workshop on Artificial Intelligence and Food, and the workshop on AI for Aging, Rehabilitation and Independent Assisted Living. This year, we also welcomed workshops that addressed issues related to responsible and explainable AI.

This volume provides a glimpse into this AI festive celebration. It focuses on 12 different workshops, representing various strands of research in AI. For each workshop there is a comprehensive summary of the workshop organizers, providing overview and goals, workshop history, main highlights, topics discussed, and insights for future research. In addition, for each represented workshop we include the extended version of the paper selected by the organizers as the best paper presented in their workshop. These papers, which were carefully reviewed by the workshop organizers and Program Committee, represent the state of the art in the specific sub-field and naturally are a good starting point for researchers interested in the related areas.

We would like to thank workshop participants and presenters, workshop program chairs and Program Committee members, the IJCAI chairs and Program Committee chairs, and the IJCAI local organization team for their invaluable contribution and support for the success of the IJCAI 2019 workshops.

April 2020
Amal El Fallah Seghrouchni
David Sarne

Organization

Workshops Chairs

Amal El Fallah Seghrouchni   Sorbonne University, LIP6, France
David Sarne   Bar-Ilan University, Israel

Web Master

Hongming Zhang   The Hong Kong University of Science and Technology, Hong Kong, China

Workshops Coordinator

Derek Fai Wong   University of Macau, Macau, China

Publication Chair

Arthur Casals   Sorbonne University, LIP6, France

Workshops Organizers

Eunika Mercier-Laurent	International Federation for Information Processing (IFIP)
Mieczyslaw Lech Owoc	Wroclaw University of Economics, Poland
Chung-Chi Chen	National Taiwan University, Taiwan
Hen-Hsen Huang	National Chengchi University, Taiwan
Hiroya Takamura	AIST, Japan
Hsin-Hsi Chen	National Taiwan University, Taiwan
Matthew Klenk	Palo Alto Research Center, USA
Diedrich Wolter	University of Bamberg, Germany
Ruben Glatt	Lawrence Livermore National Laboratory, USA
Felipe Leno da Silva	Advanced Institute for AI, Brazil
Denis Steckelmacher	Vrije Universiteit Brussel, Belgium
Patrick MacAlpine	Microsoft Research, USA
Sheng Li	University of Georgia, USA
Yaliang Li	Alibaba Group, USA
Jing Gao	University at Buffalo, USA
Yun Fu	Northeastern University, USA
Douglas Lange	Naval Information Warfare Center Pacific, USA
Luke Marsh	Defence Science and Technology Group, Australia
Takayuki Ito	Nagoya Institute of Technology, Japan
Minjie Zhang	University of Wollongong, Australia

Reyhan Aydogan	Ozyegin University, Turkey
Di Wang	Nanyang Technological University, Singapore
Ahmed Moustafa	Nagoya Institute of Technology, Japan
Takanobu Otsuka	Nagoya Institute of Technology, Japan
Zhenghua Chen	ASTAR, Singapore
Pushpak Bhattarcharya	IIT Patna, India
Niranjan Nayak	Microsoft AI, India
Manoj Kumar Chinnakotla	Bing, USA
Puneet Agrawal	Microsoft AI, India
Kedhar Nath Narahari	Microsoft AI, India
Akinori Abe	Chiba University, Japan
Hiroki Fukushima	Kyushu Women's University, Japan
Huáscar Espinoza	Commissariat à l'Energie Atomique, France
Han Yu	Nanyang Technological University, Singapore
Xiaowei Huang	The University of Liverpool, UK
Freddy Lecue	Thales, Canada
Cynthia Chen	The University of Hong Kong, Hong Kong, China
José Hernández-Orallo	Universitat Politècnica de València, Spain
Seán Ó hÉigeartaigh	University of Cambridge, UK
Richard Mallah	Future of Life Institute, USA
Parisa Kordjamshidi	Michigan State University, USA
Kristian Kersting	TU Darmstadt, Germany
Quan Guo	Michigan State University, USA
Nikolaos Vasiloglou	Relational AI, USA
Hannaneh Hajishirazi	University of Washington, USA
Dan Roth	University of Pennsylvania, USA

Contents

Artificial Intelligence for Knowledge Management and Innovation

Artificial Intelligence for Knowledge Management and Innovation

Eunika Mercier-Laurent[1] and Mieczyslaw Lech Owoc[2]

[1] IFIP TC12
eunika.mercier-laurent@univ-reims.fr
[2] IFIP TC12.6, Wroclaw University of Economics
mieczyslaw.owoc@ue.wroc.pl

Keywords: Artificial Intelligence · Knowledge Management · Smart City · Transportation · Marketing

1 Summary

The objective of this multidisciplinary seventh workshop (initiated in Montpellier on ECAI'2012) was to gather both researchers and practitioners to discuss methodological, technical and organizational aspects of Artificial Intelligence (AI) methods used for knowledge management (KM) and to share the feedback on KM applications using AI.

Accepted papers were presented in three thematically ordered sessions:

1. **Intelligent Applications** – including papers related to Knowledge Management in Smart Cities, universities, and other institutions applying suited artificial intelligence methods and techniques.
2. **Knowledge about Humans** – referring to papers on relationships between knowledge constructs and different group of users.
3. **Artificial Intelligence and Business** – embracing papers devoted to business oriented implementations.

After a warm welcome from the TC12 Artificial Intelligence Group chair prof. Eunika Mercier-Laurent, our invited talk Waltraut Ritter (Knowledge Dialogues, HK) presented the specifics and main AI solutions in the field of transportation in various countries. She also discussed specific conditions to consider, such as population, geographical aspects, existing barriers and tendency of formulation more universal approaches in solving similar transportation problems using artificial intelligence methods.

During the first session managed for the group of papers oriented on "*Intelligent Applications*" Lukasz Przysucha stressed usability and potential applications representing crowdsourcing in smart city areas. Anna Reklewska (student of Wroclaw University of Economics) tried to prove important role of Big Data technology in development of Smart City concepts.

Problems of potential generation of Robot Operation System codes taken from workflow with human behavior level were discussed by Takeshi Morita and Takahira Yamaguchi. Perspectives of the usage intelligent technology (like chatbots and automation of signing contracts were demonstrated by Mieczyslaw Owoc and Pawel Weichbroth. Minar Rawat representing India Innovation Lab focused on impact of natural language used in knowledge extraction with visual analytics option. The last presentation of this session was by Hailang Su about hyperspectral image classification based on advanced strategy involving deep learning.

The second session *"Knowledge about Humans"* begun with presentation of semantic-based support system for merging process knowledge delivered by Krzysztof Kluza. In turn, Xusheng Luo focused on development of e-commerce concept net towards user needs understanding Ali-net. Maciej Pondel discussed the problem of increasing customer loyalty supported by implementation selected machine learning techniques. Last paper of this session was those by Hafiz Suliman on stressed usability of deep neural network in labeling of outdoor scene.

The last session *"Artificial Intelligence and Business"* was initiated by Piotr Domagala who considered Internet of Things as a source of innovation for intelligent organizations. Discussion about translation embedding for knowledge graph completion in banking sector was performed by Dongxu Shao – this paper was awarded by PC. The last presentation of Helena Dudycz was devoted to potential difficulties in searching for business using semantic network visualization.

This year workshop attracted over 50 registered participants. Amid invited talk, 14 papers were presented and discussed. Electronic proceedings are available on the WG12.6 group website http://ifipgroup.com/.

The organizers invited the authors of selected papers to extend their work that will be published in Springer AICT series.

Finally, chairs of the workshop thanked for discussions and expressed hope for meeting in Yokohama during 8th workshop on IJCAI-20 in Yokohama.

Fig. 1 7th AI4KM Speakers

Translation Embeddings for Knowledge Graph Completion in Consumer Banking Sector

Dongxu Shao$^{(\boxtimes)}$ and Rajanikanth Annam

DBS Bank, Singapore, Singapore
{dongxushao,rajanikanth}@dbs.com

Abstract. Knowledge graphs have shown many successful applications such as recommendation. One essential challenge of knowledge graph is link prediction, which is to estimate the probability of a link between two nodes based on the existing graph. Most state-of-art models to solve this problem are built using embeddings. Experiments of previous works have been conducted on WN18 and FB15K datasets to compare the performance. However, both datasets have significantly different properties compared with financial data on which there is no benchmarking of link prediction models. In this paper, we run extensive experiments of recent models on real financial data, compare their performance deeply, and show the usage of a completed knowledge graph in consumer banking sector.

Keywords: Knowledge graph · Link prediction · Consumer banking

1 Introduction

Being the largest bank in Southeast Asia[1], DBS Bank has tremendous customer data from various sources such as demographics, payments, fund transfers and so on. As most of the data is inter-related, graph is a promising way to store the data, analyze the relations and extract useful insights.

Graphs storing knowledge base such as customer data are often considered as knowledge graph, where facts in the knowledge base are represented by links in the graph (edges between nodes). The nodes in a knowledge graph represent entities in knowledge base and the edges represent relations. Additionally, each node and edge could be associated with a type. For example, in the context of consumer banking, the type of a node in the graph could be customer, merchant, or building. A link (fact) in knowledge graph is a triplet $\langle h, r, t \rangle$, where h is a node representing the subject of the fact, t is a node representing the object, and r is the edge between the two nodes representing the relationship of the fact. As in the consumer banking example, the triplet $\langle Bob, transfer\_to, Carlo \rangle$ is a transaction between two customers, and the triplet $\langle Alice, with\_address, Orchard \rangle$ represents the fact that the customer $Alice$ lives in Orchard district.

As a benefit of the graphical structure, knowledge graph can capture interrelations and interactions across tremendous types of entities more effectively than traditional

---

[1] https://en.wikipedia.org/wiki/List_of_largest_banks_in_Southeast_Asia.

© Springer Nature Switzerland AG 2020
A. El Fallah Seghrouchni and D. Sarne (Eds.): IJCAI 2019 Workshops, LNAI 12158, pp. 5–17, 2020.
https://doi.org/10.1007/978-3-030-56150-5_1

Table 1. Summary of popular works

Model	Scoring function	Parameters	Time complexity	Space complexity
RESCAL [12]	$h^T M_r t$	$h, t \in \mathbb{R}^n, M_r \in \mathbb{R}^{n \times n}$	$\mathcal{O}(n^2)$	$\mathcal{O}(n^2)$
TransE [4]	$\|h + r - t\|_p$	$h, r, t \in \mathbb{R}^n$	$\mathcal{O}(n)$	$\mathcal{O}(n)$
DistMult [20]	$h^T diag(r) t$	$h, r, t \in \mathbb{R}^n$	$\mathcal{O}(n)$	$\mathcal{O}(n)$
ComplEx [18]	$Re(h^T diag(r)\bar{t})$	$h, r, t \in \mathbb{C}^n$	$\mathcal{O}(n)$	$\mathcal{O}(n)$

methods, and hence has drawn lots of attention recently. For example, Google has been using its Google Knowledge Graph [6] containing millions of facts and entities to enhance its search engine's result. DBpedia [8] is a knowledge graph extracted from data in Wikipedia useful for question answering and fact checking.

Among the various applications of knowledge graph, link prediction is one of the most widely used and researched. The aim of link prediction is to predict new links between nodes based on the existing graph. It comes from the situation that many knowledge graphs are incomplete. For example, a customer of a bank may not have credit cards in this bank. But he or she may have cards in other banks, which cannot be captured by the graph within the bank. Using link prediction, this customer could be linked with a similar card issued by the bank. As link prediction can uncover unobserved facts and intentions, it is highly useful in community detection, customer recommendation, anti-money laundering, and many more. For the same reason, link prediction is also known as knowledge graph completion.

To solve the link prediction problem, embedding-based models inspired by word embedding [10] in text mining have been increasingly popular recently. In the embedding framework, nodes and edges in a graph are all embedded into some continuous vector space. So in a triplet $\langle h, r, t \rangle$, h, r and t are represented by vectors or matrices. Then a score function is proposed to measure the probability that this triplet is a fact in the graph. Hence the embeddings are obtained by minimizing a loss function over all relations in the graph. With the learnt embeddings, the probability that h and t are linked by r can be estimated by the score of $\langle h, r, t \rangle$. Most previous works take the same embedding framework with different scoring function and loss function. One straightforward model [4] is to use vector addition to composite h and r to $h + r$ and use L_p-norm of $h + r - t$ to score the triplet. More models [5,9,13–15,18,19] have been proposed with various complicated scoring functions.

Experiments of previous works have been conducted and compared on public datasets such as WN18 about lexical relation between words and FB15k about general facts. However, it has been pointed out [17] that for many of the triplets in these two dataset, its reversion also belongs to the same dataset. For example, WN18 has two relations with large number of instances: *"has part"* and *"parts of"*. So every triplet $\langle h, has\ part, t \rangle$ corresponds to $\langle t, part\ of, h \rangle$ in the same dataset. In the consumer banking data, such inverse relation property only applies to a small portion of the data such as fund transfer. More importantly, each link in the banking knowledge graph is explicitly associated with certain types of nodes only. Hence irrelevant nodes should be excluded in the link prediction for a given link as pointed out in [14].

In this paper, we will construct a knowledge graph using real consumer banking data from DBS Bank, run experiments of popular models with node types and link types introduced, conduct comprehensive comparison of the performance drilled down to relation level, and conclude the most suitable model for different relation types. Moreover, use cases of link prediction for consumer banking will be provided.

To the best of our knowledge, this is the first work to benchmark knowledge graph completion models using real consumer data and propose a guideline to select models for different relation types.

The rest of this paper is organized as follows. We will review relevant literatures in Sect. 2 and explore the details of popular models in Sect. 3. The performance of different models on our consumer banking data will be summarized in Sect. 4. Section 5 will show some use cases and the paper will be concluded in Sect. 6.

2 Related Work

Most of the models proposed for link prediction in knowledge graph leverage embedding framework. Given a triplet $\langle h, r, t \rangle$ and embeddings of nodes into a vector space or matrix space, there are different approaches to score the probability of the existence of the triplet. Popular models are summarized in Table 1 with complexity.

2.1 Translation-Based Approaches

The structured embedding model (SE) [2] embeds edges into two matrices $L_h \in \mathbb{R}^n$ and $L_t \in \mathbb{R}^n$, where L_h is to transform h and L_t is to transform t. Then $||L_h \cdot h - L_t \cdot t||_p$ is employed as the score function, where $|| \cdot ||_p$ is the L_p-norm. The idea of this model is that if two nodes are in the same triplet, then their embedding vectors should be close in some subspace depending on the edge. The TransE model [4] took a more direct way. Instead of mapping an edge into two matrices, TransE embeds each edge into $\mathbb{R}^n$, hence the head node h can be translated by adding the edge vector r to obtain a candidate tail vector $h + r$. Then L_p-norm is adopted to measure the distance between $h + r$ and t. Although SE model has a better expressiveness, it is outperformed by TransE model.

Following the idea of TransE that the tail node t is a translation from the head node h via the edge r in the same embedding space, many models have been proposed by extending TransE from different aspects. TransH [19] first projects the embedding vectors of h and t to a hyperplane that is perpendicular to the edge embedding vector, and then uses L_p-norm to score the projected triplet. TransR [9] generalizes TransH in the sense that the node embedding vectors could be projected to arbitrary edge-related subspace. It finds a matrix M_r to each edge r and uses L_p-norm the score the transformed difference $M_r h + r - M_r t$.

2.2 Bilinear Approaches

Instead of translating from head node to tail node via the edge, bilinear approaches treat the triplets as a 3D binary tensor and score a triplet by edge-related bilinear functions whose inputs are embedding vectors of h and t. RESCAL model [12] represents the edge r by a matrix M_r in $\mathbb{R}^{n \times n}$, and scores the triplet by $h^T M_r t$.

DistMult model [20] extends RESCAL model by setting M_r to be a diagonal matrix, so the scoring function is $h^T diag(r)t$, where $diag(r)$ is the diagonal matrix whose main diagonal is r. Hence DistMult reduces the number of learning parameters significantly compared with RESCAL, and also outperforms RESCAL. However, neither of these two models have considered the difference of positioning one node as head and tail. In other words, the triplet $\langle h, r, t \rangle$ and the triplet $\langle t, r, h \rangle$ will be given the same score. To overcome this issue, ComplEx model [18] proposes to embed nodes and edges into complex vector space $\mathbb{C}^n$ instead of real space, and uses the conjugation of the embedding vector of a node when it is in tail position, so the scoring function is $Re(h^T diag(r)\bar{t})$.

2.3   Other Approaches

ConvE model [5] proposed to reshape and concatenate the embedding vectors of h and r into a 2D array, feed the array into a convolutional neural network producing a new vector, and score the output vector with t.

NTN model (Neural Tensor Network) [16] employs a normal neural network structure to score the triplets with a tensor layer using an edge-related tensor to connect head node and tail node.

A type-constrained model was proposed by [3] to refine the embedding models by excluding impossible triplets whose head node or tail node is not feasible for the edge. Similarly, TransAt model [14] introduces the attention mechanism to address the same challenge. The model first clusters nodes into several types and then only scores triplets whose node types are relevant to the relation.

3   Methodology

A knowledge graph is a directed graph $G = (V, E)$ with node type set T_V and edge type set T_E. Given the set of vertices V and the set of edges E, the node type set T_V is a cover of V so that each node is associated with at least one type in T_V. The edge type set T_E is a subset of the Cartesian product $P(T_V) \times P(T_V)$ where $P(T_V)$ is the powerset of T_V. So, each edge is associated with one type connecting from one node type to another node type. For example, the edge type *with_address* connects from *customer* nodes to *district* nodes.

3.1   Problem Statement

The knowledge graph can also be viewed as a set of triplets $\langle h, r, t \rangle$, where $h, t \in V$, $r \in T_E$ and (h, t) is an edge in E with edge type r. Triplets existing in the knowledge graph are considered as facts. But non-existing triplets could also be potential facts in two scenarios. One scenario is the knowledge graph may not be necessarily complete, so some facts could be missing in the graph. The other scenario is although h and t are not in relation r for the time being, they have high probability to be connected by r.

The link prediction problem is to estimate the probability of a triplet $\langle h, r, t \rangle$ to be a fact in the given knowledge graph. Let ϕ be a scoring function and Θ be the set of all embeddings, then the probability can be represented by:

$$Pr[\langle h, r, t \rangle | \Theta] = \sigma(\phi(\langle h, r, t \rangle | \Theta)),$$

where σ is an activation function such as sigmoid function.

3.2 Base Solutions

Different models solve the problem adopting different scoring function and different loss function. In this paper, we focus on the following three models with the lowest time complexity and space complexity.

TransE. TransE model [4] embeds all nodes and edges into $\mathbb{R}^n$, and assumes that $h + l \approx t$ if $\langle h, r, t \rangle$ is in the graph. So the scoring function is:

$$\phi(\langle h, r, t \rangle, \Theta) = ||h + r - t||_p,$$

where p is either 1 or 2.

The embeddings are learnt by minimizing the following loss function over the training set D:

$$\sum_{\langle h,r,t \rangle \in D} \sum_{\langle h',r,t' \rangle \in D'_{\langle h,r,t \rangle}} \max(\gamma + ||h + r - t||_p - ||h' + r - t'||_p, 0),$$

where γ is a margin hyperparameter and $D'_{\langle h,r,t \rangle}$ is the corruption set of $\langle h, r, t \rangle$ defined by:

$$D'_{\langle h,r,t \rangle} = \{\langle h', r, t \rangle | h' \in V\} \cup \{\langle h, r, t' \rangle | t' \in V\}.$$

DistMult. DistMult model [20] embeds all nodes and edges into $\mathbb{R}^n$, and adopts the following scoring function:

$$\phi(\langle h, r, t \rangle, \Theta) = h^T diag(r) t,$$

where $diag(r)$ is the diagonal matrix whose main diagonal is r.

This model uses the same loss function as TransE.

ComplEx. ComplEx model [18] embeds all nodes and edges into the complex vector space $\mathbb{C}^n$. In order to differentiate the head embedding and tail embedding of the same node, it adopts an asymmetrical scoring function:

$$\phi(\langle h, r, t \rangle, \Theta) = Re(h^T diag(r) \bar{t}),$$

where $Re(x)$ is the real part of a complex number x.

Given the training set D, a negative set D' is generated as a set of false facts. Then the embeddings are learnt by minimizing the following loss function:

$$\sum_{\langle h,r,t\rangle \in D} \log(1 + \exp(-\phi(\langle h, r, t\rangle, \Theta)))+$$

$$\sum_{\langle h,r,t\rangle \in D'} \log(1 + \exp(\phi(\langle h, r, t\rangle, \Theta))) + \lambda \|\Theta\|_2^2,$$

where λ is the L_2-regularization parameter.

3.3   Type Restriction

Given a relation r and all triplets with this relation in the graph, define its head candidate set as the collection of node types of the head nodes in these triplets:

$$H(r) = \{\tau \in T_V | \exists \langle h, r, t\rangle, h \in \tau\},$$

and define its tail candidate set similarly:

$$T(r) = \{\tau \in T_V | \exists \langle h, r, t\rangle, t \in \tau\}.$$

Suppose Θ has been learnt from some model whose scoring function is ϕ. When scoring a new candidate triplet $\langle h, r, t\rangle$, refine ϕ to be negative infinity if $h \notin H(r)$ or $t \notin T(r)$. In other words, if the type of h or t does not match with the type of r, then this potential link should be ignored in the knowledge graph completion process.

4   Experiments

A knowledge graph of customers in DBS Bank has been constructed where the evaluation of the three most efficient models will be conducted. The models are evaluated with different performance measurements and drilled down to relation level.

4.1   Datasets

To evaluate the models on real data, the knowledge graph constructed with DBS customers involves money transfer between customers, demographics, credit cards and merchants.

Specifically, there are 6 types of node and 6 types of relation in the knowledge graph. Node types are listed in Table 2 with description. Table 3 describes the relations with corresponding percentage in the graph, showing that 60% of the links are from relation $with\_mcc$.

The data source of the knowledge graph covers the first half year of 2018. In other words, only transactions happened between Jan 2018 and Jun 2018 are captured in the graph, and all demographics information are updated until Jun 2018.

Most of the previous works were evaluated on FB15K and WN18 datasets provided by [4], containing 14,951 and 40,943 nodes respectively. FB15K is a collection

Table 2. Node types in the knowledge graph

Node type	Description
Customer	A customer DBS
Occupation	Occupation of customers
District	A residence district
Age Group	Ages are binned into 10's
Credit Card Type	Type of credit card
Merchant Type	Type of merchant

Table 3. Relations in the knowledge graph

Relation	Percentage	Head node	Tail node	Description
with_occupation	8.44%	Customer	Occupation	The head is with this occupation
with_address	8.44%	Customer	District	The head lives in this district
with_age	8.44%	Customer	Age Group	The age of the head is in this age group
with_card	9.56%	Customer	Credit Card Type	The head has a credit card of this type
with_mcc	59.94%	Customer	Merchant Type	The head spent in merchant of this type
transfer_to	5.18%	Customer	Customer	The head transferred money to the tail

of general facts retrieved from Freebase [1] and WN18 is a collection of lexical relation between words retrieved from WordNet [11]. To compare the performance on datasets with comparable scale, our knowledge graph is built on a subset of customers and split into training, validation and testing datasets on a ratio of 8:1:1. The metadata is summarized in Table 4.

4.2 Performance Measurement

The performance of the models is evaluated by MRR, HITS@1, HITS@3 and HITS@10 as in [4]. To make this paper self-contained, the definitions of these measurements are explained below.

Let $V = \{e_j | j = 1, \cdots, m\}$ be the set of nodes in the knowledge graph, and $T = \{x_i | i = 1, \cdots, n\}$ be the testing set, where x_i is a triplet $\langle h_i, r_i, t_i \rangle$. For each test

Table 4. Datasets metadata

Dataset	# Node	# Relation	# Edge in Train/Valid/Test
FB15K	14,951	1,345	483,142/50,000/59,071
WN18	40,943	18	141,442/5,000/5,000
DBS	16,729	6	154,280/19,285/19,285

Table 5. Overall performance on DBS data

Model	MRR		HITS@1		HITS@3		HITS@10	
	Filtered	Raw	Filtered	Raw	Filtered	Raw	Filtered	Raw
TransE	0.169	0.112	0.002	0.001	0.305	**0.167**	**0.440**	**0.353**
DistMult	0.257	**0.116**	0.180	0.069	0.310	0.108	0.400	0.270
ComplEx	**0.288**	**0.116**	**0.207**	**0.070**	**0.347**	0.100	0.435	0.274
TransE (Type Restriction)	**0.324**	**0.180**	**0.237**	**0.097**	0.377	**0.208**	0.494	**0.371**
DistMult (Type Restriction)	0.310	0.149	0.216	0.084	0.368	0.145	0.492	0.341
ComplEx (Type Restriction)	0.318	0.141	0.221	0.080	**0.383**	0.129	**0.497**	0.328

triplet x_i, define its head corruption set by replacing its head node with any other node in the graph:

$$C^h(x_i) = \{\langle h, r_i, t_i \rangle | (h \in V) \wedge (h \neq h_i)\}.$$

And define its tail corruption set by replacing its tail node with any other node in the graph:

$$C^t(x_i) = \{\langle h_i, r_i, t \rangle | (t \in V) \wedge (t \neq t_i)\}.$$

Hence a good model is supposed to score x_i higher than its corruptions. Let ϕ be the scoring function, then compute the rank of x_i in its corruptions using ϕ as follows:

$$rank_i^h = 1 + \sum_{x \in C^h(x_i)} \mathbb{I}(\phi(x_i) < \phi(x)),$$

and

$$rank_i^t = 1 + \sum_{x \in C^t(x_i)} \mathbb{I}(\phi(x_i) < \phi(x)),$$

where $\mathbb{I}(\tau) = 1$ if and only if τ is true.

Then the Mean Reciprocal Rank (MRR) is defined as the harmonic mean of head rank and tail rank:

$$MRR = \frac{1}{2|T|} \sum_{x_i \in T} \left(\frac{1}{rank_i^h} + \frac{1}{rank_i^t}\right),$$

and HITS@k is defined as the portion of test triplets whose rank is no larger than k:

$$HITS@k = \frac{1}{2|T|} \sum_{x_i \in T} [\mathbb{I}(rank_i^h \leq k) + \mathbb{I}(rank_i^t \leq k)].$$

Since the target of the models is to give higher score to links existing in the graph, it should not be considered as a mistake to score a test triplet x_i lower than its corruption x if x is also valid in the graph. For this reason, a filtered version of MRR and HITS@k is defined using refined corruptions by removing valid triplets:

$$C_{filtered}^h(x_i) = \{\langle h, r_i, t_i \rangle | (h \in V) \wedge (h \neq h_i)\} \setminus G,$$

$$C_{filtered}^t(x_i) = \{\langle h_i, r_i, t \rangle | (t \in V) \wedge (t \neq t_i)\} \setminus G,$$

where G is the set of triplets in the knowledge graph.

For simplicity, the original measurements are denoted as "Raw" and the filtered ones as "Filtered".

4.3 Experiment Setup

For each model in the experiment[2], we test with different initial learning rates among {0.05, 0.01, 0.005, 0.001} and different embedding dimensions among {50, 100, 150, 200, 250, 300}, and the best combination will be selected according to MRR (Raw).

Then the performance will be compared across different models with and without type restriction at both overall level and relation level for "Raw" and "Filtered" measurements.

4.4 Comparison

The performance of TransE, DistMult and ComplEx models with and without type restriction is shown in Table 5, which is much lower than the performance on WN18 and FB15K datasets as reported in [18].

For models without type restriction, ComplEx gives the best performance on MRR and HITS@1 for both Raw and Filtered and HITS@3 Filtered, and TransE is the best for HITS@10 for both Raw and Filtered and HITS@3 Raw. It shows that without type restriction, ComplEx is better at identifying only few most possible triplets. In other words, if the aim is to obtain a small number of new links, ComplEx should be used because it has the best HITS@1 performance. On the other hand, with a larger number of new links to pick out, TransE model should be used because it has the best HITS@10 performance.

It is obvious that the performance has been uplifted significantly by type restriction. With type restriction, TransE model outperforms DistMult and ComplEx for almost all measurements except Filtered HITS@3 and Filtered HITS@10.

Table 6. Relation level filtered MRR for type restriction

Relation	TransE	DistMult	ComplEx
with_occupation	0.2731	0.2727	**0.2846**
with_address	0.0575	0.0570	**0.0605**
with_age	0.3767	**0.4164**	**0.4164**
with_card	0.3988	0.3784	**0.3996**
with_mcc	**0.3787**	0.3530	0.3606
transfer_to	**0.0062**	0.0057	0.0010

The relation level Filtered MRR performance for models with type restriction is shown in Table 6. ComplEx model has the best performance on relation

---

[2] The implementation uses public code at https://github.com/mana-ysh/knowledge-graph-embeddings with reduced running time.

with_occupation, *with_address* and *with_card*, while TransE model performs the best for relations *with_mcc* and *transfer_to* where TransE model is the best.

As in the graph each customer has only one occupation, one address and one age, so *with_occupation*, *with_address* and *with_card* are Many-to-One relations. On the other hand, as one customer could have more than one merchant type and transfer to more than on customer, and one merchant type could be linked to multiple customers, *with_mcc* and *transfer_to* are Many-to-Many relations. Hence, ComplEx is more suitable for Many-to-One relations and TransE is more suitable for Many-to-Many relations. Since the relation *with_mcc* is dominating the graph as shown in Table 3, TransE has the best overall performance.

It is worth pointing out that *transfer_to* is the only relation in the graph whose head node and tail node are from the same type, and ComplEx performs much worse than the other two models on this relation. So, ComplEx should be avoided for graphs with large portion of Many-to-Many relations or relations connecting nodes with the same type.

5   Use Case

The link prediction on a knowledge graph has many useful applications in consumer banking sector. It uncovers relations which is unobserved now but has high probability to be a fact.

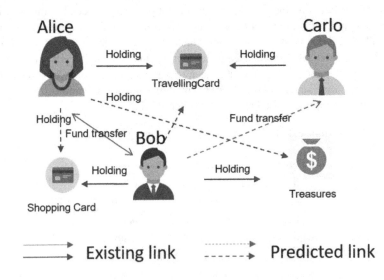

Fig. 1. Example of completed knowledge graph

Generally, there are two types of unobserved links. One type is links existing beyond DBS data. For example, there is no fund transfer between two customers within DBS, but they may have fund transfer through other banks. The other type is links to be true. For example, a customer does not have DBS credit card. But based on the connections from this customer to other customers and products, there is some card suitable for this customer. With the knowledge graph completed using link prediction, we can get a better understand about what our customers intend to do.

Suppose we have a sample knowledge graph completed using link prediction as illustrated by Fig. 1. Solid edges in the graph are existing ones and dashed edges are obtained from link prediction.

5.1 Personalized Recommendation

There are lots of products offered by the bank or partners of the bank. For each of the product, most suitable target customers need to be identified. If one predictive model is developed to identify the target customers for every product, it requires much time and resources. More efficiently, the knowledge graph provides a one-stop solution to generate target customers for all products.

Given a customer in the graph such as Bob in the example, it is straightforward to find out the products which connects to Bob by predicted link. In other words, Bob has high probability to hold a travelling credit card. As he is not holding the card now, it will be more effective to recommend travelling credit card to Bob.

The recommendation could also be real-time. Suppose Alice in the example logged in to her internet banking. With a simple query on the graph for first-degree product connections of Alice, it will be discovered that she has high probability to hold shopping credit card and treasures product. Then the internet banking system will display banners of shopping credit card and treasures product on the website she is surfing.

5.2 Member-Get-Member

Member-Get-Member (MGM) is an important channel for the bank to acquire new treasures customers. The targeting customers of MGM are customers who have treasures products and have many first-degree customer connections.

As in the example, Bob has treasures investment and he connects to Alice. Without link prediction, he has only 1 first-degree customer connection which is Alice. However, he has high probability to connect Carlo given by link prediction. There may be transfers from Bob to Carlo through other banks. So, it is more reasonable to count Bob's number of first-degree customer connections as 2.

Targeting customers with more first-degree customer connections including predicted links, it can capture intended connections of customers, making MGM more profitable.

6   Conclusions

Extensive experiments have been conducted using DBS datasets for different models. The performance is much lower than that on the public datasets.

Type restriction can improve the model performance significantly. With type restriction, ComplEx model performs best on Many-to-One relations while TransE model has the best performance on Many-to-Many relations. Additionally, ComplEx model has very low performance on relations linking nodes with the same type.

References

1. Bollacker, K.D., Evans, C., Paritosh, P., Sturge, T., Taylor, J.: Freebase: a collaboratively created graph database for structuring human knowledge. In: Proceedings of the ACM SIG-MOD International Conference on Management of Data, pp. 1247–1250 (2008)
2. Bordes, A., Weston, J., Collobert, R., Bengio, Y.: Learning structured embeddings of knowledge bases. In: Proceedings of the Twenty-Fifth AAAI Conference on Artificial Intelligence (2011)
3. Krompaß, D., Baier, S., Tresp, V.: Type-constrained representation learning in knowledge graphs. In: International Semantic Web Conference, pp. 640–655 (2015)
4. Bordes, A., Usunier, N., García-Durán, A., Weston, J., Yakhnenko, O.: Translating embeddings for modeling multi-relational data. In: Advances in Neural Information Processing Systems, NIPS, pp. 2787–2795 (2013)
5. Dettmers, T., Minervini, P., Stenetorp, P., Riedel, S.: Convolutional 2D knowledge graph embeddings. In: Proceedings of the Thirty-Second AAAI Conference on Artificial Intelligence (2018)
6. Dong, X., et al.: Knowledge vault: a web-scale approach to probabilistic knowledge fusion. In: The 20th ACM SIGKDD International Conference on Knowledge Discovery and Data Mining, pp. 601–610 (2014)
7. Ebisu, T., Ichise, R.: TorusE: knowledge graph embedding on a lie group. In: Proceedings of the Thirty-Second AAAI Conference on Artificial Intelligence (2018)
8. Lehmann, J., et al.: DBpedia - a large-scale, multilingual knowledge base extracted from Wikipedia. Semant. Web 6(2), 167–195 (2015)
9. Lin, Y., Liu, Z., Sun, M., Liu, Y., Zhu, X.: Learning entity and relation embeddings for knowledge graph completion. In: Proceedings of the Twenty-Ninth AAAI Conference on Artificial Intelligence, pp. 2181–2187 (2015)
10. Mikolov, T., Sutskever, I., Chen, K., Corrado, G.S., Dean, J.: Distributed representations of words and phrases and their compositionality. In: Advances in Neural Information Processing Systems, NIPS, pp. 3111–3119 (2013)
11. Miller, G.A.: Wordnet: a lexical database for English. Commun. ACM 38(11), 39–41 (1995)
12. Nickel, M., Tresp, V., Kriegel, H.-P.: A three-way model for collective learning on multi-relational data. In: Proceedings of the 28th International Conference on Machine Learning, ICML, pp. 809–816 (2011)
13. Nickel, M., Rosasco, L., Poggio, T.A.: Holographic embeddings of knowledge graphs. In: Proceedings of the Thirtieth AAAI Conference on Artificial Intelligence, pp. 1955–1961 (2016)
14. Qian, W., Fu, C., Zhu, Y., Cai, D., He, X.: Translating embeddings for knowledge graph completion with relation attention mechanism. In: Proceedings of the Twenty-Seventh International Joint Conference on Artificial Intelligence, IJCAI, pp. 4286–4292 (2018)
15. Shi, B., Weninger, T.: Proje: embedding projection for knowledge graph completion. In: Proceedings of the Thirty-First AAAI Conference on Artificial Intelligence, pp. 1236–1242 (2017)
16. Socher, R., Chen, D., Manning, C.D., Andrew, Y.N.: Reasoning with neural tensor networks for knowledge base completion. In: Advances in Neural Information Processing Systems, NIPS, pp. 926–934 (2013)
17. Toutanova, K., Chen, D.: Observed versus latent features for knowledge base and text inference. In: Proceedings of the 3rd Workshop on Continuous Vector Space Models and their Compositionality, pp. 57–66 (2015)
18. Trouillon, T., Welbl, J., Riedel, S., Gaussier, É., Bouchard, G.: Complex embeddings for simple link prediction. In: Proceedings of the 33nd International Conference on Machine Learning, ICML, pp. 2071–2080 (2016)

19. Wang, Z., Zhang, J., Feng, J., Chen, Z.: Knowledge graph embedding by translating on hyperplanes. In: Proceedings of the Twenty-Eighth AAAI Conference on Artificial Intelligence, pp. 1112–1119 (2014)
20. Yang, B., Yih, W., He, X., Gao, J., Deng, L.: Embedding entities and relations for learning and inference in knowledge bases. CoRR, abs/1412.6575 (2014)

Financial Technology and Natural Language Processing

Financial Technology and Natural Language Processing

Chung-Chi Chen[1], Hen-Hsen Huang[2], Hiroya Takamura[3], and Hsin-Hsi Chen[4,5]

[1] Department of Computer Science and Information Engineering,
National Taiwan University
[2] Department of Computer Science, National Chengchi University, Taiwan
[3] Artificial Intelligence Research Center, AIST, Japan
[4] Department of Computer Science and Information Engineering, National Taiwan University
[5] MOST Joint Research Center for AI Technology and All Vista Healthcare, Taiwan

Abstract. The 1st FinNLP workshop was held in conjunction with IJCAI-2019. There were 13 oral presentations, 8 posters, and 71 registered participants from both academia and industry. In this paper, we will introduce the topics in the workshop and illustrate the future research directions for NLP in FinTech applications.

1 Innovation in the 1st FinNLP Workshop

Applying artificial intelligence (AI) to improve the efficiency of humans is one of the trends recently. In this workshop, we focus on the problems of the financial industry. The followings are the topics discussed in this year FinNLP. Many works dealt with market information prediction via end-to-end models. However, if machines plan to capture the fine-grained information embedded in the documents, more in-depth works are needed. Explainable AI is one of the rise topics in the hype cycle for AI. Extracting the cause-effect is a potential approach for explaining the outcomes of the models. The best paper, entitled "Economic Causal-Chain Search using Text Mining Technology", is related to this topic. Evaluating the rationales behind the decisions is an additional issue after extracting the reason. For instance, different rationales may cause different influence to the results.

Legal issues are also important for enterprises, especially, for the department of compliance. Leveraging machine learning techniques, the enterprises can predict the possible litigations based on the multi-dimensional information of the companies. The fine-grained analysis of the contracts or other legal instruments could help understand the background knowledge of the models and thus further improve the performance. Know your customers (KYC) is also an important topic for enterprises, particularly, for the bank. Evaluating the credit and the trustworthiness of the customers is a routing work in the bank. With machine learning and natural language understanding methodologies, the accuracy of the evaluation could be improved. Anti-money laundering is a problem that combines KYC and legal issues. To design a tool for increasing the efficiency of the employees is one kind of the FinTech innovation.

The solutions of some fundamental problems in NLP may need to be tailor-made for the financial domain. For example, discovering the new terms of the business taxonomy is one of the issues in the rapidly-changing financial market. Dynamically capturing the inter-industry relations is also an essential task for real-world applications. Furthermore, the domain-specific chatbot system, fine-grained analysis of the documents, data labelling and annotation tools, and the corpora for different languages are all the important research problems for the development of NLP in the financial domain.

2   Future Research Directions of NLP in FinTech Applications

In the 1st FinNLP, most of the works focused on the formal documents, the regular textual data. The downstream researches are one of the future research directions. In addition to the formal documents, the information from the social media platforms and the Web can also provide many crucial clues for potential applications such as evaluating the brand reputation and the fine-grained KYC works. Cross-document alignment is another challenge issue for comprehending the rationales and the proof of the reasons. Not only the textual data but also the numeral information are meaningful, especially in the financial domain. Exploring the capability of numeral understanding, including numeracy and bridging the numeral in both structure data and textual data, is an important research issue for future works.

In sum, although the start-ups spring up like mushrooms recently, there are still many unsolved challenges yet. The cooperation between academia and industry could be the fastest way to advance the development of FinTech applications and turn the NLP researches into commercial products.

This workshop was partially supported by the Ministry of Science and Technology, Taiwan, under grants MOST-106-2923-E-002-012-MY3, 108-2218-E-009-051-, MOST-108-2634-F-002-008-, and MOST 107-2218-E-009-050-, and by Academia Sinica, Taiwan, under grant AS-TP-107-M05.

Economic Causal-Chain Search Using Text Mining Technology

Kiyoshi Izumi$^{(\boxtimes)}$ and Hiroki Sakaji

School of Engineering, The University of Tokyo, 7-3-1 Hongo, Bunkyo, Tokyo 113-8656, Japan
{izumi,sakaji}@sys.t.u-tokyo.ac.jp

Abstract. In this research, we extract causal information from textual data and construct a causality database in the economic field. We develop a method to produce causal chains starting from phrases representing specific events. The proposed method can offer possible ripple effects and factors of particular events or situations. Using our approach to Japanese textual data, we have implemented a prototype system that can display causal chains for user-entered words. A user can interactively edit the causal chains by selecting appropriate causalities and deleting inappropriate causalities. The economic causal-chain search algorithm can be applied to various financial information services.

Keywords: Natural language processing · Economic causal-chain · Financial text mining

1 Introduction

Economic news articles and financial reports contain various descriptions of cause and effect between economic factors such as price movements, product sales, employment, and trades. For example, "hospital operator reconsiders London IPO because of Brexit uncertainty" and "the higher prices are likely to take a toll on manufacturers as well as consumers because the economy has decelerated greatly this quarter" appeared in Bloomberg Market News on March 21, 2019.

It is beneficial to construct a database of economic causality and analyze the relationship between causality for both financial professionals and non-specialists. Such technology can support professionals' report writing and businesses. For non-specialists, technology can help them understand the implicit information about the causal relationship behind the specialized texts.

It is, however, difficult to analyze the causality between economic phenomena only by the statistical analysis of numerical data. That is because human activities produce causal relationships between economic events. Human activities are determined by mental processes such as cognition, thinking, and emotion. Thus, economic causality is influenced by social and cultural situations. It is almost impossible to extract objective and universal causality by statistical analysis of numerical data like natural scientific phenomena.

A. El Fallah Seghrouchni and D. Sarne (Eds.): IJCAI 2019 Workshops, LNAI 12158, pp. 23–35, 2020.
https://doi.org/10.1007/978-3-030-56150-5_2

In this research, we propose a method to create an economic causal-chain network from economic text data. The economic causal-chain refers to a cause and effect network structure formed by extracting a description indicating a causal relationship from the texts of financial statement summaries. In other words, it is a network that includes causal relationships that investors have recognized from financial statement summaries.

The rest of the article is organized as follows.

Section 2 presents how to construct the economic causal-chain with Japanese financial statement summaries.

Section 3 reports evaluation tests of the extraction of cause-effect expressions from Japanese economic text data.

Section 4 explains our prototype system of searching the economic causal-chain with Japanese financial statement summaries.

Section 5 discusses the potential applications of our method to create an economic causal chain network.

Section 6 reviews the related works on the cause-effect analysis of Japanese text data, and Sect. 7 concludes.

2   Technical Ideas

In this study, we analyze Japanese economic text data that seems to contain causality recognized by humans and construct a database of causality related to the economic field. For example, the Japanese sentence "円高のため、日本経済は悪化した。(*endaka no tame nihonkeizai ha akkashita*: Because of the yen's appreciation, the Japanese economy deteriorated.)" includes cause expression "円高 (*endaka*: the yen's appreciation)" and effect expression "日本経済は悪化した。(*nihonkeizai ha akkashita*: the Japanese economy deteriorated.)." Our method extracts these cause-effect expressions using clue expressions. In this case, the clue expression is "ため (*tame*: because)."

Furthermore, we develop a method to search for causal chains derived from phrases representing specific events. Using this method, we implement a system that can display causal chains for user's input words and select appropriate sequences or delete inappropriate sequences. Our method consists of the following steps.

1. Step 1 extracts sentences that include cause-effect expressions (causal sentences) from Japanese financial statement summaries using a support vector machine.
2. Step 2 obtains cause-effect expressions from the extracted sentences using syntactic patterns.
3. Step 3 constructs economic causal-chains by connecting each cause-effect expression.

Step 1 and Step 2 are implemented by a method of [1].

2.1 Step 1: Extraction of Causal Sentences

We developed a technique for extracting causal sentences from economic texts. It may be challenging to distinguish causal sentences. For instance, the Japanese clue expression "ため (*tame*: because)" is essential for extracting cause-effect expressions, but it can also be used to mean an objective. For example, the Japanese sentence "あなたのために、花を買った。(*anata no **tame** ni hana wo katta*: I bought some flowers **for** you)" includes the clue expression "ため (*tame*: because)," but it does not have a causal meaning in this context. We will, therefore, develop a method for extracting sentences that include cause and effect expressions that can cope with such situations.

This method uses a support vector machine (SVM) to acquire features for causality extraction from financial statement summaries. Our approach uses the features shown in Table 1 to extract causal sentences. We employ both syntactic and semantic features.

Table 1. Features for the extraction of causal sentences.

Kinds of features	Features
Syntactic features	Pairs of particles
Semantic features	Extended language ontology
Other features	Part of speech of morphemes just before clue expressions
	Morpheme unigrams
	Morpheme bigrams

We aim to use expressions that are frequently used in cause and effect expressions in sentences as syntactic features. For example, the Japanese sentence "半導体の需要回復を受けて半導体メーカーが設備投資を増やしている。(*handoutai no jyuyoukaifuku woukete hanndoutaime-ka-ga setsubitoushi wo fuyashiteiru*: As semiconductor demand recovers, semiconductor manufacturers are increasing their capital investment.)" has the following pattern of particles and clue expressions: "… の … を受けて … を … (*… no … woukete … wo …*)." This pattern indicates that it is highly likely to be a cause-effect expression. Our method, therefore, acquires particles that relate to clue expressions using a Japanese syntactic parser.

Besides, our method acquires words indicating causality using an extended language ontology [2]. Figure 1 shows our process of obtaining a semantic feature. Here, a **core phrase** is the last part of a phrase that includes clue expression, and a **base point phrase** is a phrase that is modified by the core phrase. First, our method acquires words that modify the core phrase or the base point phrase. Then, a tuple of concept words that are obtained by tracing extended language ontology using the words is acquired as a syntactic feature. Here, each tuple consists of two concept words, one based on the core phrase and the other based on the base point phrase.

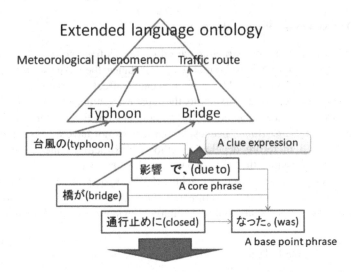

Feature : (Meteorological phenomenon, Traffic route)

Fig. 1. An example of a semantic feature.

2.2   Step 2: Extracting Cause-Effect Expressions

We employ a method by [3] to extract cause-effect expressions using four syntactic patterns. We analyzed sentence structures and used a pattern matching method with syntactic patterns is shown in Fig. 2. In Fig. 2, "Cause" indicates a *cause* expression, "Effect" denotes an *effect* expression, and "Clue" indicates a clue expression. Sakaji et al. [3] used a Japanese dependency analyzer [4] to analyze Japanese syntax, but the recall of that method is too low for our needs. However, the technique is not enough about the recall. Therefore, to improve the recall of the method, we add a new syntactic pattern (Pattern E).

Pattern A is the most basic pattern for expressing causality in Japanese. The others derive from Pattern A to emphasize either cause or effect, as represented by the arrows in Fig. 2.

To illustrate the operation of our method, we now work through examples using two of the five syntactic patterns (Patterns A and C). Figure 3 shows our method of extracting cause and effect expressions using Pattern A. It first identifies core and base point phrases using the clue expression "を背景に (*wohaikeini*: with)." Then, the cause expression "半導体メーカーの設備投資の拡大 (*handoutaime-ka-nosetsubitoushinokakudai*: expansion of capital investment by semiconductor manu-facturers)" is extracted by tracking back through the syntactic tree from the core phrase. Finally, the effect expression "半導体製造装置向け制御システムの販売が伸びた 。(*handoutaiseizousouchimukeseigyosisutemunohannbaiganobita*: sales of control sys-tems for semiconductor manufacturing equipment increased)" is extracted by tracking back through the syntactic tree from the base point phrase.

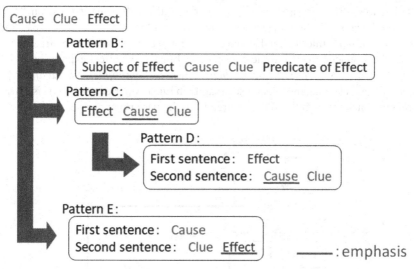

Fig. 2. A syntactic patterns list.

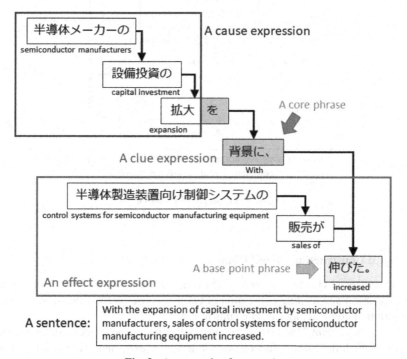

Fig. 3. An example of pattern A.

Figure 4 shows our method extracting cause and effect expressions using Pattern C. It first identifies core and base point phrases using the clue expression "ためだ 。(*tameda*: because)." Then, the cause expression "国際線が好調なのは (*kokusaisen-gakoutyounanoha*}: International airlines are doing well)" is extracted by tracking back through the syntactic tree from the core phrase. Finally, the effect expression "欧米路 線を中心にビジネス客が増えた (*oubeirosenwotyushinnibijinesukyakugafueta*}: the number of business customers increased mainly in Euro-American airlines)" is extracted by tracking back through the syntactic tree from the base point phrase.

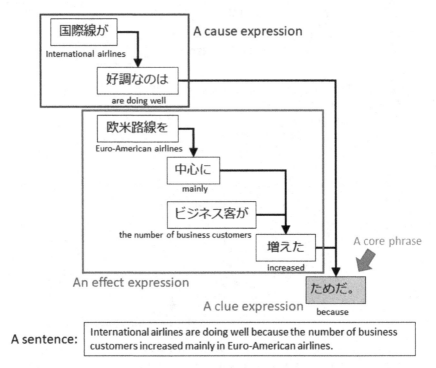

Fig. 4. An example of pattern C.

2.3 Step 3: Constructing Causal Chains

To construct causal chains, our method [5] connects an *effect* expression of a cause-effect expression and a *cause* expression of another cause-effect expression. We show an algorithm of constructing causal chains in Fig. 5.

In Fig. 5, "Company" indicates the company that issues the financial statement summary from which the cause-effect expression has been extracted. Additionally, "Date" is the date the financial statement summary was published. In Fig. 5 getSimilarity(e_i; c_i) is a function that calculates the similarity between the effect expression e_i and the cause expression c_j. Our method estimates the similarities based on vectors of word embedding. First, our method obtains word embedding average of the words included in the

Input: A list of cause–effect expressions CI
  CI_i = (Cause Expression c_i, Effect Expression e_i, Company cp_i, Date d_i)
Output: A list of causal chain LCC
 1: $LCC \leftarrow \emptyset$
 2: **for each** $(c_i, e_i, cp_i, d_i) \in CI$ **do**
 3:    **for each** $(c_j, e_j, cp_j, d_j) \in CI$ **do**
 4:       $similarity \leftarrow getSimilarity(e_i, c_j)$
 5:       **if** $similarity \geq threshold$ **then**
 6:          $LCC \leftarrow LCC + (c_i, e_i, cp_i, d_i, c_j, e_j, cp_j, d_j)$
 7:       **end if**
 8:    **end for**
 9: **end for**
10: **return** LCC

Fig. 5. Construction of causal chains.

expressions. Here, we define the average obtained from the effect expression e_i as $\tilde{W}_{e_i}$ and the average obtained from the cause expression c_j as $\tilde{W}_{c_i}$. Where $\tilde{W}_{e_i}, \tilde{W}_{c_i} \in R^m$ and m is the dimension size of word embedding. Then, our method calculates a cosine similarity between $\tilde{W}_{e_i}$ and $\tilde{W}_{c_i}$ and employs the similarity as a similarity between the effect expression e_i and the cause expression c_j. Finally, our approach acquires pairs of cause-effect expressions as a causal chain when the similarities are larger than a threshold.

3 Evaluation

In this section, we evaluate our method until Step 2. For evaluation, we use 30 pdf files of Japanese financial statement summaries and 30 documents of newspaper articles concerning business performance as test data. As a result of human tagging, the 30 pdf files include 478 cause-effect expressions, and the 30 documents include 51 cause-effect expressions. For the classification of causal sentences, we use tagged 3,360 sentences that include 1,454 causal sentences. The tagger is an individual investor with 15 years of investment experience. We use MeCab (http://taku910.github.io/mecab/) for Japanese language morphological analyzer and CaboCha for Japanese dependency parser [4]. Moreover, we employ the linear kernel as SVM kernel and SVM^{Light} as SVM.

3.1 Evaluation Results

Table 2 shows the experiment results. From Table 2, the method presents good performance for Japanese financial statement summaries and newspaper articles concerning business performance. The results of the newspaper outperform the results of financial summaries. That is because the method was developed for extracting cause-effect expressions from newspaper articles. However, the results of financial summaries satisfy sufficient performance to construct causal chains. Therefore, we think that the method performance is enough to build causal chains from economic texts.

Table 2. Evaluation results.

	Precision	Recall	F1 score	Number of extracted expressions
Financial summaries	0.82	0.62	0.71	360
Newspaper	0.93	0.75	0.83	34

4   Prototype System

Based on the above-mentioned causal-chain construction algorithm, the program of the basic framework of the economic causal-chain search system for Japanese texts was implemented. You can try this system at http://socsim.t.u-tokyo.ac.jp/. The behavior of this system is as follows.

Input of Start Text: First, the user enters the start text (Fig. 6). The user can select the search direction, from cause to result or from result to cause. It is also possible to limit the search period of textual data.

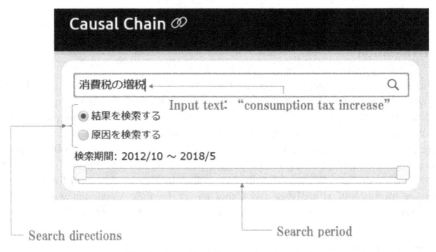

Fig. 6. A text box for entering start text.

Display of Causal Relationships: Click the search button to the right of the text box to display the causality chain from the input text (Fig. 7). By default, three causal relationships are displayed in descending order of similarities. If a user wants to see more causalities, he or she can click the "More" button to increase the display of causality nodes. If a user determines that a node of the causal relationship is not appropriate, he or she can delete the node by pressing the delete button at the upper right of each node.

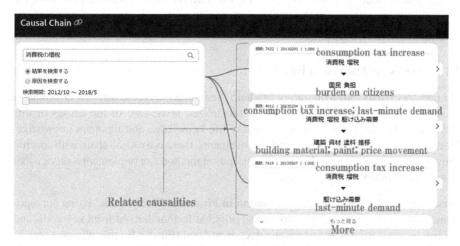

Fig. 7. Display of causal relationships

Extension of Causal Chains: If a user wants to extend the causal chain from each node, he or she can click the ">" button on the right of each node. Then the related causality is added with the clicked node as the terminal node (Fig. 8).

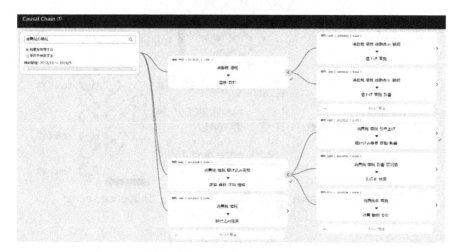

Fig. 8. Extended causal chains

By repeating the above procedures, a user can construct the required causal-chain. After the creation of the causal-chain, the user can save the causal chain in a file.

5 Application Images

Our economic causal-chain search system and the algorithm can be applied to various financial information services for both individual investors and financial professionals. We are going to implement the application service prototype program for any of the following application services.

5.1 Services for Individual Investors

For non-specialists, our technology can help them understand the implicit information about the causal relationship behind the specialized texts. One of the causes of this difficulty is the large gap between everyday life knowledge and financial knowledge. From general events to financial market movements, there is a causal-chain with specific knowledge in the economic domain. The proposed method can implement a service that provides instruction to fill this gap.

Presentation of Background Information in Financial Documents. Using our algorithm, a user can search related stocks and possible factors derived from keywords and phrases in news articles and economic document-level (Fig. 9). By the influence search, a user can know which stocks' price may be affected by specific economic events and situations denoted in the documents. By the factor search, a user can know possible causes of specific economic events and circumstances.

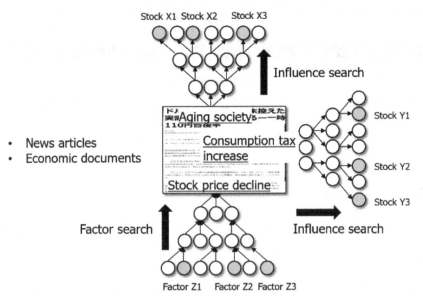

Fig. 9. Influence and factor search from financial texts

Question Answering System. Our algorithm can be applied to an interaction agent service provided by financial institutions for individual investors. Individual investors often want to ask basic questions to financial specialists and advisors. Because face-to-face advice from financial professionals is expensive, automated question answering leads to service penetration (Fig. 10).

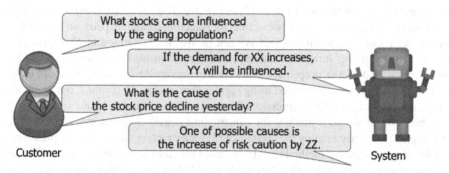

Fig. 10. Question answering system for individual investors

5.2 Supports for Financial Professionals Services

Our algorithm can be applied to a business support system for financial professionals in various departments of financial institutions such as market analysts and financial sales.

Support for Market Report Writing. The proposed method can help market analysts decide the content when writing a report. For example, they search whether there is any influence from a particular event to the market to be explained, and decides whether this event should be written in the report. Besides, for a specific price movement, it is possible to search for potential factors and check whether any information should be written in the report.

Sales Support. When salespersons of a financial institution want to sell their financial products to a customer, they can search for stocks related to the personal interests of the customer. If related stocks are searched in advance concerning the interests of the customers, they can support sales activities. Also, for questions from customers, the question answering system can provide candidates for the contents to be answered.

6   Related Work

Much work has been done on the extraction of causal information from texts. Inui et al. proposed a method for extracting causal relations (*cause, effect, pre-cond,* and *means*) from complex sentences containing the Japanese resultative connective "ため (*tame*: because)" [6], as this is a reliable indicator of causal information. Khoo et al. proposed a method to extract cause-effect information from newspaper articles by applying manually created patterns [7]. They also obtained causal knowledge from medical databases by applying their graphical patterns [8]. Chang et al. proposed a method to extract causal relationships between noun phrases using cue expressions and word pair probabilities [9]. They defined as the probability that the pair forms a causal noun phrase. Girju proposed a method for automatic detection and extraction of causal relations based on cue phrases [10], where pairs of noun phrases express causal relationships. Girju used WordNet [11] to create semantic constraints for selecting candidate pairs, so her method cannot extract unknown phrases that are not in WordNet. Bethard et al. proposed a method for classifying verb pairs that have causal relationships [12] using an SVM for classification. Sadek et al. proposed a method for extracting Arabic causal relations using linguistic patterns [13] represented using regular expressions. In contrast, our approach extract not only cause-effect expressions but also construct causal chains.

Ishii et al. proposed a method for constructing causal chains using WordNet and SVO tuples [14]. They employ the process of [3] for extracting cause-effect expressions. Alashri et al. proposed a method to extract causal relations and construct causal chains from large text corpora related to climate change [15]. However, their approach can not build causal chains when expressions consist of noun phrases. Because their method targets expressions that include Subjects, Verbs, and Objects (SVO). On the other hand, our method can construct causal chains from expressions that consist of noun phrases only.

7   Conclusions

We develop a way to produce causal chains starting from phrases representing specific events and offer possible ripple effects and factors of particular events or situations. Using our method with Japanese textual data, we have implemented a prototype system that can display causal chains for user-entered words. A user can interactively edit the causal chains by selecting appropriate causalities and deleting inappropriate causalities.

The current prototype system uses only small-sized Japanese text, earnings summaries of Japanese firms. To improve the precision and recall of acquired causal chains, the expansion of text data is necessary. As future works, we study the following two things to improve the causality database.

1. Development of a causal database using new text data such as news articles.
2. Extraction of causal information from English documents such as Form 10-k and press releases, and English database construction.

We are going to apply our method to English textual data, such as financial news articles and financial reports. The economic causal-chain search algorithm can be used for various financial information services. We want to launch some of the following services in collaboration with financial institutions or financial information vendors.

References

1. Sakaji, H., Murono, R., Sakai, H., Bennett, J., Izumi, K.: Discovery of rare causal knowledge from financial statement summaries. In: The 2017 IEEE Symposium on Computational Intelligence for Financial Engineering and Economics (CIFEr), pp. 602–608 (2017)
2. Kobayashi, A., Masuyama, S., Sekine, S.: A method for automatic ontology construction using Wikipedia. In: The IEICE Transactions on Information and Systems (Japanese edition), vol. J93-D, no. 12, pp. 2597–2609 (2010)
3. Sakaji, H., Sekine, S., Masuyama, S.: Extracting causal knowledge using clue phrases and syntactic patterns. In: 7th International Conference on Practical Aspects of Knowledge Management (PAKM), pp. 111–122 (2008)
4. Kudo, T., Matsumoto, T.: Japanese dependency analysis using cascaded chunking. In: CoNLL 2002: Proceedings of the 6th Conference on Natural Language Learning 2002 (COLING 2002 Post-Conference Workshops), pp. 63–69 (2002)
5. Nishumura, K., Sakaji, H., Izumi, K.: Creation of causal relation network using semantic similarity. In: The 32nd Annual Conference of the Japanese Society for Artificial Intelligence, p. 1P104 (2018)
6. Inui, T., Inui, K., Matsumoto, Y.: Acquiring causal knowledge from text using the connective marker tame. J. Inf. Proc. Soc. Jpn. **45**, 919–933 (2004)
7. Khoo, C., Kornfilt, J., Oddy, R., Myaeng, S.-H.: Automatic extraction of cause-effect information from newspaper text without knowledge-based inferencing. Lit. Linguist. Comput. **13**, 177–186 (1998)
8. Khoo, C., Chan, S., Niu, Y.: Extracting causal knowledge from a medical database using graphical patterns. In: Proceedings of the 38th Annual Meeting on Association for Computational Linguistics, pp. 336–343 (2000)
9. Chang, D.-S., Choi, K.-S.: Incremental cue phrase learning and bootstrapping method for causality extraction using cue phrase and word pair probabilities. Inf. Process. Manag. **42**, 662–678 (2006)
10. Girju, R.: Automatic detection of causal relations for question answering. In: ACL Workshop on Multilingual Summarization and Question Answering, pp. 76–83 (2003)
11. Fellbaum, C.: WordNet: An Electronic Lexical Database. The MIT Press, Cambridge (1998)
12. Bthard, S., Martin, J. H.: Learning semantic links from a corpus of parallel temporal and causal relations. In: Proceedings of the 46th Annual Meeting of the Association for Computational Linguistics on Human Language Technologies, pp. 177–180 (2008)
13. Sadek, J., Meziane, F.: Extracting Arabic causal relations using linguistic patterns. ACM Trans. Asian Low-Resour. Lang. Inf. Process. **15**, 1–20 (2016)
14. Ishii, H., Ma, O., Yoshikawa, M.: Incremental construction of causal network from news articles. J. Inf. Process. **20**, 207–215 (2012)
15. Alashri, S., Tsai, J.-Y., Koppela, A.R., Davulcu, H.: Snowball: extracting causal chains from climate change text corpora. In: The 2018 1st International Conference on Data Intelligence and Security (ICDIS), pp. 234–241 (2018)

Qualitative Reasoning

Qualitative Reasoning

Matthew Klenk[1] and Diedrich Wolter[2]

[1] Palo Alto Research Center, USA
matthew.klenk@parc.com
[2] University of Bamberg, Germany
diedrich.wolter@uni-bamberg.de

In 2019, the 32nd edition of the *Qualitative Reasoning Workshop* (QR) was hosted at IJCAI. Workshops in QR thus started in the previous golden years of AI, yet its original goals are fundamental questions of AI that still pose challenging and relevant research questions today. In an editorial introduction to QR research articles almost three decades ago, William and de Kleer characterized the field by stating that "the heart of the qualitative reasoning enterprise is to develop computational theories of the core skills underlying engineers, scientists, and just plain folk's ability to hypothesize, test, predict, create, optimize, diagnose and debug physical mechanisms"[1]. Such enterprise encompasses the development of means to understand the world from incomplete, imprecise, or uncertain data. This contrasts QR from purely data-driven methods such as machine learning that require a comprehensive and reliable set of training data.

QR is about developing a methodology to tackle important problems involving natural systems, social systems, and technical systems; it is also about making progress in the respective problem areas. While we have seen much progress throughout the previous 31 editions of the QR workshop, the field is not exhausted. First, the field tackles fundamental questions of AI research (e.g., model construction, inference, counterfactual reasoning). Second, QR grows with the ever-increasing repertoire of complex systems and processes developed in various (engineering) disciplines. Third (as in the following paper), QR techniques enable new capabilities in integrated intelligence systems.

In this edition of the QR workshop, we had eight papers presented that discussed aspects of theory and algorithms, as well as applications from computer games to industrial processes. In two invited talks, one by Tony Cohn and another by Masomumeh Mansouri, there was a common theme concerning the utility of hybrid representations that use qualitative spatial and temporal calculi to make inferences about real world activities. Of the technical papers at the workshop, we would like to highlight the following paper by Peng Zhang, Xiaoyu Ge and Jochen Renz of The Australian National University. This work achieves progress in an important application of robot technology, namely handling of previously unseen objects, and it also demonstrates the utility of pursuing a QR approach. The authors show that incorporating qualitative

---

[1] Qualitative Reasoning About Physical Systems – A Return to Roots. Artificial Intelligence, 51:1–9, 1991.

models about object arrangements allows them to relax constraints of state-of-the art algorithms: They are able to achieve more precise results in a more robust manner.

With ideas and applications expanding, we are looking forward to next QR and many more exciting papers!

Support Relation Analysis for Objects in Multiple View RGB-D Images

Peng Zhang$^{(\boxtimes)}$, Xiaoyu Ge, and Jochen Renz

Australian National University, Canberra, Australia
{p.zhang,xiaoyu.ge,jochen.renz}@anu.edu.au

Abstract. Understanding physical relations between objects, especially their support relations, is crucial for robotic manipulation. In this paper, we propose a method for extracting more detailed physical knowledge from a set of RGB-D images taken from the same scene but from different views using qualitative reasoning and intuitive physical models. Rather than providing a simple contact relation graph and approximating stability over convex shapes, our method is able to provide a detailed supporting relation analysis based on a volumetric representation. Specifically, true supporting relations between objects (e.g., if an object supports another object by touching it on the side or if the object above contributes to the stability of the object below) are identified. We apply our method to real-world structures captured in warehouse scenarios and show our method works as desired.

1 Introduction

Scene understanding for RGB-D images has been extensively studied recently with the availability of affordable cameras with depth sensors such as Kinect [39]. Among various scene understanding aspects [3], understanding spatial and physical relations between objects is essential for robotics manipulation tasks [25], especially when the target object belongs to a complex structure, which is common in real-world scenes. Although most research on robotics manipulation and planning focuses on handling isolated objects [5,15], increasing attention has been paid to the manipulation of physically connected objects (for example [20,36]). There are several problems that we need to deal with when analysing more complex object structures. For example, connected objects may remain stable due to support from adjacent objects rather than simple surface support from the bottom. In fact, support force may come from an arbitrary direction. Therefore, a simple bottom-up supporting relation analysis is not sufficient. Additionally, objects may hide behind other objects when observing from a certain view point.

Given that real-world objects often have irregular shapes, correctly segmenting the objects and extracting their contact relations are challenging tasks. In order to solve these problems, an efficient physical model which deals with objects with arbitrary shapes is required to infer precise support relations of a structure.

A. El Fallah Seghrouchni and D. Sarne (Eds.): IJCAI 2019 Workshops, LNAI 12158, pp. 41–61, 2020.
https://doi.org/10.1007/978-3-030-56150-5_3

In this paper, we propose a framework that takes raw RGB-D images as input and produces detailed support relations between objects in a stack. Most existing work on similar topics either assumes object shapes to be simple convex shapes [31], such as cuboid and cylinder or makes use of previous knowledge of the objects in the scene [32,34] to simplify the support analysis process. Although reasonable experimental results were demonstrated, those methods usually lack the capability of dealing with scenes that contain a lot of unknown objects. As a significant difference to existing methods, our proposed method does not assume any knowledge about the objects in a scene. After individually segmenting point clouds of each view of the scene, our method builds a volumetric representation based on Octree [18] for each view with information about hidden voxels. The octree of the whole scene combined from the input views is then constructed using spatial reasoning about the objects. This process allows us to precisely register input point clouds from different views and provide a reliable contact graph integrating all views that can then be used for a proper support relation analysis. We adopt an intuitive physical model to determine the overall stability of the structure. By iteratively removing contact force between object pairs, we can infer supporters of each object and then build the support graph. To the best of our knowledge, this is the first work that is able to explain the object support relations from a physical perspective.

2   Related Work

There has been work on scene understanding about support relations from a single view RGB-D image in both computer vision and robotics. In computer vision, scene understanding helps to produce more accurate detailed segmentation results. The work described in [14] applied an intuitive physical model to qualitatively infer support relations between objects and the experimental results showed the improvement of segmentation results on simple structures. In [32], the types of objects in indoor scenes were determined by learning from a labeled data set to get more accurate support relations. The above-mentioned papers both took a single image as input which limited the choice of the physical model since a significant amount of hidden information was not available. Shao et al. [31] attempted to recover unknown voxels from single view images by assuming the shape of the hidden objects to be cuboid and use static equilibrium to approximate the volume of the incomplete objects. In robotics, Mojtahedzadeh et al. [25] proposed a method to safely de-stack boxes based on geometric reasoning and intuitive mechanics, which was shown to be effective in their later work [36]. In [20], a simulation based method was proposed to infer stability during robotics manipulation on cuboid objects. This method includes a learning process using a large set of generated simulation scenes as a training set.

Humans look at things from different angles to gather comprehensive information for a better understanding. For example, before a Jenga player takes an action, the player will usually look around the stack from several critical views to have an overall understanding of the scene. This also applies to robots when they take images as the input source. A single input image provides incomplete information. Even when the images are taken from different views of the same static scene, the information may still be inadequate for scene understanding when using quantitative models for inferring detailed physical and spatial information, as this requires precise input. Qualitative reasoning has been demonstrated to be more suitable for modeling incomplete knowledge [17]. There are various qualitative calculi for representing different aspects of spatial entities [13,19,21,22,30]. One qualitative calculus that seems particularly useful for reasoning about spatial structures and their stability is the *Extended Rectangle Algebra (ERA)* [38] which simplifies the idea in [10] to infer stability of 2D rectangular objects. It is possible to combine ERA with an extended version of *cardinal direction relations* [26] to qualitatively represent detailed spatial relations between objects, which helps to infer the transformation between two views. It is worth mentioning that [27] proposed a framework to analyze support order of objects from multiple views of a static scene, yet this method requires relatively accurate image segmentation and the order of the images for object matching.

Models for predicting stability of a structure have been studied for many decades. Fahlman [7] proposed a model to analyze system stability based on Newton's Laws. Simulation based models were also presented in recent years [4,20]. However, Davis and Marcus [6] argue that probabilistic simulation based methods are not suitable for automatic physical reasoning due to some limitations including the lack of capability to handle imprecise input. Thus in our approach, we aim to apply qualitative spatial reasoning to combine raw information from multiple views to extract understandable and more precise relations between objects in the environment.

3   Method Pipeline

We now describe the overall pipeline of our support relation extraction method, which consists of three modules: image segmentation, view registration and stability analysis.

The image segmentation module takes a set of RGB-D images taken from different views of a static scene as input. To retain generality of our method, we do not assume any pre-known shapes of objects in the scene, that is, we do not use template matching methods that can provide more accurate segmentation results nor machine learning methods which require large amount of training data. This setting makes our method applicable in unknown environments. In the implementation, the raw RGBD data is first processed by a stream of morphology operations as described in [16] in order to fill the holes in the depth map. Notably, this hole-filling algorithm does not require any pre-training which is consistent with the no-prior-knowledge assumption in this paper. Then we use LCCP [35] for point cloud segmentation. LCCP first represents the point cloud as a set of connected supervoxels [28]. Then the supervoxels are segmented into larger regions by merging convexly connected supervoxels. Each point cloud of

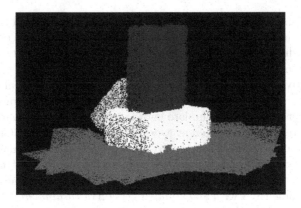

Fig. 1. Segmentation of aligned images.

a view will be segmented into individual regions. We use a *connected graph* to represent relations between the regions. Each graph node is a segmented region. The contact graph is then used to identify contact relation between objects in the structure. We use Manhattan world [9] assumption to find the ground plane. The entire scene will then be rotated such that the ground plane is parallel to the flat plane. The implementation we use is from the Point Cloud Library[1]. Figure 1 shows a typical output from this module.

In the *view registration module*, we use the iterative closest point (ICP) algorithm [2] to find the transformation between two point clouds. Notably, the initial guess for ICP algorithm is crucial. A bad initial guess may lead the registration to a local minima which provides incorrect results [29]. Due to the nature of multiple objects involving in the scene, we propose an algorithm to find an initial match for point clouds based on spatial relations between the objects. A matching between objects from two views will also be provided by this algorithm. The contact graph of each single point cloud will then be combined to produce a contact relation graph over all input images after the registration of different views.

In the *stability analysis* module, we adopt the definition of structural stability [24] and analyze static equilibrium of the structure by representing reacting forces at each contact area as a system of equations. A structure is considered stable if the equations have a solution. Given a static input scene, several schemes will be used to adjust the unseen part of the structure to make the static equilibrium hold.

The contribution of this paper is two-fold. First, we introduce a qualitative reasoning method to extract spatial relations between objects in a stack (see Sect. 4.1). We apply this information to find proper initial guess of the ICP algorithm to demonstrate its usefulness (see Sect. 4.2). Second, we propose a method for reconstructing volumetric model of objects with no prior knowledge

---

[1] http://www.pointclouds.org.

about objects (see Sect. 5.1), which is then used to analyse the true support relation of the object stack (see Sect. 5.2).

4   View Registration

In this section, we introduce a qualitative spatial reasoning approach to match objects from two scenes in order to find a proper initial guess for ICP to register the point clouds. In Subsect. 4.1, the qualitative spatial calculi and definitions related to the initial guess estimation algorithm are introduced first. In Subsect. 4.2, the algorithm is explained in detail.

4.1   Preliminaries on Qualitative Spatial Reasoning

The *extended rectangle algebra (ERA)* [38] is a qualitative spatial calculus which can be used to reason about the structural stability of connected 2D rectangular objects. For our problem, *ERA* is not expressive enough as the objects are incomplete 3D entities with irregular shapes. In Sect. 3, we mentioned that the ground plane has been detected under the Manhattan world assumption, thus it is possible to analyze spatial relations separately from vertical and horizontal directions. Although we do not assume all images be taken from the same height relative to the ground, it is reasonable to assume that images are taken from a human-eye view, not a birds-eye view. As the ground plane is detected, vertical spatial relations become stable to view changes. In contrast, horizontal spatial relations change dramatically when the view point changes. In order to analyze the horizontal spatial relations independently, all regions are projected onto the ground plane, i.e., a 2D Euclidean space.

ERA relations can be represented using *extended interval algebra (EIA)* relations (see Table 1) in each dimension in a 2D Euclidean space. EIA corresponds to Allen's interval algebra [1] with an additional center point for each interval. As a result, *EIA* has 27 basic relations (denoted by B_{eint}) which produce 27^2 *ERA* relations (see [38] for formal definitions of *ERA*). The *ERA* relation for two regions A and B can be written as $ERA(A, B) = (EIA_x(A, B), EIA_y(A, B))$. We will infer changes of direction relations with respect to horizontal view changes by applying *ERA*.

Definition 1 (region, region centroid, region radius). *Given a raw point cloud PC. Region a_l is the set of points $p_1, ..., p_n \in PC$ with the same label l from a segmentation algorithm. Let $c = (x_c, y_c, z_c)$ denote the region centroid, where*

$$x_c = \frac{\sum\limits_{i=1}^{n} x_{p_i}}{n}, \quad y_c = \frac{\sum\limits_{i=1}^{n} y_{p_i}}{n}, \quad z_c = \frac{\sum\limits_{i=1}^{n} z_{p_i}}{n} \qquad (1)$$

$dist(c, p_i)$ denotes the Euclidean distance between region centroid c and an arbitrary point $p_i \in a_l$. The region radius r of a region a is:

$$r = \max_{i \in \{1, ..., n\}} (dist(c, p_i)) \qquad (2)$$

Table 1. Some example EIA relations (adding center point to IA).

Relation	Illustration	Inverse Relation
$EIA(A, B) = lol$		$EIA(B, A) = loli$
$EIA(A, B) = mol$		$EIA(B, A) = moli$
$EIA(A, B) = lom$		$EIA(B, A) = lomi$
$EIA(A, B) = mom$		$EIA(B, A) = momi$
$EIA(A, B) = ms$		$EIA(B, A) = msi$
$EIA(A, B) = ls$		$EIA(B, A) = lsi$
$EIA(A, B) = hd$		$EIA(B, A) = hdi$
$EIA(A, B) = cd$		$EIA(B, A) = cdi$

Definition 2 (minimal bounding rectangle). *The minimal bounding rectangle of region r, denoted by $mbr(r)$, is a rectangle whose sides are parallel to the two orthogonal axes in a Cartesian coordinate system in $\mathbb{R}^2$, with the bounding lines $x = r_x^-, x = r_x^+, y = r_y^-, y = r_y^+$, where r_x^-, r_y^- are minimal x and y coordination of r, and r_x^+, r_y^+ are maximal x and y coordination of r.*

Let mbr denote the minimal bounding rectangle of a region. The mbr will change with the change of views. As a result, the EIA relation between two regions will change accordingly. By analyzing the EIA change, an approximate horizontal rotation level can be determined between two views. Before looking at incomplete regions due to occlusion or noise from the sensor, we first research how the values of $r_x^-, r_x^+, r_y^-, r_y^+$ change assuming the regions are completely sensed. We identify a conceptual neighborhood graph of EIA which includes all possible one-step changes with respect to horizontal rotation of views (see Fig. 2).

Definition 3 (view point, change of view). *The view point v is the position of the camera. Let v_1 and v_2 denote two view points, and c be the region centroid of the sensed connected regions excluding the ground plane. Assuming the point cloud has been rotated such that the ground plane is parallel to the plane defined by x-axis and y-axis of a 3D coordination system. Let v_{1xy}, v_{2xy} and c_{xy} be the vertical projection of v_1, v_2 and c to the xy plane. The change of view C is the angle difference between the line segments $c_{xy}v_{1xy}$ and $c_{xy}v_{2xy}$.*

Definition 4 (symmetric EIA relation). *Let $R \in B_{eint}$ to be an arbitrary EIA atomic relation. The symmetric EIA relation of R (denoted by $symm(R)$) is defined as R's axially symmetric atomic relation against the axis of symmetry formed by relations $\{cd, eq, cdi\}$ in the conceptual neighborhood graph given in Fig. 2. For example, $symm(mol) = lomi$. The symmetric relation of cd, eq and cdi are themselves.*

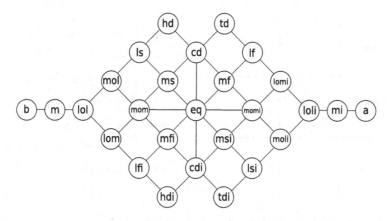

Fig. 2. Conceptual neighborhood graph for EIA based on horizontal view rotation. The axis formed by 'cd', 'eq' and 'cdi' is the axis of symmetry. The symmetric relation of each EIA relation is its symmetric relation against this axis.

Lemma 1. *Let $C_{cw\pi/2}$ denote the view change of $\pi/2$ clockwise from view point v_1 to v_2. Let $ERA_{ab_1} = (r_{x1}, r_{y1})$ and $ERA_{ab_2} = (r_{x2}, r_{y2})$ denote the ERA relations between region a and b at v_1 and v_2.*
Assuming the connected regions are fully sensed, then $r_{x2} = symm(r_{y1})$, $r_{y2} = r_{x1}$. Similarly, if the view changes by $\pi/2$ anticlockwise, then $r_{x2} = r_{y1}$, $r_{y2} = symm(r_{x1})$

The term 'fully sensed' in Lemma 1 assumes the full model of the object can be obtained from any single scan. This is by no means achievable in realistic, however, this assumption is only used to provide an ideal case for analysing the spatial relation differences due to view changing.

Proof: Lemma 1 can be simply proved by reconstructing a coordination system at each view point.

Although the conceptual neighborhood graph indicates possible relation changing path for a pair of objects in one dimension, the way the changes happen depends on the rotation direction (clockwise or anti-clockwise) and their ERA relation before the rotation. For example, $ERA(A, B) = (m, m)$ means $mbr(A)$ connects $mbr(B)$ at the bottom-left corner of $mbr(B)$, thus if the view rotates anti-clockwise, $mbr(A)$ tends to move upwards related to $mbr(B)$ regardless of the real shape of A and B, therefore $EIA_y(A, B)$ will change from 'm' to 'lol' but not 'b'. To determine the changing trend of ERA relations more efficiently, we combine ERA with *cardinal direction relations (CDR)* which describes how one region is relative to the other in terms of directional positions.

The basic CDR [33] contains nine cardinal tiles as shown in Fig. 3. 'B' represents the relation '*belong*', the other eight relations the cardinal directions N (north), NE (north-east), etc.

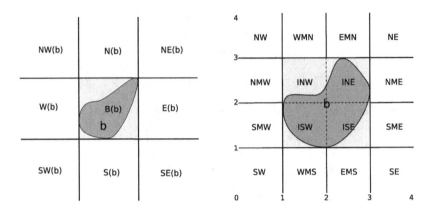

Fig. 3. Basic CDR (left) and Extended CDR (ECDR) (right). Specifically, the inner tile of basic CDR has been split into 4 relations, i.e., INW, INE, ISW and ISE. This extension allows representation about directional relation between overlapped entities, which happens frequently on the vertical projection of a stack of connected objects. Relations N, S, W and E in basic CDR are also split accordingly into more detailed relations.

Definition 5 (basic CDR relation). *A basic CDR relation is an expression* $R_1 : ... : R_k$ *with* $1 \leq k \leq 9$ *where:*

1. $R_1, ..., R_k \in \{B, N, NE, E, SE, S, SW, W, NW\}$
2. $R_i \neq R_j, \forall 1 \leq i, j \leq k, i \neq j$
3. $\forall b \in REG, \exists a_1, ..., a_k \in REG$ *and* $a_1 \cup ... \cup a_k \in REG$ *(Regions that are homeomorphic to the closed unit disk* $(x, y) : x^2 + y^2 \leq 1$ *are denoted by* REG*).*

If $k = 1$*, the relation is called a single-tile relation and otherwise a multi-tile relation.*

Similar to the extension from RA to ERA, we introduce center points to extend basic CDR to the extended CDR (denoted as $ECDR$, see Fig. 3) in order to express inner relations and detailed outer relations between regions. Notably, a similar extension about inner relations of CDR was proposed in [23]. However, as we focus on *mbr* of regions in this problem, their notions for inner relations with trapezoids are not suitable for our representation.

In [26], *rectangular cardinal direction relations (RCDR)* which combines RA and CDR was studied. As a subset of CDR, RCDR considers single-tile relations and a subset of multi-tile relations that represent relations between two rectangles whose edges are parallel to the two axes. We combine ERA and $ECDR$ in a similar way to produce the *extended rectangular cardinal direction relations (ERCDR)*. Including all single-tile and multi-tile relations, there exists 100 valid relations (not all listed in this paper) to represent the directional relation between two *mbrs*.

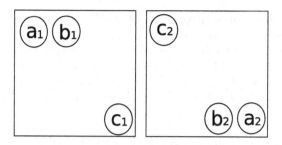

Fig. 4. An example to illustrate how to use spatial reasoning to verify object match. The spatial relation graph G_1 for the left view is {west(a_1, b_1), northwest(a_1, c_1), northwest(b_1, c_1)}, and relation graph G_2 for the right view is {east(a_2, b_2), southeast(a_2, c_2), southeast(b_2, c_2)}. If (a_1, a_2), (b_1, b_2) and (c_1, c_2) are correctly matched, by the right view by π either clockwise or anti-clockwise, an identical graph of G_1 can be achieved. If wrongly matching any object pair, the identical graph cannot be obtained.

4.2   Initial Guess Estimation for ICP

In this section, the algorithm for matching objects between two views is proposed. In Sect. 3, the point cloud has been aligned to the direction of the ground, therefore, the only two factors for initial transformation estimation are rotation against the vertical axis and the translation. With the matched objects, the task for estimating initial transformation between two point clouds for ICP algorithm is then minimising the sum of distance between all matched object pairs.

Informally, assuming a spatial relation graph is built for any two objects in the same view, if most objects in one view are correctly matched to the corresponding ones in the other view, the two spatial relation graph can be very similar (if not identical because of incomplete input) by rotating one view by a certain angle. For example, in Fig. 4, the spatial relation graph for the left view is {west(a_1, b_1), northwest(a_1, c_1), northwest(b_1, c_1)}, and for the right view is {east(a_2, b_2), southeast(a_2, c_2), southeast(b_2, c_2)}. If correctly matching all three pairs of objects, the identical graph can be obtained by rotating the right view by π from any direction. If wrongly matching any objects, the identical graph can never be obtained.

Therefore, a distance function is necessary for measuring the similarity of two relation graphs. A method about how to calculate the distance between two ERCDR relations is shown below.

Definition 6 (directional property of a single-tile relation). *Each tile t in ECDR has both a horizontal directional property $HDP(t) \in \{E, W\}$ and a vertical directional property $VDP(t) \in \{N, S\}$. The value is determined by the relative directional relation between the centroid of t and the centroid of the reference region b. For example, $HDP(INE) = E$ and $VDP(INE) = N$.*

Definition 7 (directional property of multi-tile relation). *The direc-tional property of a multi-tile relation mt is determined by majority single tile directional properties in the multi-tile relation, where $HDP(mt) \in \{E, M, W\}$ and $VDP(mt) \in \{N, M, S\}$, where M represents 'middle' which appears when the counts of the single tile directional properties are equal. For example, $HDP(WMN : EMN : INW : INE) = M$ and $VDP(WMN : EMN : INW : INE) = N$.*

Directional property can be used to estimate the trend of the relation change. Let a view point rotate clockwise, if HDP and VDP are as observed, then the change trend is as described in the following table:

HDP	VDP	change trend	change direction
E	S or M	south to north	vertical
E or M	N	east to west	horizontal
W	N or M	north to south	vertical
W or M	S	west to east	horizontal

One ERCDR relation can be transformed to the other by lifting the four bounding lines of the single/multi-tile. The distance d between two ERCDR relations is calculated from horizontal and vertical directions by counting how many grids each boundary line lifts over. The distance is related to the direction of the view point changes as well as the directional properties of the region. However, with the same angle difference, the inner tiles take much fewer changes than the outside tiles. We introduce the *quarter distance size* to represent the angle change of $\pi/2$ for normalizing the distance between ERCDR relation pairs corresponding to the angle difference.

Based on Lemma 1, we can infer the ERA relation between two regions after rotating the view point by $\pi/2$, π and $3\pi/2$ either clockwise or anticlockwise. The ERA relation can be then represented by an ERCDR tile. In order to calculate the distance between ERCDR tiles, we label each corner of the single tiles with a 2D coordinate with bottom-left corner of tile SW to be the origin $(0,0)$ (see Fig. 3).

Definition 8 (distance between ERCDR tiles). *Let t_1 and t_2 be two ERCDR tiles. x_1^- and x_1^+ are the left and right bounding lines of t_1, y_1^- and y_1^+ the top and bottom bounding lines of t_1. x_2^- and x_2^+ are the left and right bounding lines of t_2. y_2^- and y_2^+ the top and bottom bounding lines of t_2.*
The unsigned distance between t_1 and t_2 is calculated as:

$$d_{abs}(t_1, t_2) = |(x_2^+ - x_1^+) + (x_2^- - x_1^-)| + |(y_2^+ - y_1^+) + (y_2^- - y_1^-)| \quad (3)$$

The sign of d is determined by whether the change trend suggested by direc-tional property is followed. If so, $d(t_1, t_2) = |d(t_1, t_2)|$, else $d(t_1, t_2) = -|d(t_1, t_2)|$. If there is no or symmetric change on the trend direction, $d(t_1, t_2) = 0$

If there is a significant angle difference between the two tiles, the distance may not be accurate. Here we introduce three more reference tiles by rotating the original tile by $\pi/2$, π and $3\pi/2$ in turn. Figure 5 demonstrates an example of three reference tiles of a configuration. The use of reference tile can limit the distance calculation within $\pi/2$. The detailed usage of reference tiles are shown below in Definition 10.

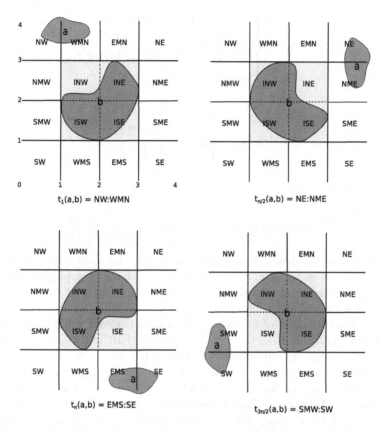

Fig. 5. An example to illustrate the reference tiles. The three reference tiles $t_{\pi/2}$, t_{π} and $t_{3\pi/2}$ are obtained by rotating the view of t_1 by $\pi/2$, π and $3\pi/2$ respectively. The use of reference tile can limit the distance calculation within $\pi/2$ to reduce the uncertainty from qualitative representation.

Definition 9 (quarter distance). *Let t_1 be an ERCDR tile and t_1' be the ERCDR tile produced by rotating t_i by $\pi/2$ or $-\pi/2$. By applying Lemma 1, the reference tiles can be easily mapped to ERCDR tiles. The quarter distance of t_1 is defined as:*

$$d_{qt} = d(t_1, t_1') \tag{4}$$

Definition 10 (normalized distance). *Let t_1 be an ERCDR tile. $t_{\pi/2}$, t_π and $t_{3\pi/2}$ denote the three reference tiles for t_1. Let t_2 be another ERCDR tile. The normalized distance $d_{norm}(t_1, t_2)$ will be calculated in two parts:*

1. *The reference tile t_{ref} and the base distance d_{base}.*
   Let $T = \{t_1, t_{\pi/2}, t_\pi, t_{3\pi/2}\}$ and $T_{ref} = \underset{t \in T}{argmin}(d_{abs}(t, t_2))$.

$$
t_{ref}(t_1, t_2) = \begin{cases} t_1 \ if \ t_1 \in T_{ref} \ and \ d(t, t_2) \geq 0 \\ t_{\pi/2} \ if \ t_{\pi/2} \in T_{ref} \ and \ t_1 \notin T_{ref} \\ t_\pi \ if \ t_\pi \in T_{ref} \ and \ t_1, t_{\pi/2} \notin T_{ref} \\ t_{3\pi/2} \ else \end{cases} \tag{5}
$$

$$
d_{base}(t_1, t_2) = \begin{cases} 0 & if & t_{ref} = t_1 \\ 1 & if & t_{ref} = t_{\pi/2} \\ 2 & if & t_{ref} = t_\pi \\ 3 & if & t_{ref} = t_{3\pi/2} \end{cases} \tag{6}
$$

2. *The normalized distance*

$$
d_{norm}(t_1, t_2) = d_{base}(t_1, t_2) + \frac{d(t_{ref}, t_2) + 1}{d_{qt}(t_1) + 1} \tag{7}
$$

Having the normalized distance for calculating the similarity between two ERCDR tiles, we now show the algorithm for identifying proper matching between objects from two different views in Algorithm 1. In brief, the idea behind Algorithm 1 is that: if objects from two views are matched in pairs properly, the variance of the collection of normalized distances between the ERCDR tile of each pair of two objects from the first view and the ERCDR tile of the matched two objects from the second view should be small.

Once the match of objects has been determined, the initial transformation can be calculated by performing local search of horizontal rotation to obtain a minimal sum of distance between two relation graphs. Then a translation is also calculated by minimising the euclidean distance of the geometric centers of the matched objects. The ICP algorithm will be performed using the calculated initial transformation.

At the end of this section, we show an example of the object initial matching pipeline.

Example 1. Considering there are two images taken from different views of the same scene. Figure 6 is the result of vertical projection of two views from the same scene. By performing the projection process and initial segmentation, we will then obtain initial matches between objects from the two views by applying the technique described in this section. The first step is to calculate d_{norm} between each possible object pairs from two different views. We will show an example of calculating d_{norm} between $tile(a_1, b_1)$ and $tile(a_2, b_2)$ from View 1 and View 2 in Fig. 6. In Fig. 7, the four reference tiles are listed. Among the four tiles, $t_{\pi/2}$

Algorithm 1. Object Matching

---

function GETMATCHEDOBJECTS

    Input:

    /*Assume $objIDList1$ and $objIDList2$ constain all object IDs from view 1 and view 2, respectively. And objIDList1.size() > objIDList2.size()*/

    $pList$ /*all permutations of the longer list, i.e. $objIDList1$ with each permutation with the length of $objIDList2$.*/

    $objIDList1$ /*the longer ID list*/

    $objIDList2$ /*the shorter ID list*/

    $relationGraph1$ /*a relation graph contains all possible ERCDR tiles from any two objects of a single view*/

    $relationGraph2$

    Output: $match$ // A set of matched object pairs

    $candidateMatch \leftarrow \{\}$

    for $i \leftarrow 0;\ i < pList.size();\ i++$ **do**

        $temList \leftarrow \{\}, curList \leftarrow pList[i]$

        for $j \leftarrow 0;\ j < objIDList2.size();\ j++$ **do**

            $temList.pushback(curList[j], objIDList2[j])$

        $candidateMatch.pushback(temList)$

    $err \leftarrow INFINITY$

    for $i \leftarrow 0;\ i < candidateMatch.size();\ i++$ **do**

        $curList \leftarrow candidateMatch[i], distList \leftarrow \{\}$

        for $m \leftarrow 0;\ m < curList.size();\ m++$ **do**

            for $n \leftarrow 0;\ n < curList.size();\ n++$ **do**

                if $m == n$ **then**

                    continue

                $r1 \leftarrow relationGraph1(curList[m][0], curList[n][0])$

                $r2 \leftarrow relationGraph2(curList[m][1], curList[n][1])$

                $distList.pushback(d_{norm}(r1, r2))$

        if $Variance(distList) < err$ **then**

            $err \leftarrow Variance(distList)$

            $match \leftarrow curList$

    return $match$

---

is used to calculate the quarter distance based on Eq. 4. Then based on Eq. 5, $t_{3\pi/2}$ is selected as the reference tile for the calculation in Eq. 7 with $d_{base} = 3$. The next step is to calculate the normalized distance between t_1 and t_2 based on $t_{3\pi/2}$ and t_2 as shown in Fig. 8.

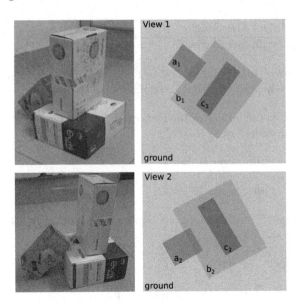

Fig. 6. An example of vertical projection of two views from the same scene. The ground label in the projected scenes in the right column is the lowest supporting surface of the stack which is self-stable without the need of other supporters. The projected scenes are then used to match the objects in two views.

By repeating the above calculation on all possible object pairs between two views, Algorithm 1 can be used to find out the matching object pairs with least variation in terms of their d_{norm}.

5   Stability Analysis

In this section, we introduce a method to complete the object with invisible voxels. Then, we show how to get support relation from the volumetric representation of the objects.

5.1   Object Completion

With the registration of multiple views, an octree representation of the scene is built. The next step is to classify invisible voxels to the objects in order to analyse the support relation. First, for each of the object, an oriented minimal bounding box OMBB is calculated. We perform Ransac [8] algorithm to fit the largest plane to the object point cloud. This plane is used as one surface and the OMBB of the object is then determined. All invisible voxels in the OMBB are then assigned to this object. As the octree is built with point clouds from different views, the set of invisible voxels are largely eliminated and the volumetric model tends to represents the intrinsic shape of the object. Figure 9 shows the process of object completion in 2D for simplicity.

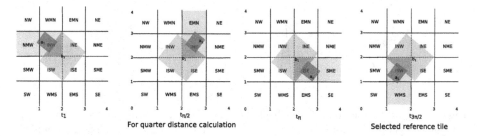

Fig. 7. Four reference tiles for calculating the distance between object pair (a_1, b_1) and (a_2, b_2) in example 1. The quarter distance described in Eq. 4 is calculated between t_1 and $t_{\pi/2}$ (tiles marked grey). Here $x_1^- = 0$, $x_1^+ = 2$, $y_1^- = 2$, $y_1^+ = 3$, $x_{\pi/2}^- = 2$, $x_{\pi/2}^+ = 3$, $y_{\pi/2}^- = 2$, $y_{\pi/2}^+ = 4$. According to Eq. 4, $d_{qt} = 4$. Also, based on Eq. 6, the reference tile used in d_{base} is $t_{3\pi/2}$, which yields a base distance of 3.

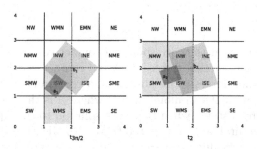

Fig. 8. $t_{3\pi/2}$ and t_2 (the tiles marked grey) are used to calculate the normalized distance between t_1 and t_2. Here $x_{3\pi/2}^- = 1$, $x_{3\pi/2}^+ = 2$, $y_{3\pi/2}^- = 0$, $y_{3\pi/2}^+ = 2$, $x_2^- = 0$, $x_2^+ = 2$, $y_2^- = 1$, $y_2^+ = 3$. Together with d_{qt} and d_{base} obtained in Fig. 7, according to Eq. 7, $d_{norm} = 3.8$.

5.2 Support Relation Analysis

We use the structural analysis method in [11] to estimate the support relation between objects in the structure. A structure is in static equilibrium when the net force and net torque of the structure equal to zero. The static equilibrium is expressed in a system of linear equations [37]:

$$A_{eq} \cdot f + w = 0$$
$$\|f^n\| \geq 0 \quad 1)$$
$$\|f^s\| \leq \mu \|f^n\| \quad 2)$$

$$(8)$$

A_{eq} is the coefficient matrix where each column stores the unit direction vectors of the forces and the torque at a contact point. To identify the contact points between two contacting objects, we first fit a plane to all points of the connected regions between the objects. We then project all points to the plane and obtain the minimum oriented bounding rectangle of the points. The resulting bounding rectangle approximates the region of contact, and the four corners of the rectangle will be used as contact points. f is a vector of unknowns representing the

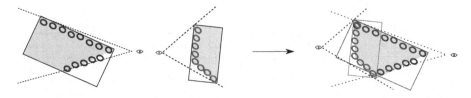

Fig. 9. Object completion. For each of the views, the voxels are classified into four categories: occupied, temporally occupied, unoccupied and unknown. The unoccupied voxels are the voxels within the range of the sensor sight but allow the rays of the sensor the go through. The occupied voxels for each view are the sensed boundary voxels. A part of the unknown voxels within its the occupied voxels' OMBB are temporally occupied voxels but subject to change during the combination of different views. The rest voxels that are not sensed are unknown voxels. By combining multiple views, the temporally occupied voxels will be re-classified into unoccupied category if they are sensed to be unoccupied in another view.

magnitude of each force at the corresponding contact vertex. The forces include contact forces f^n and friction forces f^s at the contact vertex. The constraint 1) requires the normal forces to be positive and constraint 2) requires the friction forces comply with the Coulomb model where μ is the coefficient of static friction. A structure is stable when there is a solution to the equations.

Using the structural analysis method, we can identify support relations between objects. Specifically, we are interested in identifying the core supporters [12] of each object in a scene. An object o_1 is a core supporter of another object o_2 if o_2 becomes unstable after removal of o_1. Given a contact between o_1 and o_2, to test whether o_1 is the core supporter of o_2, we first identify the direction vectors of forces and torque given by the contact on o_2, and set them to zero in Eq. 8. This is equivalent to removing all forces that o_1 imposes on o_2. If Eq. 8 has no solution, then o_1 is the core supporter. We test each pair of objects in a scene and obtain a support graph, which is defined as a directed graph with each vertex representing an object. There is an edge from v_1 to v_2 if o_1 is a core supporter of o_2.

6   Experiments

We first test our method about estimation of initial guess for ICP algorithm. Then we show the method's capability of identifying core supporters of an object in a structure. For both experiments, we test our method on two data sets as well as some single scenes for testing special configurations. *Data set 1* is from [27] which contains seven different scenes. *Data set 2*[2] is taken from a warehouse scenario of a real logistics application setting in sorting parcels. This data set consists of 5 scenes.

---

[2] Date set 2 can be provided upon request.

6.1   Initial Guess Estimation of ICP

In this experiment, we compare the initial guess from Algorithm 1 with random initial guess for ICP point cloud registration. Figure 10 shows the result qualitatively. The two images in column a are rgb photos taken different views of the same stack. Column b shows the segmentation of the point clouds of the two views. The top figure of column c is the initial guess from Algorithm 1. The angle difference between the two views is approximately 30° is this initial alignment. The bottom figure of column c is the initial guess from random guess which shows a angle difference of about 90°. Column d then shows the alignment results from ICP using both initial guesses from column c. The top figure shows the final alignment using the initial guess from Algorithm 1. The two views are corrected matched to each other without falling into local optima. However, the bottom result which used random initial guess failed to find the global optimal alignment.

In Table 2, we use the mean sum of squared error (MSE) for all point pairs to evaluate the quality of the registration on data set 2 which consists of more complex scenes.

Table 2. Initial guess results. MSE for all point pairs is used to evaluate the quality of the registration on data set 2. The results show that our method improves the initial guess which helps improve the overall quality of ICP algorithm.

	MSE (Data set 2)
Algorithm 1	1.13e–3
Random initial guess	2.29e–3

6.2   Support Graph Evaluation

For core supporter detection, we show that our method out performs the method in [27] on data set 1. As the method in [27] requires precise object models for segmentation, it does not work in unknown scenarios in data set 2. Therefore, only Algorithm 1 is tested on data set 2. The reason why support relation accuracy is slightly low is that there are more errors from segmentation which provide more false positive support relations.

In addition to data set 1 and 2, we use a single scene with special supporting relations (e.g. the top object supports the bottom object) as well as the data from [27]. Table 3 shows the core supporter detection results compared with the methods in [27]. Our algorithm is able to find most of the true support relations. In addition, our method is able to detect some special core supporter objects such as A in Fig. 11 which is difficult to be detected by statistical methods.

In Fig. 11, results of core supporter detection are presented. Notably, in the second row, we detected that even though object C is on top of object B, it contributes to the stability of B. Thus, C is a core supporter of B as well as A.

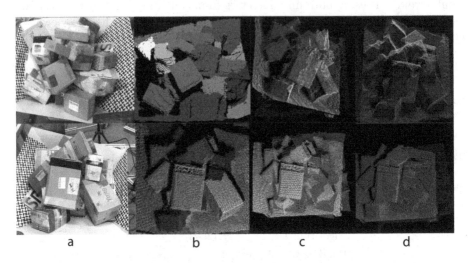

Fig. 10. Results of ICP initial guess estimation (data set 2). Col. a shows the photos of different views; col. b is the segmentation of single views; the top image of col. c is the initial guess from Algorithm 1; the bottom is the random initial guess; the top image of col. d is the registration result with initial guess from Algorithm 1; the bottom one is from random initial guess.

Table 3. Support relation results. Compared to the other listed methods in the table, our algorithm is able to find most of the true support relations.

	Accuracy(Data set 1)	Accuracy(Data set 2)
Our method	72.5	68.2
Agnostic [27]	65.0	N/A
Aware [27]	59.5	N/A

Fig. 11. Core supporter detection. Top: data set 1; bottom: single scene. As a major difference compared to [27], our method is able to detect core supporter described in Sect. 5.2. In the second row, we detected that even though object C is on top of object B, it contributes to the stability of B. Thus, C is a core supporter of B as well as A.

7 Conclusion and Future Work

In this paper, we propose a framework for identifying support relations among a group of connected objects taking a set of RGB-D images about the same static scene from different views as input. We assume no knowledge about the objects and the environment beforehand. By qualitatively reasoning about the angle change between each pair of input images, we successfully identified matching of the objects between different views and calculate the initial guess for ICP algorithm. We use static equilibrium to analyse the stability of the whole structure and extract the core support relation between objects in the structure. We can successfully detect most of the support relations. With the capability of analysing core supporting relations, the perception system is able to assist the AI agent to perform causal reasoning about consequences of an action applied on an object in a structure. Apparently this is only one aspect of physical relations that can be derived. In the future, more object features (e.g. solidity, density distribution, etc.) and relations between objects (e.g. containment, relative position, etc.) can be studied.

References

1. Allen, J.F., Koomen, J.A.: Planning using a temporal world model. In: IJCAI 1983, pp. 741–747. Morgan Kaufmann Publishers Inc., Burlington (1983)

2. Besl, P.J., McKay, N.D.: Method for registration of 3-D shapes. In: Sensor Fusion IV: Control Paradigms and Data Structures. vol. 1611, pp. 586–607. International Society for Optics and Photonics (1992)
3. Chen, K., Lai, Y., Hu, S.: 3d indoor scene modeling from RGB-D data: a survey. CVM **1**(4), 267–278 (2016)
4. Cholewiak, S.A., Fleming, R.W., Singh, M.: Visual perception of the physical stability of asymmetric three-dimensional objects. JOV **13**(4), 12–12 (2013)
5. Ciocarlie, M., Hsiao, K., Jones, E.G., Chitta, S., Rusu, R.B., Şucan, I.A.: Towards reliable grasping and manipulation in household environments. In: Khatib, O., Kumar, V., Sukhatme, G. (eds.) ISER 2014, pp. 241–252. Springer, Heidelberg (2014). https://doi.org/10.1007/978-3-642-28572-1_17
6. Davis, E., Marcus, G.: The scope and limits of simulation in automated reasoning. AIJ **233**, 60–72 (2016)
7. Fahlman, S.E.: A planning system for robot construction tasks. AIJ **5**(1), 1–49 (1974)
8. Fischler, M.A., Bolles, R.C.: Random sample consensus: a paradigm for model fitting with applications to image analysis and automated cartography. Commun. ACM **24**(6), 381–395 (1981)
9. Furukawa, Y., Curless, B., Seitz, S.M., Szeliski, R.: Manhattan-world stereo. In: CVPR 2009, pp. 1422–1429. IEEE (2009)
10. Ge, X., Renz, J.: Representation and reasoning about general solid rectangles. IJCAI **2013**, 905–911 (2013)
11. Ge, X., Renz, J., Abdo, N., Burgard, W., Dornhege, C., Stephenson, M., Zhang, P.: Stable and robust: stacking objects using stability reasoning. In: Workshop on Human-Robot Engagement in the Home, Workplace and Public Spaces, IJCAI 2017, p. 27 (2017)
12. Ge, X., Renz, J., Zhang, P.: Visual detection of unknown objects in video games using qualitative stability analysis. TCIAIG **8**(2), 166–177 (2016)
13. Guesgen, H.W.: Spatial reasoning based on Allen's temporal logic. International Computer Science Institute Berkeley (1989)
14. Jia, Z., Gallagher, A., Saxena, A., Chen, T.: 3d-based reasoning with blocks, support, and stability. CVPR **2013**, 1–8 (2013)
15. Kemp, C.C., Edsinger, A., Torres-Jara, E.: Challenges for robot manipulation in human environments [grand challenges of robotics]. RAM **14**(1), 20–29 (2007)
16. Ku, J., Harakeh, A., Waslander, S.L.: In defense of classical image processing: fast depth completion on the CPU. In: 2018 15th Conference on Computer and Robot Vision (CRV), pp. 16–22. IEEE (2018)
17. Kuipers, B.: Qualitative reasoning: modeling and simulation with incomplete knowledge. Automatica **25**(4), 571–585 (1989)
18. Laboratory, R.P.I.I.P., Meagher, D.: Octree Encoding: a New Technique for the Representation, Manipulation and Display of Arbitrary 3-D Objects by Computer (1980)
19. Lee, J.H., Renz, J., Wolter, D., et al.: Starvars-effective reasoning about relative directions. IJCAI **2013**, 976–982 (2013)
20. Li, W., Leonardis, A., Fritz, M.: Visual stability prediction for robotic manipulation. In: ICRA 2017. IEEE (2017)
21. Ligozat, G.É.: Reasoning about cardinal directions. JVLC **9**(1), 23–44 (1998)
22. Liu, W., Li, S., Renz, J., et al.: Combining RCC-8 with qualitative direction calculi: algorithms and complexity. IJCAI **2009**, 854–859 (2009)

23. Liu, Y., Wang, X., Jin, X., Wu, L.: On internal cardinal direction relations. In: Cohn, A.G., Mark, D.M. (eds.) COSIT 2005. LNCS, vol. 3693, pp. 283–299. Springer, Heidelberg (2005). https://doi.org/10.1007/11556114_18
24. Livesley, R.: Limit analysis of structures formed from rigid blocks. IJNME **12**(12), 1853–1871 (1978)
25. Mojtahedzadeh, R., Bouguerra, A., Lilienthal, A.J.: Automatic relational scene representation for safe robotic manipulation tasks. In: IROS 2013, pp. 1335–1340. IEEE (2013)
26. Navarrete, I., Sciavicco, G.: Spatial reasoning with rectangular cardinal direction relations. In: ECAI 2006, vol. 6, pp. 1–10 (2006)
27. Panda, S., Abdul Hafez, A.H., Jawahar, C.: Single and multiple view support order prediction in clutter for manipulation (2016)
28. Papon, J., Abramov, A., Schoeler, M., Worgotter, F.: Voxel cloud connectivity segmentation-supervoxels for point clouds. CVPR **2013**, 2027–2034 (2013)
29. Pomerleau, F., Colas, F., Siegwart, R., et al.: A review of point cloud registration algorithms for mobile robotics. Found. Trends® Robot. **4**(1), 1–104 (2015)
30. Randell, D.A., Cui, Z., Cohn, A.G.: A spatial logic based on regions and connection. KR **1992**(92), 165–176 (1992)
31. Shao, T., Monszpart, A., Zheng, Y., Koo, B., Xu, W., Zhou, K., Mitra, N.: Imagining the unseen: stability-based cuboid arrangements for scene understanding. TOG **33**(6), 10 (2014)
32. Silberman, N., Hoiem, D., Kohli, P., Fergus, R.: Indoor segmentation and support inference from RGBD images. In: Fitzgibbon, A., Lazebnik, S., Perona, P., Sato, Y., Schmid, C. (eds.) ECCV 2012. LNCS, vol. 7576, pp. 746–760. Springer, Heidelberg (2012). https://doi.org/10.1007/978-3-642-33715-4_54
33. Skiadopoulos, S., Koubarakis, M.: Composing cardinal direction relations. AIJ **152**(2), 143–171 (2004)
34. Song, S., Yu, F., Zeng, A., Chang, A.X., Savva, M., Funkhouser, T.: Semantic scene completion from a single depth image. arXiv preprint arXiv:1611.08974 (2016)
35. Stein, S.C., Wörgötter, F., Schoeler, M., Papon, J., Kulvicius, T.: Convexity based object partitioning for robot applications. In: ICRA 2014, pp. 3213–3220. IEEE (2014)
36. Stoyanov, T., et al.: No more heavy lifting: robotic solutions to the container unloading problem. IEEE Robot. Autom. Mag. **23**(4), 94–106 (2016)
37. Whiting, E., Ochsendorf, J., Durand, F.: Procedural modeling of structurally-sound masonry buildings. In: TOG, vol. 28, p. 112. ACM (2009)
38. Zhang, P., Renz, J.: Qualitative spatial representation and reasoning in angry birds: the extended rectangle algebra. In: KR 2014 (2014)
39. Zhang, Z.: Microsoft kinect sensor and its effect. IEEE MultiMedia **19**(2), 4–10 (2012)

Scaling-Up Reinforcement Learning

Scaling-Up Reinforcement Learning (SURL)

Trends in Reinforcement Learning Research

Ruben Glatt[1], Felipe Leno da Silva[2], Denis Steckelmacher[3],
and Patrick MacAlpine[4]

[1] Lawrence Livermore National Laboratory, USA
glatt1@llnl.gov
[2] Advanced Institute for AI, Brazil
f.leno@usp.br
[3] Vrije Universiteit Brussel, Belgium
[4] Microsoft Research, USA

Reinforcement Learning (RL) has achieved many successes in training autonomous agents to perform simple tasks over the last years. However, there are a number of major remaining challenges in RL, such as scaling it to high-dimensional, real-world applications, dealing with sample complexity, or reusing already acquired knowledge. Although many works have already focused on strategies to scale-up RL techniques and to find solutions for more complex problems with reasonable successes, many issues still exist. The second *Scaling-Up Reinforcement Learning (SURL)* workshop encouraged the discussion of diverse approaches to accelerate and generalize RL, such as the use of approximations, abstractions, hierarchical approaches, Transfer Learning, and Meta-Learning. Scaling-up RL methods has major implications on the research and practice of complex learning problems and will eventually lead to successful implementations in real-world applications. *SURL* is an effort towards bridging the gap between conventional and scalable RL approaches, providing a platform for community interaction and discussion. This workshop aims at bringing together researchers working on different approaches to scale-up RL to solve more complex or larger scale problems.

This edition of the *SURL* workshop was the second after the first one during the European Conference on Machine Learning (ECML) 2017 in Skopje. It sparked the interest of many RL researchers around the globe. With 2 invited speakers and 12 accepted high-quality contributed talks, *SURL* was the stage for discussions about opportunities and future research directions for RL research. Presenters from 3 continents shared their newest research efforts with a sizable crowd of RL enthusiasts in one of the best visited workshops of the conference.

The 2 invited speakers *Peter Stone*, from UT Austin, and *Balaraman Ravindran*, from IIT Madras, are well-known and reputed researchers who shared interesting insights on their current research.

Balaraman Ravindran talked about extending RL beyond the classical "reward-based" modeling approaches. He discussed how his group managed to enable agents to

---

solve increasingly difficult tasks through a two-level *curriculum* learning technique, and how agents can discover hierarchical structure in problems by exploiting the properties of successor representations.

Peter Stone presented his latest research on scaling-up RL to enable efficient robot skill learning. Due to the inherent restriction on performing exploration on robotic platforms, his group has been studying how to reuse knowledge gathered from simulations and human demonstrations to speed up and improve learning in this challenging domain.

Amongst the outstanding contributions (published on the workshop website), *Extending Sliding-step Importance Weighting from Supervised Learning to Reinforcement Learning* by *Tian Tian* and *Richard Sutton* was selected to represent our workshop in this special volume. Their work extends a class of elegant algorithms for importance weighting from supervised learning to the RL framework. These algorithms are much more robust in the face of highly variable importance weights in supervised learning but had not been used in RL before where importance weighting can be particularly variable due to the sampling involved in off-policy learning algorithms. The workshop chairs believe this work was well presented and covers a challenging problem in contemporary RL research. It is well therefore suited to give a taste of the insightful and creative solutions that were presented and discussed during *SURL*.

The workshop also featured many other interesting approaches from subfields including hierarchical approaches and curriculum learning, multiagent settings, multitask and subgoal challenges, and reward shaping. Experimental results were reported in applications like robotics, physics simulator, Multiplayer Online Battle Arena games, and Atari games. We highly recommend taking a look at the workshop homepage and get inspired by the great contributions.

Both the contributed and invited talks have shown that RL research has evolved far beyond the classical framework and toy problems. Varied strategies for knowledge reuse, sample-efficient learning algorithms, and smart exploration are necessary to solve the challenging domains in which RL is now applied.

Acknowledgments

We would like to thank the Artificial Intelligence Journal (AIJ) editorial board for their funding which enabled us to provide student travel grants to support the promotion and dissemination of AI research.

We also thank all unmentioned authors and presenters for their contributions: A. Remonda, S. Krebs, E. Veas, G. Luzhnica, R. Kern, Y. Deng, K. Yu, D. Lin, X. Tang, C. C. Loy, A. Ray, R. Verma, H. Khadilkar, S. Han, Y. Sung, H. Wei, K. Decker, Z. Zhang, H. Li, L. Zhang, T. Zheng, T. Zhang, X. Hao, X. Chen, M. Chen, F. Xiao, W. Zhou, A. Bassich, D. Kudenko, D. Chen, Q. Yan, S. Guo, Z. Yang, X. Su, F. Chen, H. Itaya, T. Hirakawa, T. Yamashita, H. Fujiyoshi, L. Zhang, Z. Zhang, Z. Pan, Y. Chen, J. Zhu, Z. Wang, M. Wang, C. Fan, R. Saphal, B. Ravindran, D. Mudigere, S. Avancha, and B. Kaul.

Ruben Glatt was supported by a postdoctoral fellowship at the Lawrence Livermore National Laboratory. His portion of the work was performed under the auspices of the U.S. Department of Energy by Lawrence Livermore National Laboratory under contract DE-AC52-07NA27344. Lawrence Livermore National Security, LLC. LLNL-PROC-794262. Felipe L. Silva thanks the São Paulo Research Foundation (FAPESP), grant 2015/16310-4.

Extending Sliding-Step Importance Weighting from Supervised Learning to Reinforcement Learning

Tian Tian[1]($\boxtimes$)(iD) and Richard S. Sutton[1,2]

[1] Reinforcement Learning and Artificial Intelligence, University of Alberta,
Edmonton, Canada
{ttian,rsutton}@ualberta.ca
[2] DeepMind, Edmonton, Canada

Abstract. Stochastic gradient descent (SGD) has been in the center of many advances in modern machine learning. SGD processes examples sequentially, updating a weight vector in the direction that would most reduce the loss for that example. In many applications, some examples are more important than others and, to capture this, each example is given a non-negative weight that modulates its impact. Unfortunately, if the importance weights are highly variable they can greatly exacerbate the difficulty of setting the step-size parameter of SGD. To ease this difficulty, Karampatziakis and Langford [6] developed a class of elegant algorithms that are much more robust in the face of highly variable importance weights in supervised learning. In this paper we extend their idea, which we call "sliding step", to reinforcement learning, where importance weighting can be particularly variable due to the importance *sampling* involved in off-policy learning algorithms. We compare two alternative ways of doing the extension in the linear function approximation setting, then introduce specific sliding-step versions of the TD(0) and Emphatic TD(0) learning algorithms. We prove the convergence of our algorithms and demonstrate their effectiveness on both on-policy and off-policy problems. Overall, our new algorithms appear to be effective in bringing the robustness of the sliding-step technique from supervised learning to reinforcement learning.

Keywords: Reinforcement learning · Temporal difference learning · Off-policy

1 Importance Weighting in SGD

In recent years, deep learning has dominated the field of machine learning, making advances in natural language processing, image recognition, and many other areas. At the heart of deep learning is stochastic gradient descent (SGD), which processes a series of random examples $(\boldsymbol{x}_t, y_t), t = 0, 1, 2, \ldots$ one at a time, and

2nd Scaling-Up Reinforcement Learning (SURL) Workshop, IJCAI 2019.

adjusts the weight vector $w \in \mathbb{R}^n$ in the direction that would most reduce the loss J between the target y_t and its estimate $\hat{y}(x_t; w)$:

$$w_{t+1} = w_t - \alpha \nabla J(y_t, \hat{y}(x_t; w_t)),$$

where α is the step-size parameter that controls the amount of adjustment to w in each time step t.

In many applications, some examples are more important than others. For instance, the score of a final exam is usually weighted more than midterms or quizzes. One person's consumer preference may bias towards one company more than another. Nonnegative scalars called importance weights, denoted h, are given to examples to quantify their relative importance. Importance weights appear in many machine learning algorithms, including boosting [3], covariate shift [5], active learning [1], and reinforcement learning [7,13] algorithms.

One way of incorporating importance weights into SGD is to scale the gradient by h linearly, and thus the update changes to $\alpha h \nabla J$. If α is not made sufficiently small, a large h may result in overshooting an example's target, resulting in a greater loss than before the update. This problem is illustrated in Fig. 1(a). We could use a small step-size parameter to account for updates with large importance weights, but this might make unnecessarily small updates for other examples, resulting in unreasonably slow learning.

To address this problem, Karampatziakis and Langford [6] developed a class of algorithms that are much more robust in the face of highly variable importance weights in supervised learning. Their idea, which we call "sliding step" would sub-divide w's update into k steps, each with a step-size parameter of $\alpha h/k$. In each of the k steps, we recompute the gradient and adjust the weight vector in the newly computed direction. By tending k to infinity, the step-size parameter $\alpha h/k$ becomes infinitesimal, we acquire a new class of algorithms. In Fig. 1(b), the trajectory of w_t along the loss surface can be seen to be sliding towards the optimum weight for example (x_t, y_t), giving rise to the name sliding step. Because the gradient is recomputed in each of the k steps, the gradient of the loss will tend to 0 along the k steps as the estimate tends to y_t. Thus, the estimate $\hat{y}(x_t; w_{t+1})$ will never overshoot y_t.

In this paper, we extend the sliding step idea from supervised learning to reinforcement learning, specifically, to a class of temporal difference (TD) learning algorithms. Unlike supervised learning algorithms, the target of the linear TD update is also an estimate that depends on the current value of w. We propose two new algorithms in the one-step linear function approximation setting: sliding-step TD and sliding-step Emphatic TD. We prove the convergence of sliding-step TD and demonstrate both algorithm's effectiveness on three problems: a 5-state Markov chain, a 1000-state random walk, and the off-policy "chicken problem" [4]. Our empirical results suggest our algorithms retain the robustness of the sliding-step technique from the supervised learning setting.

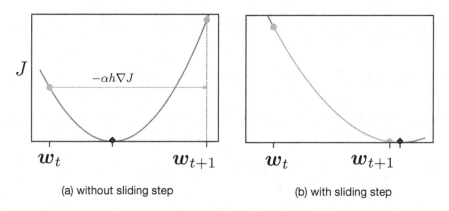

(a) without sliding step   (b) with sliding step

Fig. 1. A demonstration of the sliding-step technique on a one dimensional squared loss surface $J = \frac{1}{2}(y - \hat{y}(\boldsymbol{x}_t; \boldsymbol{w}_t))^2$. The blue diamonds indicate the optimum weight for example $(\boldsymbol{x}_t, y_t)$. (Color figure online)

2 Sliding-Step Technique in the Supervised Learning Setting

We discuss the sliding-step technique in the supervised learning setting using the linear model (i.e., $\hat{y}(\boldsymbol{x}; \boldsymbol{w}) = \boldsymbol{x}^\top \boldsymbol{w}$) and the squared loss. Recall that the sliding step idea subdivides the SGD update $\boldsymbol{w}_t + \alpha h_t(y_t - \boldsymbol{x}_t^\top \boldsymbol{w}_t)\boldsymbol{x}_t$ into k steps, where in each of the k steps, the gradient is recomputed and an intermediate update is made to the weight vector with a step-size of $\alpha h/k$. Denoting an intermediate update to $\boldsymbol{w}$ as $\tilde{\boldsymbol{w}}_i$, where the subscript corresponds to each of the k steps, we get the following procedure.

In the first step, we compute the gradient of the loss at $\boldsymbol{w}_t$, and make the first intermediate update to the weight vector with an adjustment of $\alpha h_t/k$:

$$\tilde{\boldsymbol{w}}_1 = \boldsymbol{w}_t + \frac{\alpha h_t}{k}(y_t - \boldsymbol{x}_t^\top \boldsymbol{w}_t)\boldsymbol{x}_t \tag{1}$$

In the second step, we recompute the gradient of the loss at $\tilde{\boldsymbol{w}}_1$ (i.e., $-(y_t - \boldsymbol{x}^\top \tilde{\boldsymbol{w}}_1)\boldsymbol{x}_t$), and make a second intermediate update to the weight vector along this newly computed direction with an adjustment of $\alpha h_t/k$:

$$\tilde{\boldsymbol{w}}_2 = \tilde{\boldsymbol{w}}_1 + \frac{\alpha h_t}{k}(y_t - \boldsymbol{x}_t^\top \tilde{\boldsymbol{w}}_1)\boldsymbol{x}_t \tag{2}$$

$$= \boldsymbol{w}_t + \frac{\alpha h_t}{k}(y_t - \boldsymbol{x}_t^\top \boldsymbol{w}_t)\boldsymbol{x}_t$$

$$+ \frac{\alpha h_t}{k}\left(y_t - \boldsymbol{x}_t^\top\left(\boldsymbol{w}_t + \frac{\alpha h_t}{k}(y_t - \boldsymbol{x}_t^\top \boldsymbol{w}_t)\boldsymbol{x}_t\right)\right)\boldsymbol{x}_t$$

$$= \boldsymbol{w}_t + \left(2\left(\frac{\alpha h_t}{k}\right) - \left(\frac{\alpha h_t}{k}\right)^2 \boldsymbol{x}_t^\top \boldsymbol{x}_t\right)(y_t - \boldsymbol{x}_t^\top \boldsymbol{w}_t)\boldsymbol{x}_t \tag{3}$$

To get (3), we plug (1) into $\tilde{w}_1$ of (2) and expand the recursion. After the third step, we obtain:

$$\tilde{w}_3 = w_t + \left(3\left(\frac{\alpha h_t}{k}\right) - 3\left(\frac{\alpha h_t}{k}\right)^2 x_t^\top x_t + \left(\frac{\alpha h_t}{k}\right)^3 (x_t^\top x_t)^2\right)(y_t - x_t^\top w_t)x_t.$$

After performing k intermediate weight updates and using the binomial expansion, we obtain:

$$\tilde{w}_k = w_t + \frac{1 - \left(1 - \frac{\alpha h_t}{k}x_t^\top x_t\right)^k}{x_t^\top x_t}(y_t - x_t^\top w_t)x_t \tag{4}$$

By setting $w_{t+1} = \tilde{w}_k$ and taking $k \to \infty$, we obtain:

$$w_{t+1} = w_t + \frac{1 - \exp(-\alpha h_t x_t^\top x_t))}{x_t^\top x_t}(y_t - x_t^\top w_t)x_t, \tag{5}$$

using the fact that $\lim_{k\to\infty}(1 + z/k)^k = \exp(z)$.

We could set w_{t+1} to $\tilde{w}_k$ in (4) without taking k to infinity. However, the benefit of using (5) instead of (4) is that we do not need to set a value for the k. The limit of this gradient procedure as the step-size parameter becomes infinitesimal allows us to generalize (4) to (5) with only a small additional computational cost of an exponential function.

The outcome of the sliding-step technique is the following expression replacing the step-size parameter α,

$$\frac{1 - \exp(-\alpha h x^\top x)}{x^\top x}. \tag{6}$$

By comparing (6) to:

$$\frac{\min(\alpha h x^\top x, 1)}{x^\top x}, \tag{7}$$

we see that (6) is upper bounded by (7) as illustrated in Fig. 2.

When $\alpha h \geq 1/x^\top x$, (7) truncates to $1/x^\top x$ while (6) smoothly tends to $1/x^\top x$ as αh grows. The effect of truncation bounds the size of the update to w and reduces the variance of the iterates at the expense of bias. When $\alpha h < 1/x^\top x$, (7) is αh, and we return to the original SGD update of $\alpha h \nabla J$. When αh is small, (6) will be approximately αh and the bias introduced will be small. The sliding-step expression (6) modulates the effects of importance weights.

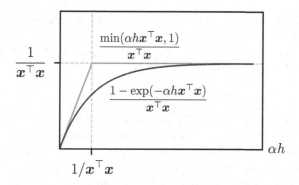

Fig. 2. Comparing the sliding-step expression $\frac{1-\exp(-\alpha h x^\top x)}{x^\top x}$ to $\frac{\min(\alpha h x^\top x, 1)}{x^\top x}$

3   Reinforcement Learning Setting

A common formalism used in reinforcement learning (RL) is the Markov decision process, which consists of a set of states $\mathcal{S}$, a set of actions $\mathcal{A}$, world probability $p : \mathcal{S} \times \mathcal{A} \times \mathcal{S} \rightarrow [0, 1]$, a set of rewards $\mathcal{R}$, and a discount factor $\gamma \in [0, 1]$. At each discrete time step t, an agent in state $S_t \in \mathcal{S}$ takes an action $A_t \in \mathcal{A}$ according to a policy $\pi : \mathcal{S} \times \mathcal{A} \rightarrow [0, 1]$. The agent then transitions from the state S_t to a new state S_{t+1} and obtains a numerical reward $R_{t+1} \in \mathcal{R} \subset \mathbb{R}$.

We are interested in making long term predictions from each $s \in \mathcal{S}$ w.r.t. the policy π:

$$v_\pi(s) \doteq \mathbb{E}_\pi[R_{t+1} + \gamma R_{t+2} + \gamma^2 R_{t+3} + \dots | S_t = s] \tag{8}$$

Temporal difference (TD) learning, a major part of RL, comprises a class of algorithms that aim to evaluate the state value (8) for each $s \in \mathcal{S}$. A key feature of TD algorithms such as TD [9] and Emphatic TD [13] is bootstrapping, where the estimate of a state value is updated based on the estimate of the value of the successor state.

There are on-policy and off-policy TD algorithms. An off-policy TD algorithm evaluates the policy π based on actions selected by a different behaviour policy, denoted μ. This results in a different state visitation distribution, and so, the frequency of the observed rewards will be different than if π were followed. We can correct this distribution mismatch via importance sampling, allowing us to compute the expectation under π. Off-policy learning algorithms such as off-policy TD [7], Emphatic TD [13] and gradient-based TD [11,12] use importance sampling ratios to correct for the mismatch in the sampling frequency. The importance sampling ratio at time step t is defined to be the ratios of the action probabilities under the two policies: $\rho_t \doteq \pi(A_t|S_t)/\mu(A_t|S_t)$, where $\mu(a|s) > 0$ for each state and action for which $\pi(a|s) > 0$. If the two policies are the same (i.e. $\rho = 1$ for all state and action pairs), then we return to the on-policy case.

For non-tabular settings where an agent only has access to a state's feature vector $x(s) \in \mathbb{R}^n$, a state value is represented by a function of the state's features, parameterized by $w \in \mathbb{R}^n$. We shall use $x(S_t)$ and x_t interchangeably throughout the rest of the paper.

If we have the values of v_π, then we can employ SGD in the supervised learning setting to update the weight vector:

$$w_{t+1} = w_t + \alpha(v_\pi(S_t) - x_t^\top w_t)x_t, \tag{9}$$

where $x_t^\top w_t$ is the linear function approximation of $v_\pi(S_t)$

The goal is to compute v_π, and we do not have access to this function. We can construct the one-step bootstrapping target $R_{t+1} + x_{t+1}^\top w_t$ in each time step since the reward and the feature vector of the next state are available. By replacing $v_\pi(S_t)$ in (9) with the one-step bootstrapping target, we obtain linear TD(0):

$$w_{t+1} = w_t + \alpha \underbrace{(R_{t+1} + \gamma x_{t+1}^\top w_t - x_t^\top w_t)}_{\text{TD error: } \delta_t} x_t, \tag{10}$$

Linear Emphatic TD(0) [13] is defined by the following stochastic update to the weight vector,

$$w_{t+1} = w_t + \alpha F_t \rho_t \delta_t x(S_t)$$
$$\text{where } F_t = \gamma \rho_{t-1} F_{t-1} + i(S_t) \text{ and } F_0 = 1 \tag{11}$$

In the one-step case, $F \in [0, \infty]$ is the emphasis, which emphasizes a state value's update based on the interest expressed for that state. An interest expressed for a state is defined as the function $i : S \rightarrow [0, \infty)$. Expressing high interest for a state will shift the accuracy of the estimate towards that state. Because F_t can take on large values due to interest and importance sampling ratios in the off-policy setting, one update to w can result in a large change if α is not made sufficiently small. This motivates the need for a way to robustly account for importance weights, especially in linear Emphatic TD(0). For the remainder of this paper, we omit writing the (0) in the following algorithms as we restrict ourselves to the one-step case.

4   Extending the Sliding Step Idea to Reinforcement Learning

We compare two ways of doing the extension in reinforcement learning, and then introduce specific sliding-step versions of (10) and (11).

At first glance, the extension seems almost straightforward. However, the target of the TD error in (10) and (11) both depend on the current value of weight vector w_t. Contrary to supervised learning, we have two ways to update the intermediate weights:

1. semi-gradient: considers only the effect of changing w_t on the prediction while ignoring the effect on the target.
2. full-gradient: considers the effect of changing w_t on both the target and prediction.

4.1   The Sliding-Step TD Algorithm

Following the sliding-step procedure outlined in Sect. 2, we apply the semi-gradient approach to the update $\delta_t \boldsymbol{x}_t$ in (10) by keeping the target constant for each of the k steps, but allow the weight vector in the prediction to change (boxed below):

$$\tilde{\boldsymbol{w}}_1 = \boldsymbol{w}_t + \frac{\alpha}{k}(R_{t+1} + \gamma \boldsymbol{x}_{t+1}^\top \boldsymbol{w}_t - \boldsymbol{x}_t^\top \boldsymbol{w}_t)\boldsymbol{x}_t$$

$$\tilde{\boldsymbol{w}}_2 = \tilde{\boldsymbol{w}}_1 + \frac{\alpha}{k}(R_{t+1} + \gamma \boldsymbol{x}_{t+1}^\top \boldsymbol{w}_t - \boxed{\boldsymbol{x}_t^\top \tilde{\boldsymbol{w}}_1})\boldsymbol{x}_t$$

$$= \boldsymbol{w}_t + \left(2\left(\frac{\alpha}{k}\right) - \left(\frac{\alpha}{k}\right)^2 \boldsymbol{x}_t^\top \boldsymbol{x}_t\right)\delta_t \boldsymbol{x}_t$$

$$\cdots$$

$$\tilde{\boldsymbol{w}}_k = \boldsymbol{w}_t + \frac{1 - \left(1 - \frac{\alpha}{k}\boldsymbol{x}_t^\top \boldsymbol{x}_t\right)^k}{\boldsymbol{x}_t^\top \boldsymbol{x}_t}\delta_t \boldsymbol{x}_t.$$

By taking $k \to \infty$, we obtain sliding-step TD:

$$\boldsymbol{w}_{t+1} = \boldsymbol{w}_t + \frac{1 - \exp(-\alpha \boldsymbol{x}_t^\top \boldsymbol{x}_t)}{\boldsymbol{x}_t^\top \boldsymbol{x}_t}\delta_t \boldsymbol{x}_t. \tag{12}$$

4.2   The Sliding-Step Emphatic TD Algorithm

Following similar steps in 4.1, we apply the semi-gradient approach to the update $F_t \rho_t \delta_t \boldsymbol{x}_t$ in (11) and obtain the sliding-step Emphatic TD algorithm:

$$\boldsymbol{w}_{t+1} = \boldsymbol{w}_t + \frac{1 - \exp(-\alpha F_t \rho_t \boldsymbol{x}_t^\top \boldsymbol{x}_t)}{\boldsymbol{x}_t^\top \boldsymbol{x}_t}\delta_t \boldsymbol{x}_t$$

$$\text{where} \quad F_t = \gamma \rho_{t-1} F_{t-1} + i(S_t) \quad \text{and} \quad F_0 = 1. \tag{13}$$

4.3   Issues with Full-Gradient Approach to TD

There are some issues with applying the full-gradient approach to TD. Applying the full-gradient approach to TD entails substituting the intermediate weights into both the target and prediction at each of the k steps (boxed below):

$$\tilde{\boldsymbol{w}}_1 = \boldsymbol{w}_t + \frac{\alpha}{k}(R_{t+1} + \boldsymbol{x}_{t+1}^\top \boldsymbol{w}_t - \boldsymbol{x}_t^\top \boldsymbol{w}_t)\boldsymbol{x}_t$$

$$\tilde{\boldsymbol{w}}_2 = \tilde{\boldsymbol{w}}_1 + \frac{\alpha}{k}(R_{t+1} + \boxed{\boldsymbol{x}_{t+1}^\top \tilde{\boldsymbol{w}}_1} - \boxed{\boldsymbol{x}_t^\top \tilde{\boldsymbol{w}}_1})\boldsymbol{x}_t.$$

After k steps and by taking $k \to \infty$, we obtain the following variant:

$$\boldsymbol{w}_{t+1} = \boldsymbol{w}_t + \frac{1 - \exp(-\alpha(\boldsymbol{x}_t - \gamma \boldsymbol{x}_{t+1})^\top \boldsymbol{x}_t)}{(\boldsymbol{x}_t - \gamma \boldsymbol{x}_{t+1})^\top \boldsymbol{x}_t}\delta_t \boldsymbol{x}_t. \tag{14}$$

Given $\boldsymbol{x}_t$ and $\boldsymbol{x}_{t+1}$ and let $c = (\boldsymbol{x}_t - \gamma \boldsymbol{x}_{t+1})^\top \boldsymbol{x}_t$, the expression $(1 - \exp(-\alpha c))/c$ is a function of $\alpha \in [0, \infty)$. For various values of c,

$$c = 0, \qquad \frac{1 - \exp(-\alpha c)}{c} \text{ is undefined}$$

$$c > 0, \qquad 0 < \frac{1 - \exp(-\alpha c)}{c} \leq \frac{1}{c}$$

$$c < 0, \qquad \frac{1 - \exp(-\alpha c)}{c} \geq \alpha$$

If c is negative, the expression is greater than α and grows exponentially, recreating the original issue of making large updates. Because c can be 0 or negative, we do not consider the variant (14) in our experiments.

5   Convergence of Tabular Sliding-Step TD with Probability 1

We prove the convergence of on-policy sliding-step TD in the tabular setting using an existing proof by Tsitsiklis [14]. In the tabular setting, the agent has access to the states rather than the feature vectors of the states. Let $V_t \in \mathbb{R}^{|\mathcal{S}|}$ denote a vector of state values of a size equal to the cardinality of state space $\mathcal{S}$. Then, each component $V_t(s), s \in \mathcal{S}$ is updated independently and asynchronously according to:

$$V_{t+1}(s) = V_t(s) + \frac{1 - \exp(-\alpha_t(s)\kappa_s)}{\kappa_s}\left(R_{t+1} + \gamma V_t(s') - V_t(s)\right), \qquad (15)$$

where s' denotes the next state and R_{t+1} is the immediate reward obtained after one state transition. The random sequence of step-size parameters $\alpha_t(s)$, one for each $s \in \mathcal{S}$, satisfies the usual step-size conditions of Robbins and Monro [8]. Algorithm (15) defines the value update for state s for time step $t = 1, 2, \ldots$. If state s is not observed at t, then $\alpha_t(s) = 0$ and no update is made to the value of state s. If state s is observed at t, then the value of state s changes while all other state values remain unchanged, similar to tabular TD. We define $\kappa_s : \mathcal{S} \to [0, \infty)$ to be analogous to $\boldsymbol{x}(s)^\top \boldsymbol{x}(s)$ of the linear sliding-step TD (12). It can be a user defined function that only depends on state s because (15) pertains to the update of value for state s.

Theorem 1. *$V_t(s)$ defined by the update rule (15) converges to $v_\pi(s)$ with probability 1 for all $s \in \mathcal{S}$ in the case of*

1. $\gamma < 1$ or
2. $\gamma = 1$, and the policy π is a proper stationary policy

under the condition that $\alpha_t(s)$ is $\mathcal{F}(t)$-measurable (i.e., $\alpha_t(s)$ is a random variable completely determined by the history: $V_0, S_0, \alpha_0(S_0), R_1, \ldots, S_t$) and satisfies *the step-size conditions [8]:*

$$\sum_{t=0}^{\infty} \alpha_t(s) = \infty, \qquad \sum_{t=0}^{\infty} \alpha_t^2(s) < \infty \quad w.p. \ 1 \tag{16}$$

Note: $(\alpha_t(s))$ is a separate sequence for each state $s \in \mathcal{S}$.

Proof. For each state $s \in \mathcal{S}$, we show the random sequence $((1 - \exp(-\alpha_t(s)\kappa_s))/\kappa_s)_{t \geq 0}$ also satisfy the step-size conditions. Then the rest follows from Tsitsiklis [14].

Let $X_n = \sum_{t=0}^{n} 1 - \exp(-\alpha_t(s)\kappa_s)$. Since the sequence $(X_n)_{n \geq 0}$ is monotonically increasing, the limit of X_n exists. To show that the limit of X_n is equal to infinity, we use $\exp(-x) \leq 1 + x^2 - x$ for $x \in [0, \infty)$:

$$1 - \exp(-\kappa_s\alpha_t(s)) \geq \kappa_s\alpha_t(s) - \kappa_s^2\alpha_t^2(s),$$

$$\sum_{t=0}^{n} 1 - \exp(-\alpha_t(s)\kappa_s) \geq \kappa_s \sum_{t=0}^{n} \alpha_t(s) - \kappa_s^2 \sum_{t=0}^{n} \alpha_t^2(s).$$

Taking the limit of the partial sum,

$$\lim_{n \to \infty} X_n \geq \kappa_s \lim_{n \to \infty} \sum_{t=0}^{n} \alpha_t(s) - \kappa_s^2 \lim_{n \to \infty} \sum_{t=0}^{n} \alpha_t^2(s) = \infty.$$

Let $Y_n = \sum_{t=0}^{n}(1 - \exp(-\kappa_s\alpha_t(s)))^2$. Since the sequence $(Y_n)_{n \geq 0}$ is monotonically increasing, the limit of Y_n exists. To show that the limit of Y_n is finite, we use $\exp(-x) \geq 1 - x$ for $x \in [0, \infty)$:

$$(1 - \exp(-\kappa_s\alpha_t(s)))^2 \leq (\kappa_s\alpha_t(s))^2$$

$$\sum_{t=0}^{n}(1 - \exp(-\kappa_s\alpha_t(s)))^2 \leq \kappa_s^2 \sum_{t=0}^{n} \alpha_t^2(s).$$

The limit of the partial sum Y_n is finite:

$$\lim_{n \to \infty} Y_n \leq \lim_{n \to \infty} \kappa_s^2 \sum_{t=0}^{n} \alpha_t^2(s) < \infty.$$

Since κ_s is a constant given a state, so is $1/\kappa_s$, and the scaled sequence $((1 - \exp(-\alpha_t(s)\kappa_s))/\kappa_s)$ is also a sequence of step-size parameters that satisfy (16) for each $s \in \mathcal{S}$.

6   Convergence Result of Linear Sliding-Step TD

If the feature vectors are all of the same magnitude, the on-policy sliding-step TD in the linear function approximation setting (12) converges to the fixed point of linear TD defined by (10) with probability 1. We replace the constant α of (12) with α_t (e.g., $\alpha_t = 1/t, t = 1, 2, \ldots$) and let $\boldsymbol{x}(s)^\top \boldsymbol{x}(s) = C$ for all $s \in \mathcal{S}$, then $(1 - \exp(-\alpha_t C)))/C$ is a sequence that satisfy the step-size conditions by similar arguments made in the proof of Theorem 1. Thus, sliding-step TD is linear TD with a special step-size of form $(1 - \exp(-\alpha_t C))/C$, and (12) converges to the fixed point of linear TD following from the results from Tsitsiklis and Van Roy [15]. Some examples of feature vectors that have the same magnitude include the basis unit vectors and normalized feature vectors (i.e., $\boldsymbol{x}(s)/\sqrt{\boldsymbol{x}(s)^\top \boldsymbol{x}(s)}$ for all $s \in \mathcal{S}$).

In general, the behaviour of sliding-step TD depends on the choice of α. When α is small, the expression $(1 - \exp(-\alpha \boldsymbol{x}(s)^\top \boldsymbol{x}(s)))/\boldsymbol{x}(s)^\top \boldsymbol{x}(s)$ is approximately α, and sliding-step TD should behave similarly to linear TD. For an α that is not sufficiently small, the expression $(1 - \exp(-\alpha \boldsymbol{x}(s)^\top \boldsymbol{x}(s)))/\boldsymbol{x}(s)^\top \boldsymbol{x}(s)$ is a different constant in $[0, \infty)$ for different feature vectors $\boldsymbol{x}$. Although the direction of the update is determined by $\delta_t \boldsymbol{x}_t$, same as TD, the iterate $\boldsymbol{w}_t$ of sliding-step TD are not averaged the same way as TD. We demonstrate the effect of α by the following two-state Markov chain experiment:

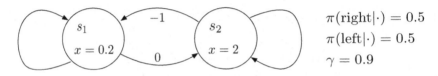

$\pi(\text{right}|\cdot) = 0.5$
$\pi(\text{left}|\cdot) = 0.5$
$\gamma = 0.9$

Fig. 3. The probability of taking the left or right action is 0.5. Taking the left action in any state results in a reward of -1 and taking the right action in any state results in a reward of 0.

Since we are interested in how well $\boldsymbol{x}^\top \boldsymbol{w}$ approximate v_π, we use the root-mean-squared value error:

$$\text{RMSVE}(\boldsymbol{w}) = \sqrt{\sum_{s \in \mathcal{S}} d_\pi(s) \left(v_\pi(s) - \boldsymbol{x}^\top \boldsymbol{w} \right)^2} \tag{17}$$

as a measure of the performance of the algorithms. The policy π induces a Markov chain whose steady-state distribution d_π weighs the squared error term in (17). In this example, we can compute d_π and v_π exactly.

Given that both states are represented by scalar values, the feature matrix is of rank 1, smaller than the number of states. Thus, the true state values cannot be represented exactly. Given that we know the world probability and the policy, we can compute the fixed point of TD exactly to be -0.59, which produces a RMSVE of 4.38. This matches our observation for TD in Fig. 4(a) for optimal $\alpha = 0.256$. However, the RMSVE of sliding-step TD with optimal $\alpha = 2.048$ fluctuated around 3.9 instead, which is statistically lower than 4.38. As α decreases (e.g., $\alpha = 0.128$), we saw the performance of sliding-step TD matching that of the TD as seen in Fig. 4(b), as expected.

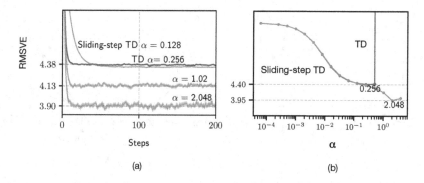

Fig. 4. Illustration of the fixed point of TD and sliding-step TD. Learning curve (a) shows the RMSVE as a function of w_t plotted against steps t for various α's. Sensitivity graph (b) shows the optimal α to be 0.256 for TD and 2.048 for sliding-step TD. The α is searched in powers of 2. The RMSVE for the learning curves are averaged over 500 runs. The RMSVE for the sensitivity graphs are averages of 200 steps and then averaged over the 500 runs. All figures in this section include error bars for standard error, but they are smaller than the line width in display.

7   Experiments

We examine the performance of sliding-step TD and sliding-step Emphatic TD with different feature representations and step-size parameter settings. We focus on three problems to allow straight forward study of the algorithms. Particularly, we are interested in the accuracy of the learned estimates, as well as the rate of learning in each evaluation. To measure how well the state value estimates approximate v_π, we use the RMSVE as a performance measure. All figures in this section include error bars for standard error, but they are smaller than the line width in display.

7.1   Five-State Markov Chain

In this on-policy experiment, we test sliding-step TD with various feature representations with varying magnitude in the feature vectors (i.e., $x^\top x$). This experiment has five states, and the state transitions and rewards are illustrated in Fig. 5. The setting of this experiment is similar to the setup in Bradtke and Barto [2] with $\gamma = 0.9$. However, the rewards consist of both positive and negative values covering a larger range of values.

Of note, the rank of matrices X_1 and X_2 equals the number of states, while the rank of matrices X_3 and X_4 is less than the number of states. In X_3 and X_4, linear functions would not represent all of the state values exactly. The magnitude of the feature vectors of matrices X_1 and X_4 are roughly the same but large, while that of matrices X_2 and X_3 vary considerably. We ran each experiment for 100,000 steps, and results are averaged over 50 independent runs.

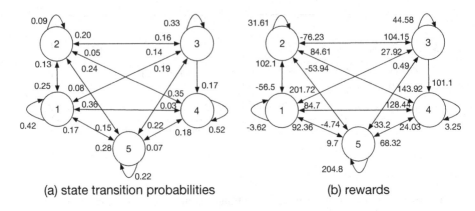

Fig. 5. The state transitions and rewards of the five-state Markov chain.

$$
\begin{bmatrix}
-160.59 & -117.66 & 80.84 & -158.6 & 61.56 \\
177.58 & 210.62 & -128.85 & -29.88 & 54.83 \\
-55.58 & -86.12 & -24.54 & 149.71 & -75.27 \\
46.78 & -96.32 & 78.13 & -8.75 & -122.62 \\
-92.71 & 33.7 & -31.62 & 1.8 & -115.98
\end{bmatrix}
\quad
\begin{bmatrix}
0.31 & 18.51 & 1.22 \\
-1.91 & -2.51 & 2.21 \\
-0.16 & 7.3 & 3.07 \\
0.04 & 8.6 & 0.04 \\
0.55 & 33.84 & 1.54
\end{bmatrix}
$$
$$X_1 \qquad\qquad X_3$$

$$
\begin{bmatrix}
0.31 & 1.55 & 18.51 & -0.6 & 1.22 \\
-1.91 & 1.77 & -2.51 & 0.71 & 2.21 \\
-0.16 & 0.23 & 7.3 & -1.04 & 3.07 \\
0.04 & 1.95 & 8.6 & 0.23 & 0.04 \\
0.55 & 0.46 & 33.84 & -1.18 & 1.54
\end{bmatrix}
\quad
\begin{bmatrix}
-160.59 & 80.84 & 61.56 \\
177.58 & -128.85 & 54.83 \\
-55.58 & -24.54 & -75.27 \\
46.78 & 78.13 & -122.62 \\
-92.71 & -31.62 & -115.98
\end{bmatrix}
$$
$$X_2 \qquad\qquad X_4$$

Fig. 6. Four different feature representations of the five-state Markov chain, each chosen to represent different broad scenarios. Each row of the feature matrix is a feature vector of a state.

Discussion: With various feature representations of varying magnitude, we observed evidence of robustness in sliding-step TD w.r.t α in Fig. 7. As a bonus, we observed a speedup in sliding-step TD when the magnitude of the feature vectors varied significantly. This is observed in Fig. 7(i–l) for feature matrices X_2 and X_3. In the case when the magnitude of the feature vectors is all large, sliding-step TD still needs a small α so not to diverge. With small α's, we found no statistically significant speedup in sliding-step TD, which is consistent with the analysis in Sect. 6.

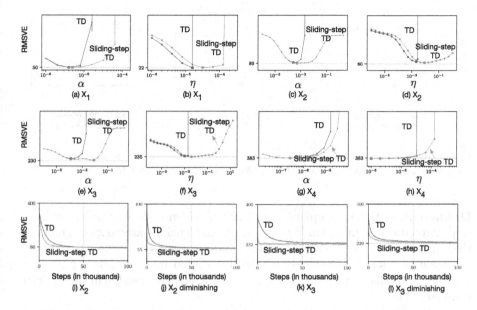

Fig. 7. Five-state Markov chain: sensitivity graphs (a, c, e, g) are shown w.r.t. constant α. Sensitivity graphs (b, d, f, h) are optimized for τ and shown w.r.t. η of diminishing $a(t) = \frac{\eta}{1+t/\tau}$. Learning curve (i, k) are shown with optimized constant α while (j,l) are shown with optimized η, τ for the diminishing case. The RMSVE of the learning curves are averaged over 50 runs. The RMSVE of the sensitivity graphs are averages of 100 thousand steps and then averaged over 50 runs. All figures include error bars.

7.2   1000-State Random Walk

In this on-policy experiment, we test sliding-step Emphatic TD (13) in the presence of large importance weights. The original experiment [10] consists of states numbered 1 through 1000, with terminal states to the left of state 1 and the right of state 1000. The agent starts in state 500 and takes the left or right action with equal probability. Once committed to an action, the agent transitions to one of its 100 neighbours with equal probability. The rewards are all 0 except −1 when reaching the left terminal state and +1 when reaching the right terminal state. We looked at two instances of the problem with transitions to 50 neighbours and 20 neighbours, varying the lengths of the random walk. Treating it as an undiscounted task with an interest of 1 for each state, longer episodes will result in larger emphasis.

We consider two feature representations: tile coding and Fourier basis [10]. For tile coding, there are 50 tilings, where each tiling is offset by four states. Every 100 states are tiled together. We run each experiment for 5000 episodes and then repeat for 30 independent runs.

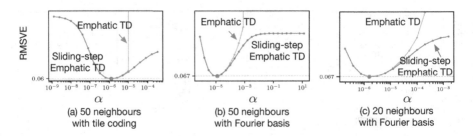

Fig. 8. 1000-state random walk: RMSVE of the sensitivity graphs are averages of 5000 episodes and then averaged over 30 runs. All figures include error bars.

Discussion: With large emphasis, we observed evidence of robustness in sliding-step Emphatic TD w.r.t. α in Fig. 8. Going from 50 neighbours to 20 neighbours, the emphasis on average increases. In response to the larger value in emphasis, the optimal α for sliding-step Emphatic TD shifted from an order of 10^{-5} to 10^{-6}. With small α's, we found no statistically significant speedup in sliding-step Emphatic TD.

7.3   The Chicken Problem

In this off-policy experiment of Ghiassian *et al.* [4], we test sliding-step Emphatic TD in the off-policy setting. This experiment consists of 8 states with 1 terminal state, and the agent starts in the first four states with equal probability. If the agent is within the first four states, then the behaviour and target policies are the same, and the agent goes forward. If the agent has passed the first four states, the behaviour policy chooses to go forward or go back to the first four states with equal probability. The target policy, however, will always choose to

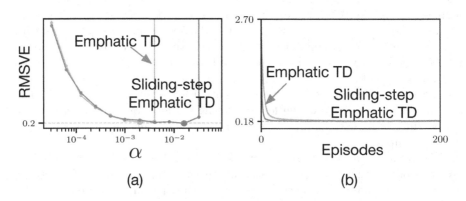

Fig. 9. Chicken problem: learning curve is shown with optimized α. The RMSVE of the learning curve is averaged over 100 runs. The RMSVE of the sensitivity graph is averages of the 500 episodes and then averaged over 100 runs. All figures include error bars.

go forward. If the agent goes forward and makes it to the terminal state, then it receives a reward of 1 and terminates. All other rewards are 0, and a discount rate of $\gamma = 0.9$ was used.

We ran each experiment for 5000 episodes, and the results are averaged over 100 independent runs. For each run, we randomly generated a new set of feature vectors to represent the eight states. Each feature vector is $\{0, 1\}^6$. To maintain a feature matrix of rank 6, no feature vectors are all zeros.

Discussion: In the off-policy setting, we observed evidence of robustness in sliding-step Emphatic TD w.r.t. α in Fig. 9. Each with their optimized α, sliding-step Emphatic TD learned slightly faster than Emphatic TD as evident in Fig. 9(b).

8   Conclusion

We have shown multiple generalizations of the sliding-step idea to temporal difference learning and derived a class of sliding-step TD algorithms: sliding-step TD and sliding-step Emphatic TD.

Sliding-step TD is similar in form to TD, but differs in the expression $(1 - \exp(-\alpha x^\top x))/x^\top x$ replacing the usual step-size parameter α:

$$\text{Sliding-step TD:} \qquad w_{t+1} = w_t + \frac{1 - \exp(-\alpha x_t^\top x_t)}{x_t^\top x_t} \delta_t x_t$$

$$\text{TD:} \qquad w_{t+1} = w_t + \alpha \delta_t x_t$$

We prove that the tabular sliding-step TD in the on-policy setting converges with probability 1. We also showed that for the linear case, if the feature vectors are all of the same magnitudes, sliding-step TD is TD with a special step-size expression and converges to the fixed point of TD with probability 1. For the general case where the magnitude of the feature vectors is not the same, we found that the behaviour of sliding-step TD depends on the choice of α.

We give substantial evidence for the robustness of sliding-step TD methods in several experiments with multiple representations and an off-policy example with sliding-step Emphatic TD. In the experiment when the magnitude of the feature vectors varied significantly, we observed a speedup in sliding-step TD. A possible explanation for this speedup could be due to sliding-step's step-size expression bounding the size of the update made to the weight vector.

References

1. Beygelzimer, A., Dasgupta, S., Langford, J.: Importance weighted active learning. In: Proceedings of the 26th International Conference on Machine Learning (ICML), pp. 49–56 (2009)
2. Bradtke, S.J., Barto, A.G.: Linear least-squares algorithms for temporal difference learning. Mach. Learn. **22**, 33–57 (1996)

3. Freund, Y., Schapire, R.E.A.: A decision-theoretic generalization of on-line learning and an application to boosting. J. Comput. Syst. Sci. **55**, 119–139 (1995)
4. Ghiassian, S., Patterson, A., White, M., Sutton, S. R., White, A.: Online off-policy prediction. ArXiv:1811.02597 (2018)
5. Huang, J., Alexander, J.S., Arthur, G., Karsten, M.B., Bernhard, S.: Correcting sample selection bias by unlabeled data. Adv. Neural Inf. Process. Syst. **19**, 601–608 (2006)
6. Karampatziakis, N., Langford, J.: Online importance weight aware updates. In: Proceedings of the 27th Conference on Uncertainty in Artificial Intelligence (UAI), pp. 392–399 (2011)
7. Precup, D., Sutton, R.S., Dasgupta, S.: Off-Policy temporal-difference learning with function approximation. In: Proceedings of the 18th International Conference on Machine Learning (ICML), pp. 417–424 (2001)
8. Robbins, H., Monro, S.: A stochastic approximation method. Ann. Math. Stat. **22**, 400–407 (1951)
9. Sutton, R.S.: Learning to predict by the methods of temporal differences. Mach. Learn. **3**(1), 9–44 (1988)
10. Sutton, R.S., Barto, A.G.: Reinforcement Learning: An Introduction. MIT Press, Cambridge (1998)
11. Sutton, R.S., et al.: Fast gradient-descent methods for temporal-difference learning with linear function approximation. In: Proceedings of the 26th Annual International Conference on Machine Learning (ICML), pp. 993–1000 (2009)
12. Sutton, R.S., Maei, H.R., Szepesvári, C.: A convergent O(n) temporal-difference algorithm for off-policy learning with linear function approximation. In: Advances in Neural Information Processing Systems 21 (NIPS), pp. 1609–1616 (2008)
13. Sutton, R.S., Mahmood, R.A., White, M.: An emphatic approach to the problem of off-policy temporal-difference learning. J. Mach. Learn. Res. **17**(73), 1–29 (2016)
14. Tsitsiklis, J.N.: Asynchronous stochastic approximation and Q-Learning. Mach. Learn. **16**(3), 185–202 (1994)
15. Tsitsiklis, J.N., Van Roy, B.: An analysis of temporal-difference learning with function approximation. IEEE Trans. Automatic Control **42**(5), 674–690 (1997)

Bringing Semantic Knowledge into
Vision and Text Understanding

Bringing Semantic Knowledge into Vision and Text Understanding

Sheng Li[1], Yaliang Li[2], Jing Gao[3], and Yun Fu[4]

[1] University of Georgia, Athens, GA, USA
sheng.li@uga.edu
[2] Alibaba Group, Bellevue, WA, USA
yaliang.li@alibaba-inc.com
[3] University at Buffalo, Buffalo, NY, USA
jing@buffalo.edu
[4] Northeastern University, Boston, MA, USA
yunfu@ece.neu.edu

The First International Workshop on Bringing Semantic Knowledge into Vision and Text Understanding, in conjunction with IJCAI 2019 in Macao, China, provides a forum for researchers to review the recent progress of vision and text understanding, with an emphasis on novel approaches that involve a deeper and better semantic understanding of vision and text data. The workshop received a number of high-quality submissions in the formats of long papers (up to 7 pages), short papers (up to 4 pages) and demo papers (up to 4 pages). Finally, we accepted 6 submissions as long papers, 2 submissions as short papers, and 1 submission as demo paper. Besides, we have also arranged two invited talks that attracted many audiences.

Generally speaking, extracting and understanding the high-level semantic information in vision and text data is considered as one of the key capabilities of effective artificial intelligence (AI) systems, which has been explored in many areas of AI, including computer vision, natural language processing, machine learning, data mining, knowledge representation, etc. Due to the success of deep representation learning, we have observed increasing research efforts in the intersection between vision and language for a better understanding of semantics, such as image captioning, visual question answering, etc. Besides, exploiting external semantic knowledge (e.g., semantic relations, knowledge graphs) for vision and text understanding also deserves more attention: The vast amount of external semantic knowledge could assist in having a "deeper" understanding of vision and/or text data, e.g., describing the contents of images in a more natural way, constructing a comprehensive knowledge graph for movies, building a dialog system equipped with commonsense knowledge, etc.

Among the accepted papers, five papers focus on vision understanding with semantic knowledge. John and Mita exploited deep features for vehicle semantic understanding in their paper *Vehicle Semantic Understanding for Automated Driving in Multiple Lane Urban Roads using Deep Vision-based Features*. The proposed method leverages both image-based features and a rule-based system. Tang studied *Pedestrian Detection via Combined Cascades*, and this new method obtains a good balance between accuracy and speed. Weng presented innovative ideas based on the Universal

Turing Machines (UTM) in his paper *Meanings of "Data" and "Rules" Emerge as Actions through Auto-Programming for General Purposes*. This work breaks the artificial barrier between "rules" and "data" in the UTM. Hu and Wang proposed a novel adversarial inference model for video prediction in their paper *Conformal-Cycle-Consistent Adversarial Model for Video Prediction with Action Control*. This paper is selected as the best paper of our workshop. Moreover, Sun *et al.* presented a *System Demo for Transfer Learning across Vision and Text using Domain Specific CNN Accelerator for On-Device NLP Applications*, which attracted a lot of attention from the audience.

The other four accepted papers study how to utilize various external information or knowledge to enhance the text semantic understanding. To be more specific, Shen *et al.* incorporated dependency information into the entity relation classifier to gain a better understanding of medical texts, as described in their paper *Discovering Medical Entity Relations from Texts using Dependency Information*. In the paper *Automatic Query Correction for POI Retrieval using Deep and Statistical Collaborative Model*, Zhu *et al.* combined deep learning methods to strengthen the representation ability of the statistical method Hidden Markov Model, and the proposed method achieves better performance on automatic query text correction. In the paper *Transfer Learning with Domain-aware Attention Network for Item Recommendation in E-commerce*, Qiu *et al.* proposed a new adversarial regularizer to learn domain invariant and domain-specific features via attention networks for item recommendation in e-commerce. In the paper *Compressive Multi-document Summarization with Sense-level Concepts*, Shen *et al.* investigated a compressive multi-document summarization model which integrates the sense-level concepts of words and entities.

The workshop attracted a broad audience of students, researchers and practitioners in computer vision, natural language processing, machine learning, and data mining. Many inspiring ideas were discussed during the workshop, as well as potential research directions, such as knowledge-guided explainable learning for text and vision understanding.

Generative Adversarial Networks for Video Prediction with Action Control

Zhihang Hu and Jason T. L. Wang[(✉)]

New Jersey Institute of Technology, Newark, NJ 07102, USA
{zh245,wangj}@njit.edu

Abstract. The ability of predicting future frames in video sequences, known as video prediction, is an appealing yet challenging task in computer vision. This task requires an in-depth representation of video sequences and a deep understanding of real-word causal rules. Existing approaches for tackling the video prediction problem can be classified into two categories: deterministic and stochastic methods. Deterministic methods lack the ability of generating possible future frames and often yield blurry predictions. On the other hand, although current stochastic approaches can predict possible future frames, their models lack the ability of action control in the sense that they cannot generate the desired future frames conditioned on a specific action. In this paper, we propose new generative adversarial networks (GANs) for stochastic video prediction. Our framework, called VPGAN, employs an adversarial inference model and a cycle-consistency loss function to empower the framework to obtain more accurate predictions. In addition, we incorporate a conformal mapping network structure into VPGAN to enable action control for generating desirable future frames. In this way, VPGAN is able to produce fake videos of an object moving along a specific direction. Experimental results show that a combination of VPGAN and pre-trained image segmentation models outperforms existing stochastic video prediction methods.

Keywords: Video prediction · Deep learning · Cycle-consistency

1 Introduction

Acquiring an in-depth understanding of videos has been a cornerstone problem in computer vision. This problem has been studied by various researchers from different perspectives, among which video prediction has attracted much attention. Video prediction aims to generate the pixels of future frames given a sequence of context frames [20,23]. This task finds many applications ranging from autonomous driving, robotic planning, to object tracking. In practice, unlabeled video sequences can be gathered autonomously from a sensor or recording device. A machine capable of predicting future events using these video sequences in an unsupervised manner will have gained extensive and deep knowledge about its physical environment and surroundings [2,19].

© Springer Nature Switzerland AG 2020
A. El Fallah Seghrouchni and D. Sarne (Eds.): IJCAI 2019 Workshops, LNAI 12158, pp. 87–105, 2020.
https://doi.org/10.1007/978-3-030-56150-5_5

However, despite its appealing prospects, accurate video prediction remains an open problem. The major challenge is the inherent uncertainty in the dynamics of the world [7]. A typical example is that the future trajectory of a ball hitting the ground is inherently random. Deterministic methods [23,25,30] are unable to handle this inherent uncertainty. Furthermore, the improper loss functions adopted in many of the deterministic methods often result in blurry predictions.

With the advent of models such as generative adversarial networks (GANs) [12] and variational auto-encoders (VAEs) [24], the quality of prediction results has been improved. Furthermore, stochastic methods based on these models are able to generate multiple future frames using some randomly sampled noise [2,7,19]. However, the adversarial loss functions in GANs tend to be difficult to tune, and these networks suffer from the mode collapse problem, i.e., they select a few prominent modes without being able to adequately cover the space of possible predictions [2,19]. Moreover, the stochastic methods lack the understanding and control of latent-variable space, rendering action control impossible. Hence, they are unable to generate desirable future frames.

To tackle these problems, we present in this paper a new GAN-based framework, named VPGAN, for stochastic video prediction. The main contributions of our work include the following:

- We introduce a new adversarial inference model designed for stochastic video prediction and incorporate a novel cycle-consistency loss into the model to better learn actions that take place in video sequences for enhancing the quality of predicted frames.
- We incorporate a conformal mapping [1] network structure into our VPGAN framework to enable action control for generating desirable future frames.
- We combine pre-trained image segmentation models [3,26] with our VPGAN framework to exploit their effectiveness in image understanding. Having more semantic understanding of the frames in video sequences would enable VPGAN to generate more accurate predictions.

To the best of our knowledge, this is the first work to incorporate action control into the video prediction task so as to generate specific future frames. In addition, the combination of our VPGAN framework and the pre-trained image segmentation models outperforms existing stochastic video prediction methods as shown in our experimental results reported in the paper.

2   Related Work

A wide range of deterministic methods for video prediction have been developed in the past. Many of these methods worked by generating future frames from the latent states of a deep learning model such as recurrent neural networks (RNNs) [22] and convolutional long short-term memory networks (ConvLSTMs) [28]. Ranzato et al. [25] designed an RNN-like network for natural language processing, which was able to predict future frames in a discrete space of patch clusters. Srivastava et al. [30] applied long short-term memory (LSTM) networks to capture long-term pixel dynamics of videos. Oh et al. [23] adapted an encoder-decoder model to encode action movement into the encoder and generate frames conditioned on the action movement. All these deterministic methods suffered from the inherently blurry predictions obtained from the standard mean squared error (MSE) loss function.

Mathieu et al. [20] developed a stochastic GAN-based model for video prediction. This model used an adversarial loss function instead of least absolute deviations (L_1 loss) and least square errors (L_2 loss). Tulyakov et al. [31] described a MoCoGAN framework, which decomposed a video into a content part and a motion part. They trained two GANs together, one of which was a motion GAN and the other was a content GAN, for video generation. Similar decomposition schemes have been used in [8] and [32]. These decomposition methods borrow the idea from background subtraction techniques [15] and work well in rather simple scenarios. However, the GAN-based models suffer from problems such as mode collapse and instability [12]. These problems have been addressed by several researchers. For example, Gulrajani et al. [13] proposed to use the Wasserstein distance to handle training instability. Mescheder et al. [21] provided some training mechanisms and tricks to overcome such problems.

Apart from GAN-based models, another popular technique for generative models is the VAE-based framework [24]. This framework aims to minimize the reconstruction loss and regularization term (KL divergence between a posterior distribution and a prior). It employs a Bayesian support vector machine, permitting efficient Bayesian inference. VAE-based models have acquired great success in image generation [24,33]. However, they suffer from the same problem when used in video prediction. Specifically, the L_2 reconstruction loss function used by these models tends to produce blurry results as it generates the expected value of all the possibilities for each pixel independently [2,19]. Hence, few works have applied VAEs directly to video prediction.

The fact that GANs lack Bayesian inference while VAEs suffer from an inappropriate loss function leads to combining GANs with VAEs. State-of-the-art VAE-GAN hybrids include SVG-LP [7] and SV2P [2], both of which perform stochastic video prediction. Notice that VAE-GAN hybrids are not the only type of models that incorporate inference mechanisms into GANs. There are many other efforts such as ALI [10] and BiGANs [9]. In particular, the adversarial learned inference (ALI) model jointly learns a generation network and an inference network using an adversarial process, and has been successfully applied to some semi-supervised learning tasks.

In this paper, we propose a new adversarial inference model in the spirit of ALI and designed specifically for video prediction, and incorporate it into our VPGAN framework. This adversarial inference model is totally different from the Bayesian inference used in the VAE-GAN hybrids such as SVG-LP [7] and SV2P [2]. Furthermore, VPGAN employs a cycle-consistency loss function to enhance the quality of prediction results. We show experimentally that a combination of our VPGAN and pre-trained image segmentation models [3,26] outperforms the existing VAE-GAN hybrids including SVG-LP and SV2P.

3   Method

The task of stochastic video prediction can be formalized as learning a multi value function $f : R^{N \times M \times T} \mapsto R^{N \times M}$ from a collection of T context frames $X_0, \ldots, X_{T-1}$, each of which is a matrix of N rows and M columns of pixels, to some possible future frames $\{X_T\}$.

It is natural to think that the transformation from frame X_{t-1} to frame X_t is caused by some variation Z_t. In [8,31,32], the latent variable Z_t is considered as the motion of objects. However, in practice, Z_t contains not only object motion, but also variations of the physical environment and surroundings. In fact, due to adding some constraints to the latent variable, Z_t is the accumulation of multiple factors, i.e., $Z_t = Z_t^1 + Z_t^2 + \ldots + Z_t^k$. Furthermore, because the variation between frames is small as environmental changes usually don't take place in a sudden, we assume that the prior distribution of Z_t is a standard Gaussian $N(\mathbf{0}, \mathbf{I})$. Based on this assumption, the video data can be described as a sequence of pairs $(X_0, Z_0), \ldots, (X_t, Z_t)$, $0 \leq t < T$.

3.1   Adversarial Inference

Let X represent the frames and let Z represent the variations under consideration. Let $p_{data}(X)$ represent the true distribution of X. We wish to construct a joint distribution $q(X, Z)$ such that $q(X, Z)$ is a good approximation of $p_{data}(X)$. In practice, it is hard to match $q(X, Z)$ with $p_{data}(X)$. On the other hand, because the video data can be described as a sequence of pairs $(X_0, Z_0), \ldots, (X_t, Z_t)$, we can consider matching $q(X, Z)$ with the joint distribution of (X_t, Z_t), denoted $p(X, Z)$. When $q(X, Z)$ and $p(X, Z)$ are matched, their marginal distributions are also matched. However, performing the matching using a traditional loss such as MSE and L_1 would result in blurry predictions. Instead, we incorporate a new adversarial inference model into our framework. By playing a min-max game between the true evidence (X_t, Z_t) and generated fake sample (X_t', Z_t'), we can match $q(X, Z)$ with $p(X, Z)$.

Figure 1 illustrates the VPGAN learning process during training. VPGAN employs two generators: $p_\psi = G_\psi(X, Z)$ and $q_\theta = G_\theta(X, Z)$. Let $X_{t-n:t-1}$ denote the frames $X_{t-n}, \ldots, X_{t-1}$ and let $Z_{t-n:t-1}$ denote the variations $Z_{t-n}, \ldots, Z_{t-1}$. Intuitively, past variations should have a 'momentum impact' on the present variation. Thus, we generate the variation at time t, Z_t, conditioned on the past frames $X_{t-n}, \ldots, X_{t-1}$ and past variations $Z_{t-n}, \ldots, Z_{t-1}$. That is to say, $Z_t \sim p_\psi(Z|X_{t-n:t-1}, Z_{t-n:t-1})$. Variations $Z_{t-n:t-1}$ are contained in the frames $X_{t-n:t-1}$ but specifying them explicitly through the input would help p_ψ focus more on the 'momentum impact.' The generator p_ψ in this case could be viewed as an encoder that encodes the past variations $Z_{t-n}, \ldots, Z_{t-1}$ into the latent variable space.

On the other hand, we generate the fake frame at time t, X_t', conditioned on variation Z_t' sampled from a prior, $q_{prior}(Z)$, and a single past frame X_{t-1}, i.e., $X_t' \sim q_\theta(X|Z_t', X_{t-1})$. Here, conditioning on one single past frame is reasonable as Z represents the changes between frames, and conditioning on less information

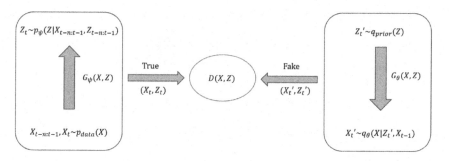

Fig. 1. Illustration of the VPGAN learning process. Both of G_ψ, G_θ are generators. Discriminator $D(X, Z)$ tries to discriminate between true (X, Z) and fake (X', Z').

would enforce Z to learn the 'true' variation efficiently. Thus, the generator q_θ serves as a decoder in our framework, which decodes the variation Z'_t and generates new frame X'_t.

The symbol $D(X, Z)$ in Fig. 1 represents the discriminator, which tries to distinguish between the true evidence (X_t, Z_t) and the generated fake sample (X'_t, Z'_t). VPGAN keeps on generating fake samples until the discriminator $D(X, Z)$ can not distinguish between the true evidence and generated fake sample, at which moment the training process terminates. When the training is completed, the two joint distributions $q(X, Z)$ and $p(X, Z)$ match with each other.

Denote $p_\psi(Z|X_{t-n:t-1}, Z_{t-n:t-1})$ by $G_\psi(X_{t-n:t-1}, Z_{t-n:t-1})$ and $q_\theta(X|Z'_t, X_{t-1})$ by $G_\theta(Z'_t, X_{t-1})$. The adversarial loss function used in the training is calculated as:

$$L_{adv} = E_{X_t \sim p_{data}(X)}[\log D(X_t, G_\psi(X_{t-n:t-1}, Z_{t-n:t-1}))] \\ + E_{Z'_t \sim q_{prior}(Z)}[1 - \log D(G_\theta(Z'_t, X_{t-1}), Z'_t)] \tag{1}$$

Figure 2 illustrates the VPGAN feed-forward inference process during testing. The figure shows how to generate or predict the next frame X_t based on the past frames $X_{t-n:t-1}$. First, the past frames $X_{t-n:t-1}$ and past encoded vectors $Z_{t-n:t-1}$ are sent to the encoder p_ψ, which generates the next encoded vector (variation) Z_t. Then the decoder q_θ takes X_{t-1} and Z_t together, and predicts the next frame X_t. Depending on different variations (latent variables) Z_t, q_θ can predict multiple possible next (future) frames $\{X_T\}$.

During training and inference, we calculate p_ψ and q_θ as follows:

$$p_\psi(Z|X_{t-n:t-1}, Z_{t-n:t-1}) \sim N(\mu_\psi(X, Z), \sigma_\psi(X, Z)\mathbf{I}) \tag{2}$$

$$q_\theta(X|Z_t, X_{t-1}) \sim N(\mu_\theta(X, Z), \sigma_\theta(X, Z)\mathbf{I}) \tag{3}$$

Based on the assumption that the prior distribution of Z is a standard Gaussian, we have:

$$q_{prior}(Z) \sim N(\mathbf{0}, \mathbf{I}) \tag{4}$$

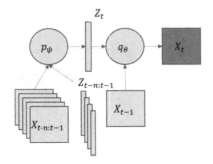

Fig. 2. Illustration of the VPGAN inference process.

The sampling procedure used in calculating p_ψ and q_θ can be computed by the reparameterization trick [17]. Specifically, instead of sampling directly from the Gaussian function with the complicated parameters, we treat the sampling procedure as a deterministic transformation of some noise such that the transformation's distribution is computable. Thus, we calculate Z_t as:

$$Z_t = \mu_\psi(X, Z) + \sigma_\psi(X, Z) \odot \xi, \ \ \xi \sim N(\mathbf{0}, \mathbf{I}) \tag{5}$$

where $\odot$ denotes the Hadamard product (element-wise product).

3.2 Cycle Consistency Loss

Cycle consistency is based on the idea of using transitivity as a way to regularize structured data. Here we propose a new cycle consistency loss function for video prediction. With the same generator in (3), we generate the frame at time $t-1$, X_{t-1}, conditioned on the opposite of Z_t and X_t. That is, we generate $\bar{X}_{t-1}$ conditioned on $-Z_t$ and X_t where $\bar{X}_{t-1}$ is approximately equal to X_{t-1} as expressed in (6) below:

$$X_{t-1} \approx \bar{X}_{t-1} \sim q_\theta(X| - Z_t, X_t) \tag{6}$$

This is reminiscent of the cycle consistency loss used for image-to-image translation in [35]. However, our cycle consistency loss function is different from that in [35] because our loss function is mainly designed for video prediction rather than image translation. Since the prior Z_t follows a standard Gaussian distribution (cf. (4)), it is natural to consider the opposite variation to be the negative of Z_t. Figure 3 illustrates how cycle consistency works in our framework. As shown in the figure, we generate the current frame X_t (right) conditioned on the previous frame X_{t-1} (left) and variation Z_t. On the other hand, with the same generator, we generate the previous frame X_{t-1} conditioned on the current frame X_t and the negative of Z_t.

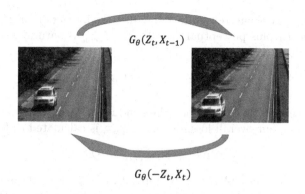

$$G_\theta(Z_t, X_{t-1})$$

$$G_\theta(-Z_t, X_t)$$

Fig. 3. Illustration of cycle consistency in our framework.

Mathematically, denote $q_\theta(X|Z_t, X_{t-1})$ by $G_\theta(Z_t, X_{t-1})$ and $q_\theta(X|-Z_t, X_t)$ by $G_\theta(-Z_t, X_t)$. Our cycle consistency loss is calculated as:

$$L^1_{cycle} = E_{X_t, X_{t-1} \sim p_{data}(X)}\{\| X_t - G_\theta(Z_t, G_\theta(-Z_t, X_t)) \|_1$$
$$+ \| X_{t-1} - G_\theta(-Z_t, G_\theta(Z_t, X_{t-1})) \|_1\} \tag{7}$$

Here, we utilize L_1 loss as the reconstruction loss. The loss function L^1_{cycle} in (7) only considers one-step cycle consistency. We can generalize the formula in (7) to take into account cycle consistency of multiple steps (more precisely, k steps) for video prediction. We first define a single-multi loss as follows:

$$l^k_{cycle} = E_{X_t, X_{t-k} \sim p_{data}(X)}\{\| X_t - G_\theta(Z_t, G_\theta(Z_{t-1}, \ldots, G_\theta(-Z_t, X_t))) \|_1$$
$$+ \| X_{t-k} - G_\theta(-Z_t, G_\theta(-Z_{t-1}, \ldots, G_\theta(Z_t, X_{t-k}))) \|_1\} \tag{8}$$

Our multi (k steps) cycle consistency loss is generalized by summing up all single-multi losses as follows:

$$L^k_{cycle} = \sum_1^k a_i \cdot l^i_{cycle} \tag{9}$$

It could be very time consuming to calculate L^k_{cycle} for $k \geq 2$ since the procedure includes iterative calculation of generator G_θ. For instance, l^2_{cycle} would require up to 8 times calculation, and the overall L^2_{cycle} would require 12 times calculation.

When using the multi-cycle consistency loss, it is natural to take into account a multi-reconstruction loss. The computational cost is mainly involved in calculating L^k_{cycle}; computing the multi-reconstruction loss takes relatively less time. Define l^k_{recon} as follows:

$$l^k_{recon} = E_{X_t, \ldots, X_{t-k} \sim p_{data}(X)}\{\varphi(X_t, G_\theta(Z_t, \ldots, G_\theta(Z_{t-k+1}, X_{t-k})))\} \tag{10}$$

Here, φ stands for the reconstruction distance between the ground truth X_t and calculated $G_\theta(Z_t, \ldots, G_\theta(Z_{t-k+1}, X_{t-k}))$. Generally, L_2 loss is applied, but in order to obtain more accurate results and reduce the impact of 'future averaging,' we let φ be the L_1 plus perceptual loss. Then, L_{recon}^k is naturally defined as:

$$L_{recon}^k = \sum_1^k b_i \cdot l_{recon}^i \tag{11}$$

Combining the multi-cycle consistency loss and multi-reconstruction loss defined in this subsection, our overall loss, denoted L_{loss}, is calculated as follows:

$$L_{loss} = \alpha L_{adv} + \beta L_{cycle}^k + \lambda L_{recon}^k \tag{12}$$

The perceptual loss [16] is widely applied in evaluating the reconstruction quality of images. It could be the distance on the Kth feature map, for some K, of some convolutional neural network, such as VGG16 [29] and ResNet [14] pre-trained on ImageNet [6]. In our paper, we applied the simple ResNet [14] to our model.

Note that, although the multi-cycle consistency loss enforcing long dependency consistency likely enables more accurate action learning and prediction, its training and inference time would be approximately k times larger than that for the one-step cycle consistency loss. Furthermore it may suffer from gradient loss. Therefore, in our VPGAN framework, we only utilize the one-step cycle consistency loss given in (7). The evaluation of different k values for L_{cycle}^k will be presented in Sect. 4.1.

3.3   Action Control

In practice, it is natural to consider the generation of desirable images or videos using GANs. Since GANs generally generate data from a random sample of the latent variable space $\mathcal{Z}$, it is hard to control the behavior of GANs. In this subsection, we propose new techniques for generating desirable frames using GANs.

In the previous subsection, we use Z_t and $-Z_t$ to represent the opposite variations in the video space $\mathcal{H}$. Specifically, for a movement dataset, Z_t should be able to learn the moving direction of an object, and then $-Z_t$ should mainly represent the object's moving in the opposite direction. That is, from the encoding space (i.e., latent variable space) $\mathcal{Z}$ to the video space $\mathcal{H}$, we preserve what we call a 'symmetry' property, meaning that if Z_1, Z_2 are symmetric in the encoding space $\mathcal{Z}$, then the corresponding generated movements should be symmetric in the video space $\mathcal{H}$.

In addition, we wish to manipulate the latent variable space $\mathcal{Z}$ so as to generate desirable moving directions, through preserving 'orthogonality,' or more precisely, through preserving angles between the encoding space $\mathcal{Z}$ and the moving direction of an object. This orthogonality property can be preserved by first enforcing the latent variable space $\mathcal{Z}$ to be a subset of R^2. Although the moving direction of an object in a video sequence is in R^2, the latent variable $Z \in \mathcal{Z} \subset R^2$ may not simply represent the moving direction of the object, for the following reasons:

- The moving direction and Z may not be in the same coordinate system, as the decoder from the latent variable space $\mathcal{Z}$ to the video space $\mathcal{H}$ may contain rotation operations.
- The latent variable Z may contain not only direction information, but also velocity, momentum, and other information.
- The latent variable Z may contain information related to environmental changes.

Thus, the angles between any two vectors in the latent variable space $\mathcal{Z}$ may not be preserved in the decoding process. To overcome this problem, we add a network to our framework to preserve such angles. This network acts as a mapping, denoted τ, which maps a latent variable from the latent variable space $\mathcal{Z}$ to the moving direction space $\mathcal{D}$. The moving direction $v(X_{t-1}, X_t)$ of an object between frames X_{t-1} and X_t can be computed by running an optical flow algorithm [4]. Thus, our modified model consists of two decoders: one from the latent variable space $\mathcal{Z} \subset R^2$ to the video space $\mathcal{H}$, and the other decoder, τ, from the latent variable space $\mathcal{Z}$ to the moving direction space $\mathcal{D}$. Figure 4 illustrates this modified model.

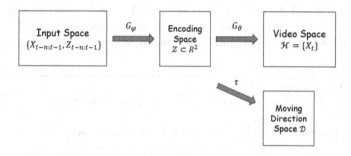

Fig. 4. Illustration of our modified model for action control.

The moving direction loss, denoted L_{moving}, is calculated as:

$$L_{moving} = \left| \frac{< \tau(Z), v(X_{t-1}, X_t) >}{|\tau(Z)| \cdot |v(X_{t-1}, X_t)|} - 1 \right| \tag{13}$$

where $< \cdot >$ represents the inner product of two vectors. Such a loss function penalizes the angle difference between two vectors. Our overall training loss is updated to take into account the moving direction loss, and is calculated as:

$$L_{loss} = \alpha L_{adv} + \beta L_{cycle}^k + \lambda L_{recon}^k + \mu L_{moving} \tag{14}$$

The Adam optimizer [18] is employed to optimize L_{loss}.

Based on a mathematical concept known as 'conformal mapping' [1], we introduce and add the network, τ, to our model. Formally, a mapping $\mathbf{f} = (f_1, \ldots, f_n)$ where $\mathbf{f} : U \to V$, $U, V \subset R^n$, is conformal (or angle-preserving) at a point

$u_0 \in U$ if it preserves the orientation and angles between directed curves through u_0. A mapping $\mathbf{f}$ is conformal iff it is homomorphic and its derivative is nowhere zero, i.e.,

$$\mathbf{J} = \frac{d\mathbf{f}}{d\mathbf{x}} = \begin{bmatrix} \frac{\partial f_1}{\partial x_1} & \cdots & \frac{\partial f_1}{\partial x_n} \\ \vdots & \ddots & \vdots \\ \frac{\partial f_n}{\partial x_1} & \cdots & \frac{\partial f_n}{\partial x_n} \end{bmatrix} \neq \begin{bmatrix} 0 & \cdots & 0 \\ \vdots & \ddots & \vdots \\ 0 & \cdots & 0 \end{bmatrix} \tag{15}$$

In our VPGAN framework, the mapping τ is implemented using a 3-layer affine transformation:

$$f^i = A^i \cdot X + B^i$$
$$f = f^1 \circ f^2 \circ f^3 \tag{16}$$

where $1 \leq i \leq 3$.

It is easy to see that such an affine transformation enforces τ to be conformal; therefore it preserves the angle between any two vectors through '0'. In this way, if we know a latent variable Z moving toward a specific direction, we can then control the generated moving direction by manipulating the latent variable Z (through rotating with some angle since the angle is preserved between the latent variable space $\mathcal{Z}$ and the moving direction space $\mathcal{D}$). Under this circumstance, we actually do not need to know details concerning Z, such as velocity, momentum and other information. Algorithm 1 depicts our action control procedure.

Algorithm 1. Action Control

1: Sample n sets of continuous frames $\{X_{t-1}, X_t\}_n$ in which objects move toward the same direction.
2: Encode the frames into $Z_t^1, \ldots, Z_t^n$ in the latent variable space $\mathcal{Z}$.
3: Calculate the mean of $Z_t^1, \ldots, Z_t^n$ and denote the mean by $\bar{Z}$.
4: Compute the angle ς between the desired direction and sampled direction.
5: Rotate $\bar{Z}$ by the angle ς in the latent variable space $\mathcal{Z}$.
6: Decode $\bar{Z}$ into the video space $\mathcal{H}$.

The advantages of our proposed action control algorithm are the following:

- It suffices to enforce a conformal mapping τ from the latent variable space $\mathcal{Z}$ to the moving direction space $\mathcal{D}$ (see Fig. 4). It is not necessary to handle the latent variables $Z_t^1, \ldots, Z_t^n$ individually.
- Even when the latent variables accumulate many different factors, such as environmental changes, momentum information and so on, our action control algorithm is still able to generate objects moving in the desired direction.

4 Experiments

A series of experiments were conducted to evaluate the performance of our VPGAN framework using different datasets, including Moving Mnist [30], BAIR

[11] and KTH [27] action datasets. Moving Mnist [30] is a simple dataset. We used it for generating desired movements. In addition, we tested our VPGAN framework on more complicated benchmark datasets, BAIR [11] and KTH [27] action dataset, to evaluate our multi (k steps) cycle consistency loss function and compare VPGAN with state-of-the-art methods. All quantitative results were obtained by calculating structural similarity (SSIM) [34] and peak-signal-to-noise ratio (PSNR) scores between ground truth and our generated frames.

4.1 Evaluation of Cycle Consistency Loss

We present in Eq. (9) the general formula of our multi (k steps) cycle consistency loss function, L_{cycle}^k. Here we show experimentally how different k values affect the performance of VPGAN. We trained VPGAN (without the action control module) using different k values on the Moving Mnist dataset [30] with the objective loss as defined in Eq. (12). The action control module was excluded because we were only interested in the impact of k on the behavior of VPGAN.

Figure 5 shows the SSIM results and running time of VPGAN for different k values on the Moving Mnist dataset. It can be seen from Fig. 5(a) that using L_{cycle}^k yields more accurate results than using L_{cycle}^{k-1}. This is understandable given that L_{cycle}^{k-1} is part of L_{cycle}^k, as shown in Eq. (9). Enforcing earlier cycle consistency is undoubtedly more important than doing it k steps later (since k-step cycle-consistency couldn't be preserved if 1-step cycle-consistency isn't preserved). We decrease the value of a_i in Eq. (9) as i becomes larger. Therefore, as shown in Fig. 5(a), there isn't a big performance gap between L_{cycle}^{k-1} and L_{cycle}^k in terms of the SSIM metric. On the other hand, using L_{cycle}^k requires much more running time than using L_{cycle}^{k-1}, as shown in Fig. 5(b). The running time difference between L_{cycle}^{k-1} and L_{cycle}^k lies in the calculation of l_{cycle}^k, which requires $4k$ iterations of calculating G_θ. The total time complexity for L_{cycle}^k is

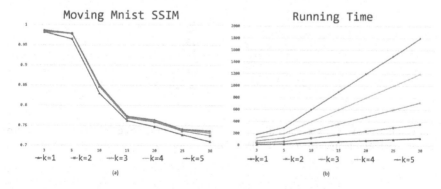

Fig. 5. Impact of k on the (a) SSIM metric and (b) running time of VPGAN on the Moving Mnist. The X-axis in the figure represents the number of generated future frames.

$O(k^2)$ iterations of calculating G_θ. Similar results were obtained on the BAIR and KTH datasets. After evaluating the trade-off between the model accuracy and running time, we decided to use L^1_{cycle} for our VPGAN framework in subsequent experiments since the accuracy difference isn't too large while the time complexity grows with square.

4.2 Results of Combining VPGAN with Image Segmentation Models

When constructing the generators G_θ and G_ψ for video prediction, as illustrated in Fig. 1, existing methods such as SVG-LP [7] and SV2P [2] employ long-short term memory (LSTM) and convolutional neural networks (CNNs) to capture the spatio-temporal information in the video data. Here we propose to further combine pre-trained image segmentation models with the generators G_θ and G_ψ. The motivation behind this combination is that when performing the video prediction task, a method needs to understand the scene and variations between frames, where the variations between frames are mainly caused by the interactions between objects. Therefore, recognizing the objects and understanding their interactions are crucial in predicting the variations.

Since there are well performed image segmentation models such as Unet [26], SegNet [3] and DeepLabv3 [5], using one of them as a feature generator stacked below the generators G_θ and G_ψ would achieve appealing results. For instance, Fig. 6 shows a combination of SegNet and the generator G_ψ in VPGAN. Here, SegNet is used as a feature extractor, and G_ψ is implemented by a convolutional long short-term memory and CNN network [15]. G_ψ takes, as input, $X_{t-n:t-1}$, $Z_{t-n:t-1}$ and the output of SegNet, and produces, as output, generated frames.

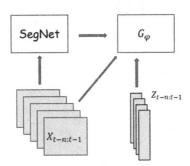

Fig. 6. Combining the pre-trained image segmentation model SegNet, used as a feature extractor, with the generator G_ψ in VPGAN.

We evaluate the different image segmentation models on Moving Mnist [30] and BAIR [11] datasets. Figure 7 presents the results where VPGAN-U represents VPGAN combined with Unet [26], VPGAN-S represents VPGAN combined with SegNet [3], and VPGAN-D represents VPGAN combined with Deep Labv3 [5]. It can be seen from Fig. 7 that combining VPGAN with the pre-trained image segmentation models performs better than VPGAN alone. Similar results were obtained on the KTH dataset. In our default framework, we employed Unet since it is a light-weight feature extractor, which takes less computational time.

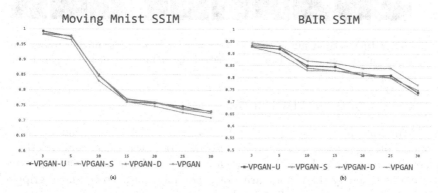

Fig. 7. Comparison of four methods VPGAN-U, VPGAN-S, VPGAN-D and VPGAN on two datasets (a) Moving Mnist and (b) BAIR respectively. The X-axis in the figure represents the number of generated future frames.

4.3 Evaluation of Action Control

In Sect. 3.3, we introduce the network τ to accomplish action control. Since τ is a conformal mapping, in theory, it preserves angles between the latent variable space and the moving direction space. However, in practice, its accuracy is affected by the training procedure. We used the Moving Mnist dataset [30] to evaluate τ. The reason for choosing this simple dataset is that we were mainly interested in the potential of action control with our techniques. Moving Mnist could well reflect the movement of a single character and doesn't involve complicated environmental changes.

Figure 8 presents some frames generated by our VPGAN on Moving Mnist. Our 'next frame' was generated by choosing a specific direction and executing Algorithm 1. By comparing the generated frames and ground truth in Fig. 8, we can see that each character in Moving Mnist is actually moving around the space randomly, but by executing Algorithm 1, we can gain action control of the character.

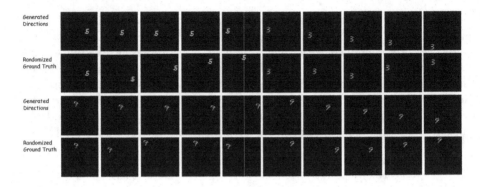

Fig. 8. Generating desired movements of Mnist characters. '5' is moving toward the left. '3' is moving downward. '7' is moving toward the right. '9' is moving right-down.

4.4   Results on the BAIR Dataset

The BAIR robot pushing dataset [11] involves a series of videos generated by a Sawyer robotic arm pushing a variety of objects. All of the videos have relatively similar surroundings (table settings) with a static background. Each video collects actions taken by the robotic arm corresponding to the commanded gripper pose. This dataset is very challenging for two reasons:

1. The movement is almost random and quite unpredictable.
2. It is a real-world video, with various objects and interactions between the robotic arm and objects (rather than a single frame-centered object with a neutral background).

The videos have a resolution of 64 × 64. Thus, our input dimension is 64 × 64 × 3. We produced 30 frames conditioned on 10 frames. The architecture we used for the generators G_θ, G_ψ in our model is composed of a convolutional long short-term memory and CNN network [15] combined with SegNet [3], as shown in Fig. 6.

Figure 9 presents some examples of frames generated by our approach on the BAIR dataset. The figure shows the potential of VPGAN in generating many possible future frames conditioned on different latent variables. It can be seen from the figure that all the random generations produced by our approach have the same good image quality as the ground truth. Figure 10 compares our method with three related methods SVL-LP [7], SV2P [19] and deterministic model on the BAIR dataset. It is clear that the proposed VPGAN framework outperforms the related methods in terms of both SSIM and PSNR measures. Similar results were obtained on the simple Moving Mnist dataset.

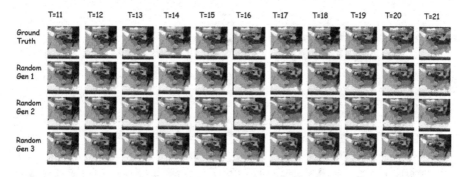

Fig. 9. Examples of generated frames on the BAIR dataset to show the potential of VPGAN in generating many possible future frames.

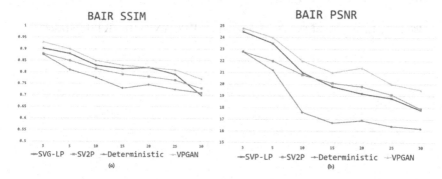

Fig. 10. Comparison of four methods SVG-LP, SV2P, deterministic model and VPGAN on the BAIR dataset based on (a) SSIM and (b) PSNR measures.

4.5   Results on the KTH Dataset

The KTH action dataset [27] contains various types of videos collected in real-world cameras. These videos include human subjects carrying out six activities (walking, jogging, running, boxing, hand waving, and hand clapping). For the first three activities, the human subject enters and leaves the frame multiple times, leaving the frame empty with a mostly static background for multiple frames at a time. Like the BAIR dataset, the videos in the KTH dataset have a resolution of 64 × 64. Therefore we employed the same architecture and trained our model in the same way as for the BAIR dataset.

Figure 11 presents some examples of frames generated by our approach on the KTH dataset. It can be seen from the figure that when T ≥ 10, the image quality of the particular 'human' drops significantly and the 'human' part becomes blurry. Nevertheless, the quality of the frames generated by our approach is as good as the ground truth for all the different T values in the figure. Figure 12 compares our method with three related methods SVG-LP [7], SV2P [19] and

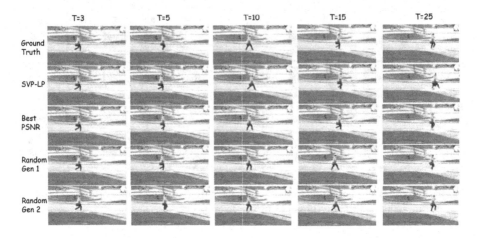

Fig. 11. Examples of frames generated by VPGAN on the KTH dataset.

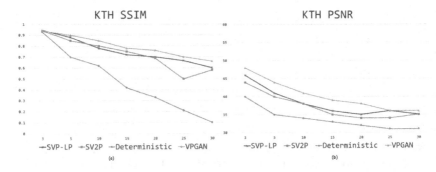

Fig. 12. Comparison of four methods SVG-LP, SV2P, deterministic model and VPGAN on the KTH dataset based on (a) SSIM and (b) PSNR measures.

deterministic model on the KTH dataset. Again, it is evident that the proposed VPGAN framework outperforms the related methods in terms of both SSIM and PSNR measures.

5   Conclusion

In this paper, we present an adversarial inference framework (VPGAN) for video prediction, and incorporate cycle consistency and conformal mapping into our VPGAN framework. Cycle consistency relieves the problem of blurry predictions to obtain more accurate results while conformal mapping enables action control through manipulating latent variables. Our experimental results show that the proposed approach works well on different datasets and outperforms existing methods.

Acknowledgments. This work was supported in part by an NJIT faculty seed grant on deep learning and by the U.S. National Science Foundation under Grant No. 1927578. We thank the reviewers of IJCAI 2019 workshops for their thoughtful comments, which helped improve this paper.

References

1. Ahlfors, L.V.: Conformal Invariants: Topics in Geometric Function Theory. McGraw-Hill, New York (1973)
2. Babaeizadeh, M., Finn, C., Erhan, D., Campbell, R.H., Levine, S.: Stochastic variational video prediction. In: 6th International Conference on Learning Representations (2018)
3. Badrinarayanan, V., Kendall, A., Cipolla, R.: SegNet: a deep convolutional encoder-decoder architecture for image segmentation. IEEE Trans. Pattern Anal. Mach. Intell. **39**(12), 2481–2495 (2017)
4. Beauchemin, S.S., Barron, J.L.: The computation of optical flow. ACM Comput. Surv. **27**(3), 433–467 (1995)
5. Chen, L.C., Papandreou, G., Kokkinos, I., Murphy, K., Yuille, A.L.: DeepLab: semantic image segmentation with deep convolutional nets, atrous convolution, and fully connected CRFs. IEEE Trans. Pattern Anal. Mach. Intell. **40**(4), 834–848 (2017)
6. Deng, J., Dong, W., Socher, R., Li, L.J., Li, K., Fei-Fei, L.: ImageNet: a large-scale hierarchical image database. In: 2009 IEEE Conference on Computer Vision and Pattern Recognition, pp. 248–255 (2009)
7. Denton, E., Fergus, R.: Stochastic video generation with a learned prior. In: Proceedings of the 35th International Conference on Machine Learning, pp. 1182–1191 (2018)
8. Denton, E.L., Birodkar, V.: Unsupervised learning of disentangled representations from video. In: Advances in Neural Information Processing Systems, pp. 4417–4426 (2017)
9. Donahue, J., Krähenbühl, P., Darrell, T.: Adversarial feature learning. In: 5th International Conference on Learning Representations (2017)
10. Dumoulin, V., et al.: Adversarially learned inference. In: 5th International Conference on Learning Representations (2017)
11. Finn, C., Goodfellow, I.J., Levine, S.: Unsupervised learning for physical interaction through video prediction. In: Advances in Neural Information Processing Systems, pp. 64–72 (2016)
12. Goodfellow, I.J., et al.: Generative adversarial nets. In: Advances in Neural Information Processing Systems, pp. 2672–2680 (2014)
13. Gulrajani, I., Ahmed, F., Arjovsky, M., Dumoulin, V., Courville, A.C.: Improved training of Wasserstein GANs. In: Advances in Neural Information Processing Systems, pp. 5769–5779 (2017)
14. He, K., Zhang, X., Ren, S., Sun, J.: Deep residual learning for image recognition. In: Proceedings of the IEEE Conference on Computer Vision and Pattern Recognition, pp. 770–778 (2016)
15. Hu, Z., Turki, T., Phan, N., Wang, J.T.L.: A 3D atrous convolutional long short-term memory network for background subtraction. IEEE Access **6**, 43450–43459 (2018)

16. Johnson, J., Alahi, A., Fei-Fei, L.: Perceptual losses for real-time style transfer and super-resolution. In: Leibe, B., Matas, J., Sebe, N., Welling, M. (eds.) ECCV 2016. LNCS, vol. 9906, pp. 694–711. Springer, Cham (2016). https://doi.org/10.1007/978-3-319-46475-6_43

17. Kingma, D.P.: Fast gradient-based inference with continuous latent variable models in auxiliary form. arXiv preprint arXiv:1306.0733 (2013)

18. Kingma, D.P., Ba, J.: Adam: a method for stochastic optimization. In: 3rd International Conference on Learning Representations (2015)

19. Lee, A.X., Zhang, R., Ebert, F., Abbeel, P., Finn, C., Levine, S.: Stochastic adversarial video prediction. arXiv preprint arXiv:1804.01523 (2018)

20. Mathieu, M., Couprie, C., LeCun, Y.: Deep multi-scale video prediction beyond mean square error. In: 4th International Conference on Learning Representations (2016)

21. Mescheder, L., Geiger, A., Nowozin, S.: Which training methods for GANs do actually converge? arXiv preprint arXiv:1801.04406 (2018)

22. Mikolov, T., Karafiát, M., Burget, L., Černockỳ, J., Khudanpur, S.: Recurrent neural network based language model. In: 11th Annual Conference of the International Speech Communication Association (2010)

23. Oh, J., Guo, X., Lee, H., Lewis, R.L., Singh, S.P.: Action-conditional video prediction using deep networks in Atari games. In: Advances in Neural Information Processing Systems, pp. 2863–2871 (2015)

24. Pu, Y., et al.: Variational autoencoder for deep learning of images, labels and captions. In: Advances in Neural Information Processing Systems, pp. 2352–2360 (2016)

25. Ranzato, M., Szlam, A., Bruna, J., Mathieu, M., Collobert, R., Chopra, S.: Video (language) modeling: a baseline for generative models of natural videos. arXiv preprint arXiv:1412.6604 (2014)

26. Ronneberger, O., Fischer, P., Brox, T.: U-Net: convolutional networks for biomedical image segmentation. In: Navab, N., Hornegger, J., Wells, W.M., Frangi, A.F. (eds.) MICCAI 2015. LNCS, vol. 9351, pp. 234–241. Springer, Cham (2015). https://doi.org/10.1007/978-3-319-24574-4_28

27. Schuldt, C., Laptev, I., Caputo, B.: Recognizing human actions: a local SVM approach. In: 17th International Conference on Pattern Recognition, pp. 32–36 (2004)

28. Shi, X., Chen, Z., Wang, H., Yeung, D.Y., Wong, W.K., Woo, W.C.: Convolutional LSTM network: a machine learning approach for precipitation nowcasting. In: Advances in Neural Information Processing Systems, pp. 802–810 (2015)

29. Simonyan, K., Zisserman, A.: Very deep convolutional networks for large-scale image recognition. arXiv preprint arXiv:1409.1556 (2014)

30. Srivastava, N., Mansimov, E., Salakhutdinov, R.: Unsupervised learning of video representations using LSTMs. In: Proceedings of the 32nd International Conference on Machine Learning, pp. 843–852 (2015)

31. Tulyakov, S., Liu, M.Y., Yang, X., Kautz, J.: MoCoGAN: decomposing motion and content for video generation. In: Proceedings of the IEEE Conference on Computer Vision and Pattern Recognition, pp. 1526–1535 (2018)

32. Villegas, R., Yang, J., Hong, S., Lin, X., Lee, H.: Decomposing motion and content for natural video sequence prediction. arXiv preprint arXiv:1706.08033 (2017)

33. Walker, J., Doersch, C., Gupta, A., Hebert, M.: An uncertain future: forecasting from static images using variational autoencoders. In: Leibe, B., Matas, J., Sebe, N., Welling, M. (eds.) ECCV 2016. LNCS, vol. 9911, pp. 835–851. Springer, Cham (2016). https://doi.org/10.1007/978-3-319-46478-7_51

34. Wang, Z., Bovik, A.C., Sheikh, H.R., Simoncelli, E.P.: Image quality assessment: from error visibility to structural similarity. IEEE Trans. Image Process. **13**(4), 600–612 (2004)
35. Zhu, J., Park, T., Isola, P., Efros, A.A.: Unpaired image-to-image translation using cycle-consistent adversarial networks. In: IEEE International Conference on Computer Vision, pp. 2242–2251 (2017)

Evaluation of Adaptive Systems
for Human-Autonomy Teaming

Evaluation of Adaptive Systems for Human-Autonomy Teaming

Douglas S. Lange[1] and Luke Marsh[2]

[1] Naval Information Warfare Center Pacific
dlange@spawar.navy.mil
[2] Defence Science and Technology Group
luke.marsh@dst.defence.gov.au

1 Workshop Overview

Human-Autonomy Teaming (HAT) describes situations where people cooperate with artificially intelligent autonomous agents to perform some function. In a general sense, we can envision heterogeneous teams composed of autonomous participants each using either human or artificial intelligence. These relationships can take on different structures depending on the level of supervision the humanscan exert and the level of intelligence and autonomy provided by the non-human agents.

2 Workshop History

In the first workshop on HAT, the IJCAI 2017 Workshop on Impedance Matching in Cognitive Partnerships, we combined invited talks by Professor Stuart Russell of Berkeley, Dr. Peter Friedland of the US Air Force Office of Scientific Research, Professor Tim Miller of the University of Melbourne, and Dr. Mike Cox of the Wright State Research Institute with a series of presentations supported by papers, and a lively panel discussion. The first workshop explored cognitive partnerships among heterogeneous autonomous team members, whether they are humanor artificial. People often struggle to work through the impedance mismatches caused by varying backgrounds, professional fields, and goals. This workshop targeted areas of impedance mismatch between humans and autonomous AI.

In the second workshop on HAT, Autonomy in Teams: Joint Workshop on Sharing Autonomy in Human-Robot Interaction, as part of the federated workshop program associated with IJCAI 2018, we continued to focus on partnerships between humans and artificial intelligence. We held a full day workshop that combined invited talks, papers, and posters. In the morning, we had discussions on the definition and critical capabilities of the partnerships. In the afternoon we focused on measurement of team performance. Among the invited speakers were Roger Woltjer the Deputy Research Director at the Swedish Defence Research Agency.

3   Workshop Content and Highlights

In this third IJCAI workshop on HAT, we delved further into the problem of evaluation. Software engineering tools and techniques for evaluating the quality of traditionally developed software capabilities are well studied and many approaches are mature. System components developed through learning from data are less easily tested for mission critical systems. Reserving a portion of the data sample for testing provides a statistical measure of quality relative to the overall sample of the particular type of data for a particular component of what may be one in a series of learned models in a complex system. The quality of theoverall system as it relates to a complex mission are less well known. Add to the problem the desire to allow models to adapt while deployed in lifelong learning approaches and complexity is further increased. Humans bring another element of quality assessment to the problem. Their interaction with the adaptive artificially intelligent components must also be evaluated in some way. Humans will adapt to the changing behaviors of the autonomy in ways that are currently unpredictable.

During the half day workshop we explored a number of key issues on the evaluation of HAT, covering invited talks from Prof. Ron Meyden of the University of New South Wales on Formal Methods for Multi-Agent Systems and Phillip Smith from Monash University on Autonomy: Considerations for Verification. The invited talks were followed by a number of engaging paper submissions on Collaborative Localisation Simulation and Assessment; and Data Communication Assistance via Swarm Robotics.

4   Selected Workshop Paper

Data Communication Assistance via swarm robotics a behaviour creation comparison, Phillip Smith et. al, was selected as best workshop paper due to its interesting approach to evaluation of behaviours in the real world by testing them in previously unseen environments.

5   Concluding Remarks and Insights for Future Research

The evaluation of adaptive systems for HAT is an on-going and challenging field of research. Techniques and approaches for evaluation need to test for resilience, competence and trustworthiness of the team as a whole. Achieving these three aims in a HAT is a challenge in itself and it is proposed that an important area of future research in HAT involves successfully training both the artificial intelligence and human agents as a team. Machine learning addresses how agents can learn models of their environment and tasks. The field of education addresses human education. A fair amount of research has gone into training all human teams to work together. In HAT, not only do the individual members of the team have to learn about their environment and tasks, they must learn to work together building models of each other's behavior and models of communication in order to develop teamwork, and they must do this across the mismatched mental models of humans and autonomous agents.

Data Communication Assistance via Swarm Robotic: A Behaviour Creation Comparison

Phillip Smith[1(✉)], Asad Khan[1], Aldeida Aleti[1], Vincent C. S. Lee[1],
and Robert Hunjet[2]

[1] Faculty of Information Technology, Monash University, Clayton, Victoria, Australia
phillip.smith@monash.edu

[2] Defence Science and Technology Group, Edinburgh, South Australia

Abstract. This paper compares two behaviour creation algorithms for Unmanned Aerial Vehicle swarms. The objective of this work is to have a self-organising robotic swarm which unintrusively assists humans in network restricted environments by facilitating data-transfer between disconnected groups. The behaviour creation algorithms explored are a well-cited approach for evolving neural networks (ENN) and our Learning Classifier System (LCS) approach. We utilise simulations in randomised, obstacle dense landscapes to validate, compare and contrast these two algorithms. We explore the algorithms both with and without the environment layout being known to the swarm *a priori*. These simulations show the ENN algorithm struggles to create appropriate behaviours for this complex data-transfer task, resulting in an unassertive swarm. Our LCS behaviours have the swarm operate with up to 61% of the fitness range above ENN in both expected and unexpected environments, resulting in the desired human assistance.

1 Introduction

Swarm robotics is a growing research field which utilises a large collection of low-complexity robotic agents to solve tasks beyond the scope of a single, high-complexity, robot [23,24]. These tasks are achieved by the interaction and cooperation of agents, forming an *emergent behaviour*. One such task for which swarms show potential the creation of a Mobile Ad-hoc NETwork (MANET) [10,12] in environments constricted both spatially and in communication. This swarm task aims to facilitate connectivity between disconnected networking devices in urban environments. More specifically, the swarm assists human operators in network restricted environments to remain in communication with one another, with minimal interaction from the humans or their devices.

In this paper, the autonomous creation of such swarm behaviours is explored via two algorithms: an algorithm which modifies a Neural Network (NN) using a Genetic Algorithm (GA), hereon referred to as Evolved Neural Network (ENN),

© Springer Nature Switzerland AG 2020
A. El Fallah Seghrouchni and D. Sarne (Eds.): IJCAI 2019 Workshops, LNAI 12158, pp. 111–126, 2020.
https://doi.org/10.1007/978-3-030-56150-5_6

and an adaption of Learning Classifier System (LCS) [15] for rule-based evolution and Reinforcement Learning (RL). The former of these approaches has seen considerable exploration within the swarm community [13,14,25]. However, it has only been implemented for trivial swarm tasks, such as locomotion. It is thus hypothesised that ENN will create insufficient behaviours for the challenging data-transfer task, which is non-deterministic, partially-observable and requires heterogeneous agent behaviours. In contrast, the latter approach, LCS, has shown significant performance in our previous data-transfer swarm work [22] and thus is further explored in this study.

The quality of the two algorithms is evaluated via virtual swarms, operating in numerous 2D landscapes with obstacles and restricted communication. Each swarm implementation is tasked with transferring data from one human-held networking device to another in the shortest time possible. This quality-evaluation is measured via task effectiveness, behaviour reliability, and behaviour creation time. These three aspects are seen as key for real-world swarm applications to be operationally viable. Additionally, the quality of the created behaviours is tested in both the environments used by the creation algorithms, and environments unseen *a priori*.

The two main contributions of this paper are:

(a) the implementation and analysis of ENN for swarm behaviours in a non-trivial task
(b) the comparison of ENN and LCS for swarm behaviour creation, in relation to swarm performance, reliability and time efficiency

The remainder of this paper is structured with Sect. 2 presenting a background on swarm ENN and LCS; the agent architecture and modification to the ENN algorithm presented in Sect. 3; Sect. 4 defines the experiments of this study; Sect. 5 presenting the results; and finally this work is concluded in Sect. 6.

2   Related Work

2.1   Swarm ANN

Since early robotic-NN works [3], shallow NNs have been evolved to connect sensor inputs, such as IR range values, with actuator controls, such as individual motor velocities. In these early works, a binary GA was used for autonomous selection of the available sensor values to be used as NN inputs. This search allowed for redundant environment data to be removed from the agents' observation. Furthermore, by evolving the *input activation* genome, the development of an agent was accelerated as this hyper-parameter did not require manual tuning or exhaustive exploration. In contrast to this input evolution, [8,18,25] had respectively: a single, a group and a swarm of robotic agent(s), equipped with fully connected, single-layer NNs. The GAs of these works created behaviours by evolving the neuron weights, connecting the input and output nodes. These agents were evaluated with simplistic tasks, such as moving to a goal location.

These two approaches have been combined in recent swarm evolution studies by Heinerman *et al.* [13,14]. In these works, a swarm was assigned the (simplistic) task of travelling about an environment at maximum speed, without collision. Three-levels of adjustment were utilised to create the required behaviour:

1. The aforementioned evolution of active inputs for the NN was evolved between implementations of the swarm.
2. The heterogeneous evolution of neuron weightings was evolved by each swarm member throughout each trial, with set evaluation windows for measuring weight genome quality.
3. Inter-swarm genome sharing was utilised to accelerate the evolution and reduce behaviour rediscovery [5] in the heterogeneous swarm.

Using multiple evolution layers allowed the swarm to create an overall behaviour genome, which could be stored and reused in later implementations. It also allowed the swarm to be adjustable during operations, overcoming unexpected environment variation. These qualities are also seen in the LCS behaviour creation of [22].

2.2   Learning Classifier System

LCS swarm behaviour creation [22] uses a combination of inter-implementation evolution and intra-implementation RL to create and adjust swarm behaviours created from a set of condition-action (or '*if-then*') rules. These rule-sets are created via the deconstruction of known swarming heuristics, and each rule reconstructed via grammar based genetic programming [19]. During operation, RL has the agents learn appropriate rule use for a given situation. After each swarm implementation, the rule-sets of low performing agents are evolved via the adoption of rules from high performing agents and the mutation of currently held rules.

3   Swarm Task, Agent Architecture and ENN implementation

In this section, the problem domain is further defined and the agent observation methods, available actions and reward function are presented. To improve comparability between ENN and LCS, both utilise the same input variables, action outputs and evaluation functions.

3.1   Problem Domain

In this study, a swarm of Unmanned Aerial Vehicles (UAVs) is simulated assisting the transfer of 125 MB of data between two human-operated devices which are separated by 500 m of random urban landscape and have no satellite connectivity. For simulation simplicity, these devices are abstracted to stationary communication devices, one being a data sink, the other a data source. Furthermore, this data is discretised into s segments.

For the most effective communication assistance the swarm aims to achieve full data-transfer in minimum time, thus behaviour solutions are evaluated via,

$$\text{fit}_r \in \mathbb{R} : (-1, 1) = \frac{s_s}{s} - \frac{T_s}{T} \tag{1}$$

where s_s is the data-segments that reached the sink within the simulation time-limit, T, and T_s is simulation time. The termination criteria of this task results in either $\frac{s_s}{s} = 1$, causing a positive fitness, or $\frac{T_s}{T} = 1$, causing a negative fitness.

These negative fitnesses are further defined as *shallow failure* and *complete failure*. In the case of shallow failure, all data does not reach the sink devices within the utilised T, but is expected to as $T \to \infty$. In contrast, when fit $\leq \frac{\Phi}{s} - 1$, where Φ is the swarm size, the solution is seen as a complete failure. This fitness suggests each agent only transferred $[0, 1]$ segments during T. Such a score has a close correlation to all agents becoming trapped by obstacles or non-cooperative behaviours emerging. In such situations, the swarm is predicted to fail the data-transfer task even as $T \to \infty$.

3.2   Observation Inputs and Action Outputs

To facilitate data-transfer, agents move toward the goal location with segments in a buffer and transmit these segments to other agents or the non-swarm devices (human communication devices).

An issue that arises with the NN swarms of literature, [14, 25], is low-level sensor reading inputs and actuator command outputs cannot realise complex actions without considerable exploration during swarm behaviour evolution. These low-level controls are referred to by Duarte *et al.* in [6] as *primitives*, which are seen as insufficient for 'complex robots in tasks beyond mere locomotion' [6]. As such, a higher level of control is proposed which utilises Low-Level Heuristics (LLH) as both inputs and outputs for the ANN. These LLH are the conditions and actions used in the LCS behaviours, as defined in [22].

For the inputs of the agents, the philosophies of swarm robotics in [4] are upheld by limiting sensor complexity. The inputs are restricted to fellow swarm agent positions, determined via signal triangulation, and network status, determined via information propagation. Agents are also aware of currently observable obstacles by simple range sensors; however, no environment mapping is utilised.

For the action outputs of the swarm agents, five networking and relative motion actions are utilised. These actions are further defined via alternative targeting, giving a total of 15 options. ENN selects from these actions by linking each to an output node; the output node with the highest activation value is executed, similar to [17]. For LCS, each rule associates an environment input condition to one of these actions, creating a discrete pool of possible actions in each rule-set. In this study these actions are:

1) collect from source
2, 3) send to closest neighbour
    – toward source
    – toward sink
4–7) move toward
    closest neighbour
    source
    sink
    wall

8–11) move away from
    – closest neighbour
    – source
    – sink
    – wall
12–15) orbit
    – closest neighbour
    – source
    – sink
    – wall

It can be observed from this action list that the swarm agents are responsible for both requesting data from the source and delivering the data to the sink. In this way, the connected devices may remain unaware of the connection being swarm-based; no swarm statuses or behaviour information is fed into the non-swarm devices nor must the non-swarm devices govern the flow of data. As such, the swarm may assist data communication transparently and without requiring the humans or connecting devices to alter their activities to interact with or assist the swarm.

3.3 Reward Function

Swarm agents evaluate local performance via a Geographical routing [11] based reward, ρ. This function is defined as,

$$\rho_\alpha = \sum_{s \in S_h} \Delta(r_{s,\text{sink}}) + \sum_{s \in S_t} \Delta(r_{s,\text{sink}}) + \sum_{s \in S_r} \Delta(r_{s,\text{sink}})$$

$$\rho_\beta = \begin{cases} 0, & |S_h| > 0 \vee |S_t| > 0 \vee |S_r| > 0 \\ \Delta(r_{i,\text{source}}), & \text{otherwise} \end{cases} \tag{2}$$

$$\rho = \log(|\rho_\alpha| + 1) \cdot \text{sgn}(\rho_\alpha) + \log(|\rho_\beta| + 1) \cdot \text{sgn}(\rho_\beta) - c$$

where

- ρ_α is the reward generated by data-segments in S_h, S_t and S_r, which are respectively the agent's collections of data-segments held, transferred and received since last scoring
- ρ_β is the reward a data-less agent receives for moving toward the source
- $\Delta(r_{s,sink})$ is the change in distance between a data segment and sink since last scoring
- $\Delta(r_{i,source})$ is equivalent for agent and source
- c is a cost value for the performed action (communication or movement), which may be weighted to encourage greater agent energy efficiency.

This reward equation encourages agents to effectively transport and transmit data in the direction of the known sink, or return to the source for further data collection.

3.4   Evolved Neural Network Architecture

In alignment with Heinerman [14], the NN structure used by ENN has no hidden layers and thus input and output nodes directly connecting with a weight set W, where the connection of input i and output o is $w_{i,o} \in W$, $w \in \mathbb{R} : (-1, 1)$. These weights are periodically evolved during the swarm implementation and *input activation* genomes, Γ_{enn}, are evolved offline, between swarm implementations. After empirical exploration, it has been found the third level of adjustment in [14], periodic inter-swarm W exchange, does not results in performance improvement in this swarm implementation. However, the additional offline evolution of *starting weights*, $\bar{W}$, and the use of Γ_{enn} and $\bar{W}$ sharing between swarm members during offline evolution shows some performance improvement. This evolution of starting weights reduces the re-evolution of similar W for each implementation.

During implementation, the current W, W_n, is evaluated via the sum of action rewards, ρ, over period T_w. After T_w, a hill-climbing acceptance function is used to replace the current best W, W_{best}, with W_n if $(\sum \rho)_{best} < (\sum \rho)_n$, or discard W_n otherwise. Should W_n be discarded, the mutation rate, ψ, is modified by a constant increment value, $\dot{\psi}$, via $\psi + \dot{\psi} \rightarrow \psi$. If W_{best} is replaced, ψ it set to $1 \cdot \dot{\psi}$. The potentially updated W_{best} is then mutated for further exploration; $\forall w_{i,o}$ being adjusted via a Gaussian with mean 0 and ψ standard deviation.

After each swarm evaluation is terminated, offline evolution is conducted on the Γ_{enn} and $\bar{W}$. As stated above, this evolution utilises behaviour sharing between swarm members. In this study, this behaviour sharing consists of high-performing swarm members transferring a copy of Γ_{enn} and $\bar{W}$ to low-performing swarm members. Agents' individual performances are measured via the number of data segments that were held by the agent for at least one time-step in the evaluation and reached the sink by implementation end. The threshold between high- and low-performance is the mean of performances over the swarm, as implemented in [21]. Each low-performance agent undergoes offline evolution via crossover and mutation, and a high-performing agent is selected via roulette-wheel to share its behaviour with the evolving agent. The offline evolution of an agent's Γ_{enn} and $\bar{W}$ consists of each genome undergoing one-point crossover. The parents of each crossover are the genome held by the agent and the shared genome. The offspring also undergos mutation via bit-wise flipping for Γ_{enn} and via digit-wise Gaussian shifting for $\bar{W}$. The offline sharing of genomes allows effective individual agent behaviours to be distributed across the swarm, as seen in [14], though the use of this genome in the evolution process allows the swarm to remain heterogeneous, and thus specialised behaviours may still emerge. Additionally, as both the input activation and starting weight evolution are conducted offline, the set of all agents' Γ_{enn} and $\bar{W}$ may be defined as a swarm behaviour solution which remains constant throughout an implementation.

For this data-transfer problem, the structure of the ENN has an input layer of 10 nodes, each with value $\mathbb{R} : [0, 1]$ which are normalised representations of internal and local environment state conditions.

4 Experiment Design

4.1 Simulation

For this study, MASON [16], a Java-based multi-agent simulator, is used for swarm implementation. In these tests, time is discretised into 200 ms time-steps and agents are assumed to travel with mean velocities of $5\,\text{ms}^{-1}$; speeds achievable by UAVs [9]. These time discretisation and agent speeds have been chosen so that 1 time-step represent 1 m of agent travel. Using this discretisation, the file transfer task is broken into 500 data-segments of 2 Mb (0.25 MB) each. Each data-segment is simulated as a single unit, and thus must be wholly transferred within a single time-step. This segment sizing assumes transfer speeds of 10 Mbps, a value within reason for modern Wi-fi [26]. Furthermore, the data-transfer process of these experiments use the Log-Distance Path Loss (LDPL) model [20], which estimates the signal power loss over distance with Gaussian shadowing. In alignment with the communication ability of common Wi-fi adaptors [1], agents have a transfer power of 12 dBm, a receiving threshold of −83 dBm, and a Signal to Noise and Interference Ratio (SNIR) of 10. These signals are transferred at 2.412 GHz (Wi-Fi channel 1 [2]), the environment has a path-loss exponent of 2.5 and Gaussian shadowing with mean 0 and standard deviation 3 dB. The source and sink are placed ∼500 m apart with randomly generated obstacles between. These obstacles attenuate the signal by 5 dB [7] per meter the signal passes through. Finally, the time-limit, T of these tests is 20,000 time-steps, which translates to just over one hour of swarm operation.

4.2 Evolution Parameters

To evolve W in ENN, T_w is set to 20 time-steps and $\dot{\psi}$ to 10^{-3}. For the crossover and mutation of input activation genomes and $\bar{W}$, the mutation rate is set to 5% (to match [14]) and the Gaussian shift of $\bar{W}$ has mean 0 and standard deviation 0.25. Finally, LCS has an evolution generation limit of 500, and ENN has a limit of 1,000. The additional ENN generations allow both algorithms to reach evolution search convergence.

4.3 Experimental Settings

To explore these two algorithms, two experiments are conducted for each: environment-specific evolution and environment-generic evolution.

In the first experiment, 10 sets of 30 environments are presented to LCS and ENN for behaviour evolution. The best-evolved fitness, according to (1), is recorded for each environment and the median and inner quartile of these best fitnesses are reported for each of the ten sets along with the results of a Mann-Whitney U-Test, with $\alpha = 0.05$, to validate the variation in performances. Each of the environments use random generation to determine the obstacle configurations and the initially generated behaviours of the swarm. These generators are uniquely seeded for each of the 30 environments, and the same seed is used for both LCS and ENN to ensure comparable results. The ten environment sets explore variation in the task settings; validating the comparison between the algorithms. In these sets, the background noise is $-85\,$dBm or $-95\,$dBm and each noise is tested with a swarm of size 1, 2, 4, 8 and 16.

In addition to the fitness results, the percentages of best-evolved solutions which *shallow fail* or *completely fail* the data-transfer task are reported, as task reliability is seen as a key attribute for evaluating the swarm behaviour. Furthermore, the evolutionary improvements of ENN and LCS are reported via the median and inner quartiles of fitness differences between first generations and best-evolved generations for each experiment set.

The second experiment of this study explores the algorithms' abilities to create generally applicable behaviours. A further 30 behaviours are evolved in this experiment with each generation evaluated by using the mean fitness in five training obstacle configurations. The resulting behaviour is tested in a further 30 alternative obstacle configuration environments, giving a total of 900 evaluations per algorithm. In this second experiment, the background noise and swarm size remain constant at $-95\,$dBm and 8, respectively. This experiment explores the generality and reusability of the created behaviours. For both algorithms, the post-evolution behaviour fitnesses and alternative environment fitnesses are presented via median and inner quartiles, and the Mann-Whitney U-Test, fail-rates and evolution progress are again reported. Additionally, the evolution fitness growth of the algorithms is explored via a moving average graph, with a window of 50 generations, and via a graph of the best-evolved solution fitness by each generation. For each algorithm, these graphs are combined for all 30 evolution runs, with the reported values being the average and 90% confidence intervals of the set.

Finally, the processing time required by ENN and LCS to create behaviours are reported. The average time over all evolutions of both above experiments are presented tabularly, along with the average number of time-steps in these evolutions. Additionally, these times and time-step results are graphically presented for further discussion and justification.

5   Results and Discussion

5.1   Environment-Specific Evolution

Shown in Fig. 1 is the median and inner quartiles of both approaches for the discussed background noise and swarm size settings. LCS produces significantly greater fitness solutions over ENN, with all sets showing no quartile overlap. Additionally, the Mann-Whitney U-tests reports values less than 0.001 for all swarm sizes and background noises, this indicates the better performance of LCS is statistically significant. The most significant fitness difference is in the high-noise environments with 8 swarm members; the median fitness difference is 61% of the fitness range ($\frac{0.35--0.872}{1--1}$).

In addition to fitness superiority, Table 1 shows LCS swarms to be more reliable in completing the data-transfer task, with LCS swarms never completely failing the task. In contrast, ENN swarms see some complete failure cases for most swarm sizes with -85 dBm and for 1-agent swarms with -95 dBm background noise.

Figure 2 shows the median and inner quartile for the evolutionary fitness-improvement. These graphs show the evolution fitness-improvement of both LCS and ENN follow bell-shaped relations to the swarm size, though the algorithms in the two noise settings demonstrate different aspects of this relation. Firstly, ENN demonstrates the lower limit of the relation; for high noise environments, with swarm size ≤ 4, no fitness-improvement is seen. In contrast, ENN swarms of 8 to 16 agents in -85 dBm noise shows a positive relation between swarm size and fitness increase. Likewise, all LCS swarms in -85 dBm noise and all ENN swarms in -95 dBm show a steady increase in fitness-improvement for sizes 1 to 8. An improvement plateau then occurs for these swarms (LCS in -85 dBm and ENN in -95 dBm) when the swarm size increases from 8 to 16. These plateaus have similar fitness-improvements for all swarm sizes and Fig. 1 reports similar or greater final fitnesses. This represents the saturation limit of the fitness-improvement possible by the evolutionary searches; further swarm size increments are predicted to not produce greater fitnesses. Finally, LCS swarms of 8 to 16 agents in -95 dBm noise show a decline in fitness-improvement although Fig. 1 reports these settings both produce high fitness swarms. This suggests the data-transfer task has been simplified by the low noise and large swarm size, and thus requires little (or no) evolution by LCS; the RL of LCS and the variation of rule-sets in the large heterogeneous swarm allows first generation swarms to complete the data-transfer task with significant throughput.

From this pattern observation, LCS leads ENN relative to swarm size impacting fitness-improvement; LCS reaches improvement plateau as ENN begins increasing, and undergoes improvement decline as ENN reaches the plateau. Additionally, it can be observed that both LCS and ENN swarms in -95 dBm, with sizes of 8 and 16, have saturated evolution improvements, yet, Fig. 1 reports

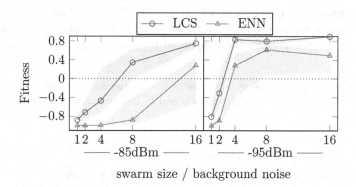

Fig. 1. Median & inner quartiles for each algorithm after evolution. LCS has significantly higher *median*, with no quartile overlap, compared to ENN for all experiment settings.

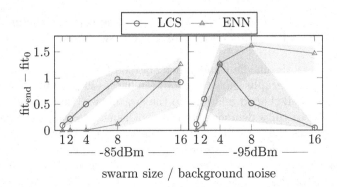

swarm size / background noise

Fig. 2. Median and inner quartile for fitness-improvement during evolution. Both algorithms have little growth when the swarm size is small or when the task is more challenging due to extra background noise.

LCS to produce swarms of greater fitness. Therefore, LCS still dominates ENN with both in optimal conditions. In these optimal settings, LCS has a median fitness of 0.89, which translates to a data-transfer time of 7 min, 20 s or an average transfer of 2.27 Mbps. In contrast, the peak median fitness of ENN is 0.615, which equates to 25 min, 40 s or 650 kbps. It can therefore be concluded, the agent architecture of LCS , particularly the online adjustment of RL rather than periodic weight evolution, allows for overall greater swarm performance.

5.2   Environment-General Evolution

Figure 3 shows the median and inner quartile fitness for the best-evolved behaviours in the training environments, and in the 900 unseen evaluation environments. Additionally, this figure includes evolutionary fitness-improvements.

The LCS swarm shows relatively small reductions in evolution performance when comparing the environment-specific results, Fig. 1, and multi-environment, Fig. 3, results; a median fitness reduction of only 4% is seen. In contrast, the evolution of ENN is significantly impacted by evaluating each generation with

Table 1. Shallow and complete failure rates for environment-specific tests. Fail-rates show LCS never completely fails the task and is less impacted by swarm size than ENN.

		\-85 dBm					\-5 dBm				
		1	2	4	8	16	1	2	4	8	16
LCS	Shallow failure (%)	100	100	66.7	30	6.7	100	66.7	3.3	6.7	0
	Complete failure (%)	0	0	0	0	0	0	0	0	0	0
ENN	Shallow failure (%)	100	100	100	86.7	46.7	100	100	36.7	20	16.7
	Complete failure (%)	26.7	10	0	10	3.3	13.3	0	0	0	0

multiple environments; the median fitness of ENN reduces by 72.5% of the fitness range $(\frac{0.71-(-0.74)}{1--1})$ and is below fitness 0.

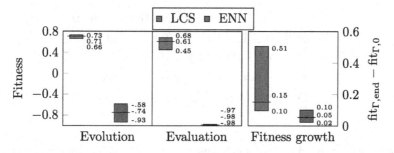

Fig. 3. Median and inner quartile results of best fitnesses during evolution (left), fitness-improvement during evolution (right) and behaviours implemented in unseen environments (centre). Significantly lower evolution progress by ENN results in complete failure in alternative environments.

Furthermore, the created behaviours of LCS prove effectively general with the median fitness of the 900 alternative environments being relatively high at 0.61. This shows even in inexperienced situations the LCS swarm may still transfer data with effective throughput. Additionally, the shallow failures, reported in Table 2, remain relatively low at 13.5% and only 5.2% of cases showed complete data-transfer failure. In comparison, ENN shows considerably lower performance in alternative environments, with all trials being shallow failures, and 36.7% of trials completely failing. As a result of this, a fitness difference of 79.5% arises between ENN and LCS, and LCS produces more reliable solutions. As can be expected from these results, the Mann-Whitney U-tests again reports statistically significant differences, with values less than 0.001. Initially, this poor ENN performance was speculated to be the result of acceptable, but over specialised, behaviours evolving for the five evolution environments and thus not being reusable in the alternative environments. However, the low evolution fitness in Fig. 3 (left) and low evolution improvement in Fig. 3 (right) shows this over specialisation failure is more significant; the ENN evolution cannot createNN which are generally applicable to all five evolution environments, even when given 1000 generations to do so, much less be reusable in the unseen environments. To further explore this failure, Fig. 4 presents the fitness change during evolution for both LCS and ENN via a moving average fitness over the generations, and the best-found fitness during evolution. These graphs show the LCS evolution often finds low-performing solutions, though intermittently discovers high-performing solutions which allow the average maximum fitness to rise to 0.6 by generation 10. In contrast, ENN sees little improvement and no NN configurations are found to solve the task in all evaluation environments. This evolution failure is due to the neural weights requiring specialised settings for each environment. In contrast, the condition-action rules of LCS observe the

Table 2. Shallow and complete failure rates for environment-general tests, both after evolution and when evaluated in alternative environments. Fail-rates show LCS has minor shallow and complete failures, while ENN has over seven times the complete failures and all trials resulted in shallow failure.

		Evolution	Evaluation
LCS	Shallow failure (%)	0	13.2
	Complete failure (%)	0	5.2
ENN	Shallow failure (%)	100	100
	Complete failure (%)	0	36.7

environmental state via hyper-plane dissection, and allow wider application of each rule. Thus the LCS rules has greater applicability during evolution and unseen evaluation.

In relation to transfer speeds in the unseen environments, LCS achieves a median transfer time of 26 min or 641 kbps. Although this value is considerably lower than in environment-specific cases, ENN sees greater reductions with a median of 10 data segments transferred in T, giving an average throughput of 500 bps. It can thus be concluded that ENN is incapable of evolving generally applicable solutions for the application of data-transfer, and thus can only be utilised when an environment is known *a priori*. Additionally, it can be noted that LCS behaviours in unknown environments and ENN in known environments achieve relatively similar performances. This strengthens the argument

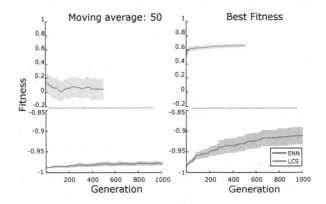

Fig. 4. ENN and LCS average generation fitnesses during environment-general behaviour creation. Left graphs are rolling average fitness with window size of 50 generations. Right graphs are best fitness by generation. Each graph averaged over 30 evolution instances with the averages shown by solid line and 95% confidence intervals shown by shaded areas. LCS has low average fitness but high performing solutions are intermittently discovered. ENN remains low throughout the evolution. As stated in Sect. 4, ENN is evolved for twice the generations of LCS.

for LCS being capable of producing behaviours which are generally applicable in environments unseen before.

5.3 Execution Time

To finalise this study, the average execution time for ENN and LCS are listed in Table 3 for both environment-specific and environment-general behaviour creation. Furthermore, to examine these time differences, the average time-steps are also listed in this table, and the two values are graphically presented in Fig. 5. For both environment-specific and environment-general evolution, ENN requires longer execution time than LCS. For the environment-specific evolution, an execution time 3.7 times that of LCS is observed and when multiple environments are used for evaluation, this multiplier grows to 5.2. This difference is due to two main factors: the lower fitness of ENN throughput evolution requiring more time-steps, and the evolution process of ENN being generally slower than LCS.

In relation to the additional time-steps, a lower fitness directly attributes to longer execution time as each evaluation with a fitness in the range $[-1, 0]$ operates for T time-steps while a solution with positive fitness requires $T_s = T \cdot (1 - Fit)$ steps. In Table 3, ENN is shown to perform, on average, 3.1 and 3.8 times the time-steps of LCS (for specific and general evolution, respectively).

Table 3. Average real-world evolution time (in minutes) and average time-steps for LCS and ENN (multiplied by $T = 20,000$). LCS is more time effective in both experiments.

	Env. Specific		Env. General	
	LCS	ENN	LCS	ENN
Average execution time (min)	60	220	120	620
Average time-steps ($\times T$)	319	988	471	1778

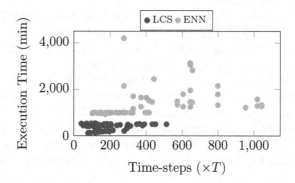

Fig. 5. ENN and LCS graphical depiction of execution time versus time-steps. ENN has have higher execution time, irrespective of time-steps.

After accounting for ENN performing twice the evolution generations of LCS, these time-step ratios are confirmed to contribute to the longer evolution time.

To demonstrate the evolution operations of ENN are generally slower than LCS, Fig. 5 shows the two algorithms hold relatively constant execution times for the time-step range 0 to 300. In this range ENN shows a constant execution time 245% that of LCS. After accounting for the additional evolution generations in ENN, this ratio confirms the evolution and operation of LCS to be generally faster and thus more efficient than ENN.

Table 3 and Fig. 5 shown that LCS is a more efficient behaviour creating algorithm within the context of the data-transfer task of this study. This efficiency is due to both the higher performance throughout evolution allowing faster evaluations and the evolution process for genome alteration being significantly faster.

6   Conclusion and Further Work

In this paper, we have explored two algorithms for creating behaviours which allow a swarm of robots to assist humans in communication restricted, urban environments by facilitating data-transfer between them; a challenging task by swarm robotic standards. Furthermore, these behaviours are required to have the swarm unintrusively interact with the communication devices in a way that the devices (and human operators) do not need to adjust their activities to have the swarm assist.

The two algorithms explored are a well-cited technique for evolving neural networks, ENN, and our own LCS-based algorithm.

This investigation has shown our LCS approach to be significantly superior for this real-world application, in regards to swarm performance and reliability while also creating the behaviours in less time. When the environment conditions are explicitly evolved, we see the LCS swarms achieved an average transfer-rate of 2.27 Mbps in optimal conditions, while the ENN swarm reached only 0.65 Mbps. Additionally, we see ENN has a far higher probability of failing to evolve a valid behaviour for a given environment.

For environments not known *a priori*, ENN shows complete failure to create generally applicable behaviours while LCS sees only minor performance reduction. Finally, it has been shown that LCS evolves these behaviours in far less time, showing it is both more effective and efficient.

From this, our hypothesis is validated that ENN, which is seen as state of the art in swarm literature, is better suited to trivial problems, such as locomotion, while our LCS approach may be applied to this real-world task.

In relation to future work, three areas will be explored for this behaviour creation development: further exploring NN driven swarms, further evaluating the behaviours created by these algorithms, and implementing life-long behaviour learning in the swarm.

Firstly, we aim to further explore the potential of neural network-driven swarms. This exploration will examine more traditional approaches of neural networks, such as offline batch training of NN via expert behaviour data. These techniques have seen significant success in non-swarm robotic behaviour creation and thus show potential for swarm implementation.

Secondly, this exploration has evaluated the algorithms in resulting swarm fitness (which includes task efficiency), reliability and behaviour creation time. Additionally, by evaluating the swarms in conditions unseen during training, the reusability of the created behaviours was assessed. However, for real-world swarm implementations, it is acknowledged that further evaluation work is required. This includes evaluating the energy efficiency of the behaviours, the emergent behaviours' robustness to member loss and mid-operation condition changes, and assessing the predictability of the agents to either improve robot-human cooperation or reduce the swarm's venerability to malicious attack.

Finally, this study has revealed that although LCS creates environment-general behaviours with greater performance than ENN, some performance reduction is still present compared to environment-specific behaviours. To overcome such reduction, our final future work will explore life-long learning in the form of adding each evolved behaviour to a repertoire. During deployment, agents may select from this repertoire in place of evolving new solutions. In doing so, we aim to see the performance of environment-specific behaviours with the wide applicability of environment-general behaviours.

Acknowledgement. Funding for this research was provided by Cyber and Electronic Warfare Division, Defence Science and Technology Group, Commonwealth of Australia.

References

1. RN-XV Data Sheet. https://cdn.sparkfun.com/datasheets/Wireless/WiFi/WiFly-RN-XV-DS.pdf
2. IEEE standard for information technology–telecommunications and information exchange between systems local and metropolitan area networks–specific requirements - Part 11: wireless LAN medium access control (mac) and physical layer (phy) specifications. IEEE Std 802.11-2016 (Revision of IEEE Std 802.11-2012), pp. 1–3534, December 2016. https://doi.org/10.1109/IEEESTD.2016.7786995
3. Balakrishnan, K., Honavar, V.: On sensor evolution in robotics. In: Conference on Genetic Programming, pp. 455–460. MIT Press (1996)
4. Brambilla, M., Ferrante, E., Birattari, M., Dorigo, M.: Swarm robotics: a review from the swarm engineering perspective. Swarm Intell. **7**(1), 1–41 (2013)
5. D'Ambrosio, D.B., Lehman, J., Risi, S., Stanley, K.O.: Evolving policy geometry for scalable multiagent learning. In: International Conference on Autonomous Agents and Multiagent Systems, vol. 1, pp. 731–738 (2010)
6. Duarte, M., Gomes, J., Oliveira, S.M., Christensen, A.L.: Evolution of repertoire-based control for robots with complex locomotor systems. IEEE Trans. Evol. Comput. **22**(2), 314–328 (2018)
7. Faria, D.B.: Modeling signal attenuation in IEEE 802.11 wireless LANs. Computer Science Department, Stanford University 1 (2005)
8. Floreano, D., Mondada, F.: Automatic creation of an autonomous agent: genetic evolution of a neural network driven robot. In: From Animals to Animats 3: International Conference on Simulation of Adaptive Behavior, pp. 421–430. The MIT Press (1994)

9. Fotouhi, A., Ding, M., Hassan, M.: Dronecells: Improving 5g spectral efficiency using drone-mounted flying base stations. arXiv preprint arXiv:1707.02041 (2017)

10. Fraser, B., Szabo, C., Hunjet, R.: Simulating the effect of degraded wireless communications on emergent behaviour. In: Proceedings of the 2017 Winter Simulation Conference (2017)

11. Ghafoor, K.Z., Lloret, J., Sadiq, A.S., Mohammed, M.A.: Improved geographical routing in vehicular ad hoc networks. Wireless Pers. Commun. **80**(2), 785–804 (2014). https://doi.org/10.1007/s11277-014-2041-3

12. Hauert, S., Zufferey, J.C., Floreano, D.: Evolved swarming without positioning information: an application in aerial communication relay. Auton. Robots **26**(1), 21–32 (2009)

13. Heinerman, J., Drupsteen, D., Eiben, A.E.: Three-fold adaptivity in groups of robots: the effect of social learning. In: Conference on Genetic and Evolutionary Computation, pp. 177–183. ACM (2015)

14. Heinerman, J., Rango, M., Eiben, A.E.: Evolution, individual learning, and social learning in a swarm of real robots. In: Symposium Series on Computational Intelligence, pp. 1055–1062. IEEE (2015)

15. Holland, J.H., Reitman, J.S.: Cognitive systems based on adaptive algorithms. ACM Sigart. Bull. **63**, 49–49 (1977)

16. Computer Science & Engineering Laboratory: The GMU Center for Social Complexity: Mason. http://cs.gmu.edu/~eclab/projects/mason/

17. Liu, C., Zhu, E., Zhang, Q., Wei, X.: Modeling of agent cognition in extensive games via artificial neural networks. IEEE Trans. Neural Networks Learn. Syst. **99**, 1–12 (2018)

18. Nelson, A.L., Grant, E., Henderson, T.C.: Evolution of neural controllers for competitive game playing with teams of mobile robots. Robot. Auton. Syst. **46**(3), 135–150 (2004)

19. O'Neill, M.: Grammatical evolution: evolutionary automatic programming in an arbitrary language. Kluwer Academic Publishers, Boston (2003)

20. Rappaport, T.S., et al.: Wireless communications: principles and practice, vol. 2. Prentice Hall, PTR (1996)

21. Smith, P., Hunjet, R., Aleti, A., Barca, J.C., et al.: Data transfer via UAV swarm behaviours: Rule generation, evolution and learning. Aust. J. Telecommun. Dig. Econ. **6**(2), 35 (2018)

22. Smith, P., Hunjet, R., Khan, A.: Swarm learning in restricted environments: an examination of semi-stochastic action selection. In: International Conference on Control, Automation, Robotics and Vision, pp. 848–855. IEEE (2018)

23. Soleymani, T., Trianni, V., Bonani, M., Mondada, F., Dorigo, M.: Bio-inspired construction with mobile robots and compliant pockets. Robot. Auton. Syst. **74**, 340–350 (2015)

24. Timmis, J., Ismail, A.R., Bjerknes, J.D., Winfield, A.F.: An immune-inspired swarm aggregation algorithm for self-healing swarm robotic systems. Biosystems **146**, 60–76 (2016). https://doi.org/10.1016/j.biosystems.2016.04.001, https://www.ncbi.nlm.nih.gov/pubmed/27178784

25. Trianni, V.: Evolutionary swarm robotics: evolving self-organising behaviours in groups of autonomous robots, vol. 108. Springer (2008)

26. Vassis, D., Kormentzas, G., Rouskas, A., Maglogiannis, I.: The IEEE 802.11 g standard for high data rate WLANs. IEEE network **19**(3), 21–26 (2005)

Agent-Based Complex Automated Negotiations

Agent-Based Complex Automated Negotiations

Takayuki Ito[1], Minjie Zhang[2], Reyhan Aydoğan[3], Di Wang[4],
Ahmed Moustafa[1], and Takanobu Otsuka[1]

[1] Nagoya Institute of Technology, Japan
{ito.takayuki, ahmed.moustafa,
takanobu.otsuka}@nitech.ac.jp
[2] University of Wollongong, Australia
minjie@uow.edu.au
[3] Özyeğin University, Turkey
reyhan.aydogan@ozyegin.edu.tr
[4] Nanyang Technological University, Singapore
WangDi@ntu.edu.sg

Complex Automated Negotiations have been widely studied and are one of the emerging areas of research in the field of Autonomous Agents and Multi-Agent Systems. These days AI systems have been developed by many different companies and organizations. In the near future, if a lot of heterogeneous AI systems are acting in a society, then we do need to have coordination mechanisms based on automated negotiation technologies. It must be complex and also autonomous because of the complexity of our society.

The complexity in an automated negotiation depends on several factors: the number of negotiated issues, dependencies between these issues, representation of the utility, negotiation procedural and protocol, negotiation form (bilateral or multi-party), time constraints negotiation goals, and so on. Complex automated negotiation scenarios are concerned with negotiation encounters where we may have for instance, a large number of agents, a large number of issues with strong interdependencies, real time constraints, concurrent and inter-depended negotiation, and etc. Many real world negotiation scenarios present one or more of the mentioned elements. Software agents can support the automation of complex negotiations, by negotiating on the behalf of their owners and providing adequate strategies to their owners to achieve realistic, win-win agreements. In order to provide solutions in such complex automated negotiation scenarios, research has focused on incorporating different technologies including search, CSP, graphical utility models, Bayesian nets, auctions, utility graphs, optimization and predicting and learning methods. The applications of complex automated negotiations could include e-commerce tools, decision-making support tools, negotiation support tools, collaboration tools, as well as knowledge discovery and agent learning tools.

ACAN2019 will discuss, among others, the following aspects and topics of such complex automated negotiations within the field of Autonomous Agents and Multi-Agent Systems, which have distinct relationships with IJCAI main conference topics:

- Complex Automated Negotiations Frameworks and Mechanisms.
- Bilateral and Multilateral Negotiations, High dimension Multi-Issue Negotiations, Large Scale Negotiations, Concurrent Negotiations, Multiple Negotiations, Sequential Negotiations, Negotiations under Asymmetric Information, and so on

- Complex Automated Negotiations Frameworks and Mechanisms.
- Bilateral and Multilateral Negotiations, High dimension Multi-Issue Negotiations, Large Scale Negotiations, Concurrent Negotiations, Multiple Negotiations, Sequential Negotiations, Negotiations under Asymmetric Information, and so on
- Prediction of Opponent's Behaviors and Strategies in Negotiations
- Machine Learning in Negotiations
- Simulation Models and Platforms for Complex Negotiations
- Coordination Mechanisms for Complex Negotiations
- Matchmaking and Brokering Mechanisms
- 2-Sided Matching
- Utility and Preference Elicitation Technologies in Negotiations
- Utility and Preference Representations in Negotiations
- Computational Complexity of Multi-Issue Negotiations
- Real-life Aspects of Electronic Negotiations
- Negotiations with Humans, Negotiations in Social Networks etc.
- Knowledge management in Automated Negotiations.
- Moral consideration for automated negotiations.
- Applications for Automated Negotiations (e.g. cloud computing, smart grid, electronic commerce etc.)

A considerable number of researchers in various sub-communities of autonomous agents and multi-agent systems are actively working on these and related issues. They are, for instance, being studied in agent negotiations, multi-issue negotiations, auctions, mechanism design, electronic commerce, voting, secure protocols, matchmaking and brokering, argumentation, co-operation mechanisms and distributed optimization.

The goal of this workshop is to bring together researchers from these communities to learn about each other's approaches to the complex negotiation problems, encourages the exchange of ideas between the different areas, and potentially fosters long-term research collaborations to accelerate progress towards scaling up to larger and more realistic applications.

Automated Negotiating Agents Competition (ANAC) Special Session from 2010 has been tightly cooperating with ANAC (Automated Negotiating Agents Competition). This year, we had an ANAC special session, in which we explained and discussed the research challenges addressed in ANAC 2018.

This year, we had 11 submissions. 7 papers were accepted as full papers (acceptance rate = 64 %). The other paper were accepted as short papers. Each paper was reviewed by at least three PC members or experts in the field. Acceptance standards included its technical soundness, novelty, impact and readability. We selected the following paper as the best paper, which was nominated based on the scores of the reviews, and finally selected by the organizers[1].

- (Best Paper Award) Ryuta Arisaka and Takayuki Ito. Numerical Abstract Persuasion Argumentation for Expressing Concurrent Multi-Agent Negotiations.

---

[1] Since Takayuki Ito is one of the authors, he was not included in this selection process.

Numerical Abstract Persuasion Argumentation for Expressing Concurrent Multi-Agent Negotiations

Ryuta Arisaka$^{(\boxtimes)}$ and Takayuki Ito

Nagoya Institute of Technology, Nagoya, Japan
ryutaarisaka@gmail.com,ito.takayuki@nitech.ac.jp

Abstract. A negotiation process by 2 agents e_1 and e_2 can be interleaved by another negotiation process between, say, e_1 and e_3. The interleaving may alter the resource allocation assumed at the inception of
the first negotiation process. Existing proposals for argumentation-based
negotiations have focused primarily on two-agent bilateral negotiations,
but scarcely on the concurrency of multi-agent negotiations. To fill the
gap, we present a novel argumentation theory, basing its development
on abstract persuasion argumentation (which is an abstract argumentation formalism with a dynamic relation). Incorporating into it numerical information and a mechanism of handshakes among members of the
dynamic relation, we show that the extended theory adapts well to concurrent multi-agent negotiations over scarce resources.

1 Introduction

Agent negotiations may be modelled by game-theoretical approaches, heuristic-
based approaches or argumentation-based approaches [18]. For obtaining rational
explanations as to why agents (have) come to a deal, the last, argumentation-
based methods (e.g. [3,12–14,18]), with their intrinsic strength to handle information in conflict, have been shown to offer some research perspective and direction.

However, the focus of argumentation-based formal approaches has been primarily on bilateral negotiations involving only two parties so far: extension to
more general multiagent negotiations is not automatic when demand and supply
of scarce resources being negotiated over can change in the middle of a negotiation due to negotiation process interleaving. Consider the following with agents
e_1, e_2, e_3.

Of e_1: She owns an electronics shop. She has recently obtained two Nintendo
Switch. Her ask price for the console is $300 each. She has $0.

Of e_2: He and his brother have been a big Nintendo fan. He has heard that it
is now available at e_1's store. He plans to buy two of them, one for himself,
and the other for his brother. His budget is $650. He currently does not have
a Nintendo Switch.

© Springer Nature Switzerland AG 2020
A. El Fallah Seghrouchni and D. Sarne (Eds.): IJCAI 2019 Workshops, LNAI 12158, pp. 131–149, 2020.
https://doi.org/10.1007/978-3-030-56150-5_7

Of e_3: He is a reseller for profit. He has heard Switch consoles are now at e_1's shop for \$300. He has also heard that e_2 is looking for the console. He plans to buy them up from e_1 and resells them to e_2 for \$400 each. He has \$600, and no Nintendo Switch.

Suppose the preference of each agent is such that:

- e_1 likes to sell both of the Switch consoles. The price per console (\$300) is not negotiable.
- e_2 likes to obtain two Switch consoles. In case of multiple offers, he chooses the cheapest one. If there is only one seller, his default action is to accept any ask price, except when he cannot afford it, in which case he asks the seller to lower the price to the amount he possesses.
- e_3 likes to obtain as many Switch consoles from e_1 for \$300 as his budget allows him, and likes to resell them to e_2 for \$400 so long as e_2 accepts the deal. He is willing to negotiate over the price if e_2 complains at the ask price. However, he will not lower the price below \$300.

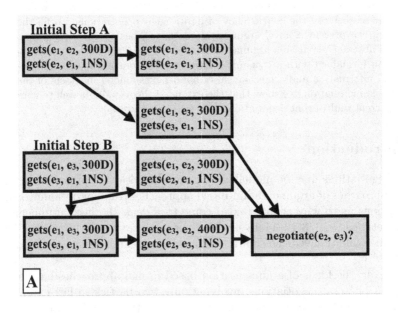

Suppose e_2 and e_3 are the only ones who would visit e_1 for Switch consoles and that both of the consoles would be eventually sold to one of them, the steps indicated in $\boxed{A}$ cover all possible situations that could result. gets(e_x, e_y, nD) means for e_x to get n dollars from e_y, gets(e_x, e_y, nNS) means for e_x to get n Nintendo Switch from e_y, and negotiates(e_x, e_y)? means for e_x to negotiate over the price of 1 Switch with e_y.

Initially, either e_2, as in **Initial Step A** in $\boxed{A}$, or e_3, as in **Initial Step B**, gets 1 Switch from e_1 for \$300. One of the following holds in the end.

1. e_2 gets 2 Switch from e_1 for \$600, and e_3 gets none.

2. e_2 gets 1 Switch from e_1 for \$300, e_3 then gets 1 Switch from e_1 for \$300, and e_3 tries to sell it to e_2 for \$400. Since e_2 at that point has only \$350, he tries to haggle over the price, to settle at \$350.
3. e_3 gets 1 Switch from e_1 for \$300, e_2 then gets 1 Switch from e_1 for \$300, and e_3 tries to sell it to e_2 for \$400. Since e_2 at that point has only \$350, he tries to haggle over the price, to settle at \$350.
4. e_3 gets 2 Switch from e_1, and tries to sell them to e_2 for the total price of \$800. e_2 gets 1 Switch from e_3 for \$400, but for the second Switch, e_2 haggles over the price, to settle at \$250, which fails due to e_3's preference.

Whereas, if a bilateral negotiation can progress uninterrupted till the end, the resource reallocation that the two agents negotiate over will be based on the resource allocation at the inception of the negotiation, a common business negotiation process is often not bound by the tight protocol guaranteeing no interruptions [15,19]. In the above example, even if e_2 wishes to buy 2 Switch consoles from e_1 as in the situation 1., e_3 may pick up a Switch from a shelf by the time e_2 manages to take one of them, leading to the situation 2. or 3.

The argumentation-based negotiation methodologies considered in the literature, mostly for two-party - and not for interleaved - negotiations, do not immediately scale up to addressing this concurrency issue. To adapt to it, in this work we propose a novel argumentation-based negotiation framework. We base the development on abstract persuasion argumentation (APA) [7] which is a dynamic argumentation formalism that conservatively extends Dung abstract argumentation [10]. It accommodates a dynamic relation called persuasion in addition to attack relation (an argument a_1 attacks an argument a_2) of abstract argumentation. Such a relation as: an argument a_1 converts an argument a_2 into another argument a_3 is expressible in APA. Also, it extends the notion of defence against an attack in Dung argumentation to a persuasion. Changes in resource allocation as a result of a successful negotiation can be modelled as a successful persuasion. Failure of a successful negotiation can be modelled as an unsuccessful persuasion, on the other hand.

We introduce the following new features to APA.

- **Quantification of arguments:** We express a resource as a quantified argument. To describe that there are 2 Nintendo Switch, we will have an argument: there is a Nintendo Switch, to which we assign a numerical value 2 indicating the quantity of the resource.
- **Handshakes between persuasions:** an agent often tries to obtain a resource from another agent who requires a resource from the first agent in exchange. While the two relations may each be expressed as a persuasion in APA, it has no explicit mechanism to enforce two persuasions to be considered always together for a dynamic transition. As a resolution, we introduce a handshake function.
- **Numerical constraints for attacks and persuasions:** It matters in negotiation how many (much) of one of the resources are to be exchanged for how many (much) of the other resource. It can also happen that an agent attacks another agent's argument with its argument only under a certain condition.

To intuitively express them, we allow both attacks and persuasions to be given numerical constraints.

- **Multi-agency:** each agent has its own argumentation scope, and may also apply its own criteria to choose acceptable arguments within it. We explicitly introduce the notion of agents into APA.

1.1 Key Contributions

- **Argumentation-based negotiation for interleaved negotiations:** As far as we are aware, this is the first negotiation theory in the line of abstract argumentation [10] that adapts to interleaved multi-agent negotiations over scarce resources.
- **Finer control over dynamic transitions:** While APA dynamics is already Turing-complete [6], it does not mean that APA's interpretation of transition relation [7] (detail is in Sect. 2.2) can deterministically simulate a handshake of two persuasions for a transition. Numerical APA consolidates the synchronisation, accommodating a finer control over how a dynamic transition takes place. Also, it is rather cumbersome to have to deal with quantities without explicit use of numbers. Numerical APA is an improvement on this aspect.
- **Explainable preference:** In relevant theories (e.g. [3,12–14]), the use of preference relation [2,8] over arguments to control directionality of the attack (and other) relations is ubiquitous. However, the preference is often external to the underlying argumentation with no concrete explanation given as to what formulates it. In this work, we instead rely upon numerical constraints to achieve conditionalisation of attack (and persuasion) relations. Since they concern quantities of resources, we can understand more explicitly why some attack (persuasion) may not be present.

1.2 Related Work

Studies around concurrent negotiations are emerging, e.g. [16,20]. However, the problems we described above with argumentation-based approaches have not been considered in the literature, as far as our awareness goes.

Argumentation-based negotiation (Cf. [18] for an early survey) was proposed to obtain rational explanations as to why agents have or have not come to a deal.

In [17], a kind of agents' interaction during a bilateral negotiation through common goals was studied, under the assumption that there be no resource competition among agents. While we do not explicitly study cooperation among agents in this work, we allow resource competition, as was illustrated early in this section. We further allow interleaving of bilateral negotiations.

In [3,4], agents negotiate over potential goals. Say, negotiation is over resource allocation, then each goal describes a possible resource allocation, represented as an argument. At each negotiation turn, new arguments and relations among them (such as attacks and supports) may be inserted into agents' scopes, to assist them make judgement as to which goal(s) should be accepted, with their preferences. There are other studies, e.g. [9], that focus on some specific aspects of the theoretical framework. These works do not consider interleaved negotiations, however, for which the use of the goal arguments can be in fact problematic, as we are to illustrate later in Sect. 3.1. Also, we approach towards agents' preferences via numerical information, as we described above.

In [12], a structural argumentation [11] was applied to contract-negotiations, where features express properties of items including quantities. Yet again, it does not cover interleaved negotiations.

In the rest, we will present: technical preliminaries (in Sect. 2); numerical abstract persuasion argumentation with the above-introduced features (in Sect. 3); and examples (in Sect. 4), before drawing conclusions.

2 Technical Preliminaries

2.1 Abstract Argumentation

Let $\mathcal{A}$ be a class of abstract entities that we understand as arguments, whose member is referred to by a with or without a subscript, and whose finite subset is referred to by A with or without a subscript. A finite argumentation framework is a tuple (A, R) with a binary relation over A [10]. In this work, we assume $A \neq \emptyset$. We denote the set of all finite argumentation frameworks by $\mathcal{F}$.

The following definitions apply to any $(A, R) \in \mathcal{F}$. $a_1 \in A$ is said to attack $a_2 \in A$ if and only if, or iff, $(a_1, a_2) \in R$. $(a_1, a_2) \in R$ is drawn graphically as $a_1 \rightarrow a_2$. $A_1 \subseteq A$ is said to defend $a_x \in A$ iff each $a_y \in A$ attacking a_x is attacked by at least one member of A_1. $A_1 \subseteq A$ is said to be: conflict-free iff no member of A_1 attacks a member of A_1; admissible iff it is conflict-free and it defends all the members of A_1; complete iff it is admissible and includes any argument it defends; preferred iff it is a set-theoretically maximal admissible set; and grounded iff it is the set intersection of all complete sets of A.

Let Sem be $\{co, pr, gr\}$, and let D be Sem $\times \mathcal{F} \rightarrow 2^{2^{\mathcal{A}}}$. Given a finite argumentation framework (A, R), we denote by D(sem, (A, R)) the set of all (A, R)'s: complete sets iff sem $=$ co; preferred sets iff sem $=$ pr; and grounded sets iff sem $=$ gr. By definition, $|D(gr, (A, R))| = 1$. There are many other types of semantics, but the three are quite typical semantics related (roughly) by complete sets.

2.2 APA: Abstract Persuasion Argumentation

Let $2^{(A,R)}$ denote $\{(A_1, R_1) \mid A_1 \subseteq A$ and $R_1 = R \cap (A_1 \times A_1)\}$.[1] APA [7] is a tuple $(A, R, R_{\mathbf{p}}, A_{\mathbf{0}}, \hookrightarrow)$ for $A_{\mathbf{0}} \subseteq A$; $R_{\mathbf{p}} \subseteq A \times (A \cup \{\epsilon\}) \times A$; and $\hookrightarrow$: $2^A \times (2^{(A,R)} \times 2^{(A,R)})$. It extends abstract argumentation (A, R) conservatively. $(a_1, \epsilon, a_2) \in R_{\mathbf{p}}$ is drawn graphically as $a_1 \multimap a_2$; and $(a_1, a_3, a_2) \in R_{\mathbf{p}}$ as $a_1 \overset{a_1}{\dashrightarrow} a_3 \multimap a_2$.

---

[1] "and" instead of "and" is used when the context in which the word appears strongly indicates truth-value comparisons. It follows the semantics of classical logic conjunction.

The following definitions apply to any APA tuple $(A, R, R_\mathbf{p}, A_\mathbf{0}, \hookrightarrow)$. Let $F(A_1)$ for some $A_1 \subseteq A$ denote $(A_1, R \cap (A_1 \times A_1))$. $F(A_1)$ for any $A_1 \subseteq A$ is said to be a state. $F(A_\mathbf{0})$ is called the initial state in particular. In any state $F(A_x)$, any member of A_x is said to be visible in $F(A_x)$, while the other members of A are said to be invisible in $F(A_x)$. A state $F(A_1)$ is said to be reachable iff $F(A_1) = F(A_\mathbf{0})$ or else there is some $F(A_2)$ such that $F(A_2)$ is reachable and that $(A_x, (F(A_2), F(A_1))) \in \hookrightarrow$, written alternatively as $F(A_2) \hookrightarrow^{A_x} F(A_1)$ for some $A_x \subseteq A$. Such A_x the transition is dependent upon was termed a reference set in [7], but to make clearer its association to an agent, we call it an *agent set* instead.

$a_1 \in A$ is said to attack $a_2 \in A$ in a state $F(A_1)$ iff $a_1, a_2 \in A_1$ and $(a_1, a_2) \in R$. For $a_1, a_2, a_3 \in A$, a_1 is said to be: inducing a_3 in a state $F(A_1)$ iff $a_1 \in A_1$ and $(a_1, \epsilon, a_3) \in R_\mathbf{p}$; and converting a_2 into a_3 in $F(A_1)$ iff $a_1, a_2 \in A_1$ and $(a_1, a_2, a_3) \in R_\mathbf{p}$.

$(a_1, \alpha, a_3) \in R_\mathbf{p}$ for $\alpha \in A \cup \{\epsilon\}$ is said to be possible in $F(A_1)$ with respect to an agent set $A_x \subseteq A$ iff a_1 is either inducing a_3 or converting α into a_3 in $F(A_1)$ and a_1 is not attacked by any member of A_x in $F(A_1)$. The set of all members of $R_\mathbf{p}$ that are possible in $F(A_1)$ with respect to an agent set $A_x \subseteq A$ is denoted by $\Gamma^{A_x}_{F(A_1)}$.

Interpretation of $\hookrightarrow$. The interpretation given of $\hookrightarrow$ in [7] is: (1) any subset Γ of $\Gamma^{A_x}_{F(A_1)}$ can be simultaneously considered for transition from $F(A_1)$ into some $F(A_2)$; (2) if $\Gamma \subseteq \Gamma^{A_x}_{F(A_1)}$ is considered for transition into $F(A_2)$, then: (2a) if either (a_1, ϵ, a_3) or (a_1, a_2, a_3) is in Γ, then $a_3 \in A_2$; (2b) if (a_1, a_2, a_3) is in Γ, then a_2 is not in A_2 unless it is judged to be in A_2 by (2a); and (2c) if $a \in A_1$, then $a \in A_2$ unless it is judged not in A_2 by (2b).

In other words, for $A_1 \subseteq A$ and for $\Gamma \subseteq R_\mathbf{p}$, let $\mathsf{neg}^{A_1}(\Gamma)$ be $\{a_x \in A_1 \mid \exists a_1 \in A_1 \; \exists a_3 \in A.(a_1, a_x, a_3) \in \Gamma\}$, and let $\mathsf{pos}^{A_1}(\Gamma)$ be $\{a_3 \in A \mid \exists a_1, \alpha \in A_1 \cup \{\epsilon\}.(a_1, \alpha, a_3) \in \Gamma\}$. For $A_x \subseteq A$, $F(A_1)$ and $F(A_2)$, we have: $F(A_1) \hookrightarrow^{A_x} F(A_2)$ iff there is some $\emptyset \subset \Gamma \subseteq \Gamma^{A_x}_{F(A_1)} \subseteq R_\mathbf{p}$ such that $A_2 = (A_1 \backslash \mathsf{neg}^{A_1}(\Gamma)) \cup \mathsf{pos}^{A_1}(\Gamma)$.

State-Wise Acceptability Semantics. $A_1 \subseteq A$ is said to be conflict-free in a (reachable) state $F(A_a)$ iff no member of A_1 attacks a member of A_1 in $F(A_a)$. $A_1 \subseteq A$ is said to defend $a \in A$ in $F(A_a)$ from attacks iff, (if $a \in A_a$, then) every $a_u \in A$ attacking a in $F(A_a)$ is attacked by at least one member of A_1 in $F(A_a)$ (counter-attack). $A_1 \subseteq A$ is said to be proper in $F(A_a)$ iff $A_1 \subseteq A_a$. In [7], there is another criterion of no-elimination: $A_1 \subseteq A$ is said to defend $a \in A$ in $F(A_a)$ from eliminations iff, if $a \in A_a$, there is no state $F(A_b)$ such that both $F(A_a) \hookrightarrow^{A_1} F(A_b)$ and $a \notin A_b$ at once (no elimination). Such condition can be made general: $A_1 \subseteq A$ is said to defend $a \in A$ in $F(A_a)$ from k-step eliminations, $k \in \mathbb{N}$, iff, if $a \in A_a$, then for every $0 \le i \le k$ and for every $\underbrace{F(A_a) \hookrightarrow^{A_1} \cdots \hookrightarrow^{A_1}}_{i} F(A_i)$, it holds that $a \in A_i$.

$A_1 \subseteq A$ is said to be: k-step admissible in $F(A_a)$ iff A_1 is conflict-free, proper and defends every member of A_1 in $F(A_a)$ from attacks and k-step eliminations;

complete in $F(A_a)$ iff A_1 is admissible and includes every $a \in A$ it defends in $F(A_a)$ from attacks and k-step eliminations; preferred in $F(A_a)$ iff A_1 is maximally k-step complete in $F(A_a)$; and grounded in $F(A_a)$ iff it is the set intersection of all k-step complete sets in $F(A_a)$.

In the rest of the paper, we assume k to be always 0, for technical simplicity.

2.3   Abstract Argumentation with Agents

In the context of argumentation-based negotiations, it is common to consider argumentation per agent. We can extend abstract argumentation (A, R) with $A \neq \emptyset$ into $(A, R, E, f_{\mathbf{E}}, f_{\mathsf{sem}})$ with: E a set of agents; a function $f_{\mathbf{E}} : E \to (2^A \backslash \emptyset)$ which is such that, for $e_1, e_2 \in E$, if $e_1 \neq e_2$, then $f_{\mathbf{E}}(e_1) \cap f_{\mathbf{E}}(e_2) = \emptyset$; and $f_{\mathsf{sem}} : E \to \mathsf{Sem}$. Intuitively, any $a \in f_{\mathbf{E}}(e)$ is understood to be in the scope of the agent $e \in E$, and each agent $e \in E$ has its own semantics $f_{\mathsf{sem}}(e)$.

3   Numerical Abstract Persuasion Argumentation

As per our discussion in Sect. 1, we extend APA with (1) numerical information, (2) a mechanism of handshakes, and (3) multi-agency. Prior to formally defining the theory, we provide intuition for the first two components through examples.

3.1   Numbers and Numerical Constraints

Numbers and numerical constraints as always are powerful enrichment to a formal system. In the context of this paper, the following are the merits of having them.

Numbers Help us Better Organise Scarce Resource Allocations. Without them, it takes some effort to describe availability of resources in an argument. With goal arguments [4], each of all possible allocations of resources presently negotiated over is defined as an argument. For example, if e_1 and e_2 commence their negotiations over 2 Switch and \$650, the allocation that 2 Switch and \$0 are with e_1 and 0 Switch and \$650 are with e_2 is one argument a_u, while the allocation that 2 Switch and \$0 are with e_2 and 0 Switch and \$650 are with e_1 is another argument a_v, and similarly for all the other possibilities. Bundling together every resource location in one big argument is not necessarily desirable in concurrent multi-agent negotiations, as availability of resources can change in the middle of the negotiation due to interruption by another negotiation, say between e_1 and e_3. Such a change can entail disappearance of some of resource allocations that were initially feasible.

With numbers, the need for maintaining those big arguments is precluded. To describe the idea, we can have an argument *There is a Switch.* in the scope of e_1 (the argument a_1) and an argument *There is a Switch.* in the scope of e_2 (the argument a_2). Similarly, we can have an argument *There is a dollar.*

In the scope of e_1 (the argument a_3) and *There is a dollar.* in the scope of e_2 (the argument a_4). Then, we can have a set N^a of partial functions $\mathcal{A} \to \mathbb{N}$ mapping an argument for a resource into its quantity in non-negative integer, e.g. $n^a \in N^a$ can be such that $n^a(a_1) = 2$ (e_1 has 2 Switch), $n^a(a_2) = 0$ (e_2 has 0 Switch), $n^a(a_3) = 0$ (e_1 has \$0) and $n^a(a_4) = 650$ (e_2 has \$650). These numerical information let us infer the earlier-mentioned big argument a_u. When there is any change to the quantities of the resources, we can replace n^a with another $n_1^a \in N^a$ which differs from n^a in mapping only for those resources (as arguments) affected by it. In the meantime, arguments themselves will stay the same. Making the overall resource allocation an inferrable - rather than hard-coded - information makes adaptation to interleaved negotiations simpler and more intuitive.

Numerical Constraints Help us Express Conditional Attacks and Persuasions. Whether an agent attacks or attempts a persuasion (such as to solicit a concession of an offer) in a state could very well depend on the specific resource allocation in the state. An illustrative example is: e_2 thinks of \$300 already too expensive for an electronics device, but, say the money in his possession is \$350, at least not so much as him being unable to buy a Switch. Thus, according to his preference (see on the second page of this paper), he is not happy but he does not complain (attack) at the seller for the ask price. This changes clearly when the ask price is \$400, since he would not be able to purchase it out of his pocket. There, the chance is that he actually complains (attacks) at the seller.

Numerical constraints can help model this situation intuitively by allowing attacks to conditionally occur. Assume:

- Three arguments: *Dollars required.* in e_1's scope (a_1); *There is a dollar.* in e_2's scope (a_2); and *That costs a lot.* in e_2's scope (a_3).
- $n^a(a_1) = n_1$ and $n^a(a_2) = n_2$.
- An attack $a_3 \to a_1$ with a numerical constraint $n_2 < n_1$ given to it.

What these intend is that a_3 attacks a_1 when e_1's ask price n_1 exceeds dollars n_2 in e_2's possession. Numerical constraints can be similarly used for a persuasion, not only for an attack.

Whether they are for an attack or a persuasion, constraints may be left unspecified if irrelevant. However, it is rather inflexible to just allow constant numbers in a constraint, since we may like to express a condition: *if the quantity of a_1 is greater than that of a_2*, which depends on a chosen $n^a \in N^a$. We therefore define a formal object for expressing a constraint, its synatx and semantics:

Definition 1 (Constraint objects: syntax). *Let* Nums, exp, *and* num *with or without a subscript be recognised in the following grammar. We assume n to be a member of $\mathbb{N}$, a to be a member of $\mathcal{A}$, and r to be some (a_1, a_2, a_3) with $a_1, a_2, a_3 \in \mathcal{A}$. Any* Nums *(with or without a subscript) recognised in this grammar is assumed to be a finite set, and is called a constraint object.*

$$Nums := Nums, exp \mid \emptyset.$$
$$exp := num = num \mid num < num.$$
$$num := n \mid \star a \mid \star r.$$

Let S^{Nums} be the class of all constraint objects, and let $g : S^{Nums} \to S^{Nums}$ be such that $g(Nums) = Nums$ iff no $\star a$ for some $a \in \mathcal{A}$ or $\star r$ for some $r \in \mathcal{A} \times \mathcal{A} \times \mathcal{A}$ occurs in $Nums$. We denote the subclass of S^{Nums} that contains all $Nums \in S^{Nums}$ with $g(Nums) = Nums$ but nothing else by S^{Nums^G}. We call $Nums \in S^{Nums^G}$ a ground constraint object.

For the semantics, we define an interpretation function from S^{Nums} to S^{Nums^G}.

Definition 2 (Interpretation of constraint objects). *Let* S^{num} *denote the set of all distinct num, and let* $n^r : (\mathcal{A} \times (\mathcal{A} \cup \{\epsilon\}) \times \mathcal{A}) \to S^{num}$ *be a partial function such that* $n^r(r)$, *if defined, is some* $n \in \mathbb{N}$ *or* $\star a$ *for some* $a \in \mathcal{A}$. *Let* $\mathcal{I}^t : S^{num} \times N^a \to S^{num}$ *be such that* $\mathcal{I}^t(x, n^a)$ *is:* x *if* $x \in \mathbb{N}$; $n^a(a)$ *if* $x = \star a$; $n^r(r)$ *if* $x = \star r$ *and* $n^r(r) \in \mathbb{N}$; $\mathcal{I}^t(n^r(r), n^a)$ *if* $x = \star r$ *and* $n^r(r)$ *is* $\star a$ *for some* $a \in \mathcal{A}$; *and undefined, otherwise.*

Let $\mathcal{I} : S^{Nums} \times N^a \to S^{Nums^G}$ *be such that* $\mathcal{I}(Nums, n^a)$ *is* $Nums_1$, *where* $Nums_1$ *is as the result of replacing every occurrence of* $x \in S^{num}$ *in Nums with* $\mathcal{I}^t(x, n^a)$. $\mathcal{I}(Nums, n^a)$ *is defined iff* $\mathcal{I}^t(x, n^a)$ *is defined for every occurrence of* $x \in S^{num}$ *in Nums.*

For any $Nums \in S^{Nums}$ *and for any* $n^a \in N^a$, *we say that* $\mathcal{I}(Nums, n^a)$ *is interpretation of Nums with respect to* n^a.

Definition 3 (Constraint objects: semantics). *We define a predicate* $sat : S^{Nums} \times N^a \to \{true, false\}$ *to be such that* $sat(Nums, n^a)$ *iff, for every* $n_1 < n_2 \in \mathcal{I}(Nums, n^a)$, n_2 *is greater than* n_1, *and for every* $n_1 = n_2 \in \mathcal{I}(Nums, n^a)$, n_1 *is equal to* n_2.

The purpose of sat is to judge if the numerical constraints in $Nums \in S^{Nums}$ are satisfied for a given $n^a \in N^a$.

Numbers Help us Express the Quantity Needed of a Resource for a Dynamic Transition. Suppose e_2 has \$650, and that e_1 tries to obtain \$300 from e_2. After a successful transaction, e_2's budget decreases, not to 0, however. This scenario is not concisely expressed in APA: if (1) $\{(a_1, a_2, a_3)\} = R_{\mathbf{p}}$, (2) both a_1 and a_2 are visible in a state (see Sect. 2), and (3) (a_1, a_2, a_3) is possible in the state, then in the next state a_2 is invisible. However, with numbers, suppose:

- Three arguments: *Dollars required.* in e_1's scope (a_1); *There is a dollar.* in e_2's scope (a_2); and *There is a dollar.* in e_1's scope (a_3).
- $n^a(a_2) = 650$ and $n^a(a_3) = 0$.
- $(a_1, a_2, a_3) \in R_{\mathbf{p}}$, with n^r assigning 300 to (a_1, a_2, a_3), i.e. $n^r((a_1, a_2, a_3)) = 300$, signifying how many dollars e_1 will require.

Then the conversion (a_1, a_2, a_3), provided it is possible in a given state, will update n^a to $n_1^a \in N^a$ such that $n_1^a(a_2) = 350$; and $n_1^a(a_3) = 300$, without mandatorily eliminating a_2.

3.2   Handshakes Among persuasion Relations

Suppose: *Dollar required.* in the scope of e_1 (argument a_1); *There is a dollar.* in the scope of e_2 (argument a_2); *There is a dollar.* in the scope of e_1 (argument a_3); *Switch required.* in the scope of e_2 (argument a_4); *There is a Switch.* in the scope of e_1 (argument a_5); and *There is a Switch.* in the scope of e_2 (argument a_6).

Suppose the following two persuasions over them: one is (a_1, a_2, a_3), another is (a_4, a_5, a_6). To enforce a handshake between them, we introduce a function $\mathsf{hs} : R_{\mathbf{p}} \to 2^{R_{\mathbf{P}}}$ such that (1) if $r_2 \in \mathsf{hs}(r_1)$, then $r_1 \in \mathsf{hs}(r_2)$, and that (2) if $\mathsf{hs}(r_1) \neq \emptyset$, then it is not considered for transition unless there is some $r_2 \in \mathsf{hs}(r_1)$ that is considered for transition simultaneously with it (see Sect. 2 for what it means for a persuasion to be considered for transition). The interpretation of $|\mathsf{hs}(r_2)| > 1$ is that r_2 may be considered together with a member (and not all the members) of $\mathsf{hs}(r_2)$.

3.3   Numerical Abstract Persuasion Argumentation

Denote the class of all partial functions $(\mathcal{A} \times (\mathcal{A} \cup \{\epsilon\}) \times \mathcal{A}) \to S^{num}$ by N^r, every member of which is such that, if defined, the output is some $n \in \mathbb{N}$ or $\star a$ for some $a \in \mathcal{A}$.

Definition 4 (Numerical Abstract Persuasion Argumentation). *We define a Numerical Abstract Persuasion Argumentation (Numerical APA) to be a tuple* $(A, R, R_{\mathbf{p}}, E, f_{E}, f_{sem}, A_0, \mathsf{hs}, \Rightarrow, n_0^a, n^r, cst)$, *with: (1)* $\mathsf{hs} : R_{\mathbf{p}} \to 2^{R_{\mathbf{P}}}$; *(2)* $n_0^a \in N^a$; *(3)* $n^r \in N^r$; *(4)* $cst : (R \cup R_{\mathbf{p}}) \to S^{Nums}$; *and (5)* $\Rightarrow$: $2^A \times ((2^{(A,R)} \times N^a) \times (2^{(A,R)} \times N^a))$.

All the others, i.e. A, R, $R_{\mathbf{p}}$, E, f_E, f_{sem} *and* A_0 *are as defined in Sect. 2, i.e.* $A \subseteq_{fin} \mathcal{A}$, $R \subseteq A \times A$, $R_{\mathbf{p}} \subseteq A \times (A \cup \{\epsilon\}) \times A$, E *a set of agents,* $f_E : E \to (2^A \backslash \emptyset)$ *with* $f_E(e_1) \cap f_E(e_2) = \emptyset$ *if* e_1 *is not* e_2, $f_{sem} : E \to$ *Sem, and* $A_0 \subseteq A$. *We assume* $A \neq \emptyset$.

The following definitions apply to any Numerical APA $(A, R, R_{\mathbf{p}}, E, f_{\mathbf{E}}, f_{sem}, A_0,$ $\mathsf{hs}, \Rightarrow, n_0^a, n^r, cst)$.

Definition 5 (States). *Let* $F(A_1, n_1^a)$ *for some* $A_1 \subseteq A$ *and some* $n_1^a \in N^a$ *denote* $((A_1, R \cap (A_1 \times A_1)), n_1^a)$. *We call any such* $F(A_1, n_1^a)$ *a (Numerical APA) state. We call* $F(A_0, n_0^a)$ *the initial state in particular.*

In state $F(A_x, n_x^a)$, *we say any member of* A_x *visible in* $F(A_x, n_x^a)$, *while the other members of* A *invisible in* $F(A_x, n_x^a)$.

We say that $F(A_1, n_1^a)$ *is reachable iff* $F(A_1, n_1^a) = F(A_0, n_0^a)$ *or else there is some* $F(A_2, n_2^a)$ *such that* $F(A_2, n_2^a)$ *is reachable and that* $F(A_2, n_2^a) \Rightarrow^{A_y}$ $F(A_1, n_1^a)$ *for some* $A_y \subseteq A$.

Exactly how $\Rightarrow$ is interpreted is left unspecified at this point, which will be detailed later in Subsect. 3.7.

3.4   Restrictions

In this work, we will restrict our attention to a subset of all Numerical APA tuples. Specifically,

1. We divide A into arguments that denote resources, and the other arguments as ordinary arguments. We assume that no resource arguments become ordinary arguments, or vice versa via state transitions.
2. We assume any resource argument with quantity 0 is invisible. In particular, there is no $a \in A_0$ such that $n_0^a(a) = 0$.
3. We assume that $n^r \in N^r$ does not update by dynamic transitions. This seems reasonable, however, since $R_\mathbf{p}$ and updates on n^a together easily simulate updates on n^r.
4. We assume that n^r is defined at most for members of $R_\mathbf{p}$ that are conversions. We assume that $n^r((a_1, a_2, a_3))$ for $(a_1, a_2, a_3) \in R_\mathbf{p}$ with $a_1, a_2, a_3 \in A$ is defined iff a_2 and a_3 are a resource argument. This is for our intended purpose, that $n^r((a_1, a_2, a_3))$ represents the number (amount) of resources a_1 asks of from a_2 which changes the number (amount) of resources a_3. We further assume that if $n^r((a_1, a_2, a_3))$ for $(a_1, a_2, a_3) \in R_\mathbf{p}$ is defined, then for every $a_4, a_5 \in A$, if $(a_4, a_2, a_5) \in R_\mathbf{p}$, then $n^r((a_4, a_2, a_5))$ is defined and vice versa.

Formal definitions follow.

Definition 6 (Resource and ordinary arguments). *We say that $a \in A$ is a resource argument in $F(A_1, n_1^a)$ iff $n_1^a(a)$ is defined. We say that $a \in A$ is an ordinary argument in $F(A_1, n_1^a)$ iff a is not a resource argument in $F(A_1, n_1^a)$.*

Definition 7 (Type rigidity). *We say that A is type rigid iff for every $F(A_x, n_x^a)$, $a \in A$ is a resource argument in $F(A_0, n_0^a)$ iff a is a resource argument in $F(A_x, n_x^a)$.*

Definition 8 (Normal relations). *We say that $R_\mathbf{p}$ is normal iff for every $F(A_1, n_1^a)$:*

- *for every $(a_1, a_2, a_3) \in R_\mathbf{p}$ with $a_1, a_2, a_3 \in A$, $\mathcal{I}^t(n^r((a_1, a_2, a_3)), n_1^a)$ is defined iff a_2 and a_3 are a resource argument in $F(A_1, n_1^a)$.*
- *If $\mathcal{I}^t(n^r((a_1, a_2, a_3)), n_1^a)$ for $(a_1, a_2, a_3) \in R_\mathbf{p}$ is defined, then for any $a_4, a_5 \in A$, $(a_4, a_2, a_5) \in R_\mathbf{p}$ iff $\mathcal{I}^t(n^r((a_4, a_2, a_5)), n_1^a)$ is defined.*

In the rest, we assume a restricted class of Numerical APA tuples with type-rigid A and normal $R_\mathbf{p}$, and which are moreover such that n^r remains constant through state transitions.

3.5   Attacks and Persuasions

Some attacks and persuasions may not satisfy constraint objects attached to them in a state, in which case we simply ignore their influence in the state, as embodied in:

Definition 9 (Constraint-adjusted relations). *We say:*

- *R' is an attack relation constraint-adjusted in $F(A_1, n_1^a)$ iff $R' = \{(a_1, a_2) \in R \cap (A_1 \times A_1) \mid \text{sat}(\text{cst}((a_1, a_2)), n_1^a)\}$.*
- *$R'_{\mathbf{p}}$ is a persuasion relation constraint-adjusted in $F(A_1, n_1^a)$ iff all the three conditions 1., 2. and 3. hold good for every $r \in R'_{\mathbf{p}}$.*
  1. *If $r \equiv (a_1, \epsilon, a_3)$ for some $a_1, a_3 \in A$, then $a_1 \in A_1$ and $\text{sat}(\text{cst}(r), n_1^a)$.*
  2. *If $r \equiv (a_1, a_2, a_3)$ for some $a_1, a_2, a_3 \in A$, then $a_1, a_2 \in A_1$ and $\text{sat}(\text{cst}(r), n_1^a)$.*
  3. *There exists no $R''_{\mathbf{p}}$ such that $R'_{\mathbf{p}} \subset R''_{\mathbf{p}}$ and that $R''_{\mathbf{p}}$ satisfies both of the conditions 1. and 2. above.*

We denote the attack relation constraint-adjusted in $F(A_1, n_1^a)$ by $f_R(F(A_1, n_1^a))$ ($\subseteq R \cap (A_1 \times A_1)$), and the persuasion relation constraint-adjusted in $F(A_1, n_1^a)$ by $f_{R_{\mathbf{p}}}(F(A_1, n_1^a))(\subseteq R_{\mathbf{p}} \cap (A_1 \times (A_1 \cup \{\epsilon\}) \times A))$.

We use the constraint-adjusted relations to characterise attacks and persuasions in a state.

Definition 10 (Attacks and persuasions in a state). *We say $a_1 \in A$ attacks $a_2 \in A$ in a state $F(A_1, n_1^a)$ iff $(a_1, a_2) \in f_R(F(A_1, n_1^a))$. We say $a_1 \in A$ is inducing $a_2 \in A$ in a state $F(A_1, n_1^a)$ iff $(a_1, \epsilon, a_2) \in f_{R_{\mathbf{p}}}(F(A_1, n_1^a))$. We say $a_1 \in A$ is converting $a_2 \in A$ to $a_3 \in A$ in a state $F(A_1, n_1^a)$ iff $(a_1, a_2, a_3) \in f_{R_{\mathbf{p}}}(F(A_1, n_1^a))$.*

3.6 State-Wise Agent Semantics

We say $A_1 \subseteq A$ is conflict-free in $F(A_a, n_a^a)$ iff no member of A_1 attacks a member of A_1 in $F(A_a, n_a^a)$. We say $A_1 \subseteq A$ defends $a \in A$ in $F(A_a, n_a^a)$ from attacks iff, if $a \in A_a$, then every $a_u \in A_a$ attacking a in $F(A_a, n_a^a)$ is attacked by at least one member of A_1 in $F(A_a, n_a^a)$. We say $A_1 \subseteq A$ is proper in $F(A_a, n_a^a)$ iff $A_1 \subseteq A_a$.

As was stated in Sect. 2, in this work we will not deal with defence from eliminations. With this simplification, each agent semantics in a given state is knowable without consideration over dynamic transitions.

Definition 11 (State-wise agent admissibility). *We say that $A_1 \subseteq A$ is: admissible in $F(A_a, n_a^a)$ for $e \in E$ iff $A_1 \subseteq f_E(e)$ and A_1 is conflict-free and A_1 is proper and A_1 defends every member of A_1 from attacks in $F(A_a, n_a^a)$; complete in $F(A_a, n_a^a)$ for $e \in E$ iff A_1 is admissible in $F(A_1, n_1^a)$ for e and A_1 includes every $a \in f_E(e)$ it defends from attacks in $F(A_a, n_a^a)$; preferred in $F(A_a, n_a^a)$ for $e \in E$ iff A_1 is a maximal complete set in $F(A_a, n_a^a)$ for e; and grounded in $F(A_a, n_a^a)$ for $e \in E$ iff A_1 is the set intersection of all complete sets in $F(A_a, n_a^a)$ for e.*

Together with the choice of a semantic type $f_{\text{sem}}(e)$ by each agent $e \in E$, we obtain:

Definition 12 (State-wise agent semantics). *Let* $S : 2^A \times N^a \times E \to 2^{2^A}$ *be such that* $S(A_1, n_1^a, e_1)$ *is the set of all:*

- *complete sets in* $F(A_1, n_1^a)$ *for* e_1 *if* $f_{sem}(e_1) = co.$
- *preferred sets in* $F(A_1, n_1^a)$ *for* e_1 *if* $f_{sem}(e_1) = pr.$
- *grounded sets in* $F(A_1, n_1^a)$ *for* e_1 *if* $f_{sem}(e_1) = gr.$

For every $F(A_1, n_1^a)$ *and every* $e \in E$, *we call* $S(A_1, n_1^a, e)$ e's *semantics in* $F(A_1, n_1^a)$.

3.7   Interpretation of $\Rightarrow$

As in APA (see Sect. 2), we then characterise possible persuasions with respect to some agent set.

Definition 13 (Possible persuasions). $(a_1, \alpha, a_2) \in R_\mathbf{p}$ *for* $\alpha \in A \cup \{\epsilon\}$ *is said to be possible in* $F(A_1, n_1^a)$ *with respect to an agent set* $A_x \subseteq A$ *iff there is some* $e_1 \in E$ *such that* $A_x \in S(A_1, n_1^a, e_1)$ *(note that* A_x *may be an empty set; see Sect. 2) and* a_1 *is either inducing* a_2 *or converting* α *into* a_2 *in* $F(A_1, n_1^a)$ *and* a_1 *is not attacked by any member of* A_x *in* $F(A_1, n_1^a)$. *We denote by* $\Gamma^{A_x}_{F(A_1, n_1^a)}$ *the set of all members of* $R_\mathbf{p}$ *that are possible in* $F(A_1, n_1^a)$ *with respect to an agent set* $A_x \subseteq A$.

There may be more than one agent in a Numerical APA; some persuasions must always be together due to hs; and, on the other hand, some persuasions cannot be together due to the quantity change of a resource otherwise going below 0. We thus obtain a multi-agent version of Definition 13:

Definition 14 (Multi-agent possible persuasions). *We say that* $A_x \subseteq A$ *is a multi-agent union set in* $F(A_1, n_1^a)$ *iff* $(A_x \cap f_E(e)) \in S(A_1, n_1^a, e)$ *for every* $e \in E$.

(Explanation: every agent may have more than one set of arguments in its semantics in $F(A_1, n_1^a)$. *While any one of them may be chosen by the agent, not two distinct ones can they choose at the same time. Therefore, when we obtain the set union of one member of every agent's semantics, it should trivially hold that the set intersection of the union set and* $f_E(e)$ *is a member of* e's *semantics in* $F(A_1, n_1^a)$.)

For each multi-agent union set A_x *in* $F(A_1, n_1^a)$, *let* $\Lambda^{A_x}_{F(A_1, n_1^a)}$ *denote* $\bigcap_{e \in E} \Gamma^{A_x \cap f_E(e)}_{F(A_1, n_1^a)}$ *(denoting possible persuasions with respect to each* $A_x \cap f_E(e)$ *(* $e \in E$ *)), we say that* $(\emptyset \subset) \Lambda \subseteq \Lambda^{A_x}_{F(A_1, n_1^a)}$ *is a multi-agent possible persuasion set in* $F(A_1, n_1^a)$ *with respect to* A_x *iff both of the following conditions hold:*

1. *For every* $r_1 \in \Lambda$, *if* $hs(r_1) \neq \emptyset$, *then there exists one and only one* $r_2 \in hs(r_1)$ *such that* $r_2 \in \Lambda$. *(**Handshake-compatibility**)*
2. *Let* $dec, inc : 2^A \times N^a \times 2^{R_\mathbf{p}} \times A \to \mathbb{N}$ *be such that:*
    - $dec(A_1, n_1^a, \Gamma, a) = \{(a_1, a, a_3) \in \Gamma \mid n^r((a_1, a, a_3))$ *is defined.*$\}$.

- $inc(A_1, n_1^a, \Gamma, a) = \{(a_1, a_2, a) \in \Gamma \mid n^r((a_1, a_2, a))$ is defined.$\}$.

(Explanation: $dec(A_1, n_1^a, \Gamma, a)$ returns the set of conversions in Γ on a, and $inc(A_1, n_1^a, \Gamma, a)$ returns the set of conversions in Γ that induce a.)

Then, for $a \in A_1$, if a is a resource argument, $n_1^a(a) + \Sigma_{r \in inc(A_1, n_1^a, \Lambda, a)} \mathcal{I}^t(n^r(r), n_1^a) - \Sigma_{r \in dec(A_1, n_1^a, \Lambda, a)} \mathcal{I}^t(n^r(r), n_1^a) \geq 0$. **(Resource-safety)**

A multi-agent union set defined above involves every $e \in E$, to express defence by every agent against dynamic transitions with the set of arguments it chooses. Finally:

Definition 15 (Interpretation of $\Rightarrow$). *We define: $F(A_1, n_1^a) \Rightarrow^{A_x} F(A_2, n_2^a)$ iff (1) A_x is a multi-agent union set and (2) there is some multi-agent possible persuasion set Λ in $F(A_1, n_1^a)$ with respect to A_x such that:*

- $n_2^a(a) = n_1^a(a) + \Sigma_{r \in inc(A_1, n_1^a, \Lambda, a)} \mathcal{I}^t(n^r(r), n_1^a) - \Sigma_{r \in dec(A_1, n_1^a, \Lambda, a)} \mathcal{I}^t(n^r(r), n_1^a)$
  for every resource argument $a \in A$.
- *Let $neg(\Lambda)$ and $pos(\Lambda)$ be:*
  - $neg(\Lambda) = \{a_x \in A_1 \mid \exists a_1 \in A_1 \ \exists a_3 \in A.(a_1, a_x, a_3) \in \Lambda$ and $(n_2^a(a_x) = 0$ or $n_2^a(a_x)$ is undefined.$)\}$.
  - $pos(\Lambda) = \{a_3 \in A \mid \exists a_1, \alpha \in A_1 \cup \{\epsilon\}.(a_1, \alpha, a_3) \in \Lambda$ and $(n_2^a(a_3) \neq 0$ or $n_2^a(a_3)$ is undefined.$)\}$.
  Then $A_2 = (A_1 \backslash neg(\Lambda)) \cup pos(\Lambda)$.

4   Example Modelling of Concurrent Multi-Agent Negotiations

We illustrate Numerical APA with our running example. We assume the following graphical conventions in all figures.

- $a \in A$ is generally drawn as a. As an exception, for $a \in A$ with a defined $n_1^a(a)$ in $F(A_1, n_1^a)$, it may be drawn more specifically as $n_1^a(a) : a$, or as in any form that puts the quantity before the argument.
- A visible argument is bordered, an argument that is not visible is not bordered.
- $(a_1, a_2) \in R$ with $cst((a_1, a_2)) = $ Nums is drawn as $a_1 \xrightarrow{\text{Nums}} a_2$. Nums may be omitted if Nums $= \emptyset$, and brackets to indicate a set of constraints may be omitted if it is a singleton set.
- $(a_1, \epsilon, a_3) \in R_\mathbf{p}$ with $cst((a_1, \epsilon, a_3)) = $ Nums is drawn as $a_1 \overset{\text{Nums}}{\multimap} a_3$. Nums may be omitted if Nums $= \emptyset$, and brackets may be omitted if it is a singleton set.
- $(a_1, a_2, a_3) \in R_\mathbf{p}$ with $cst((a_1, a_2, a_3)) = $ Nums and a defined $n^r((a_1, a_2, a_3)) = x \ (\in S^{num})$ is drawn as $a_1 \overset{\text{Nums}}{\underset{x}{\dashrightarrow}} a_2 \overset{a_1}{\multimap} a_3$. Nums may be omitted if Nums $= \emptyset$, and brackets may be omitted if it is a singleton set. If $n^r((a_1, a_2, a_3))$ is not defined, then x is not stated.

Let us reflect back on the negotiation example of Sect. 1, more specifically on the stage of the negotiation in $\boxed{A}$ right after **Initial Step B** (e_1 gives 1 Switch to e_3 for \$300) is taken. There are 16 arguments in total that appear in at least one of the 3 figures below. Out of them, a_{12-16} are e_1's arguments, a_{7-11} are e_2's arguments, and a_{1-6} are e_3's arguments. $\boxed{B}$, $\boxed{C}$, and $\boxed{D}$ represent an argumentation-based bilateral negotiation for e_3(left column)-e_2(right column), e_1(left column)-e_2(right column), and e_1(left column)-e_3(right column), respectively. Some attacks and persuasions may not be drawn in those figures if they are not contained within the bilateral negotiation. Formally, they represent the following Numerical APA. What exactly $\mathsf{Nums}_1, \mathsf{Nums}_2$ and Nums_4 in $\boxed{B}$ and $\boxed{C}$ are also stated below.

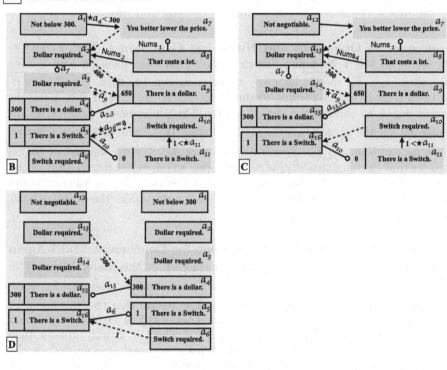

- $A \equiv \{a_1, \ldots, a_{16}\}$.
- $E = \{e_1, e_2, e_3\}$.
- $R \equiv \{(a_8, a_2), \quad (a_1, a_7), \quad (a_{12}, a_7), \quad (a_8, a_{13}), \quad (a_{11}, a_{10})\}$.
- $R_{\mathbf{p}} \equiv \{(a_2, a_9, a_4), \quad (a_3, a_9, a_4), \quad (a_7, a_2, a_3),$
  $(a_8, \epsilon, a_7), \quad (a_{10}, a_5, a_{11}), \quad (a_7, a_{13}, a_{14}), \quad (a_{13}, a_9, a_{15}),$
  $(a_{14}, a_9, a_{15}), \quad (a_{10}, a_{16}, a_{11}), \quad (a_{13}, a_4, a_{15}), \quad (a_6, a_{16}, a_5)\}$.
- $f_{\mathbf{E}}(e_1) = \{a_{12}, \ldots, a_{16}\}, \qquad f_{\mathbf{E}}(e_2) = \{a_7, \ldots, a_{11}\}, \qquad f_{\mathbf{E}}(e_3) = \{a_1, \ldots, a_6\}$.
- $f_{\mathsf{sem}}(e_1) = f_{\mathsf{sem}}(e_2) = f_{\mathsf{sem}}(e_3) = \mathsf{pr}$ (for this example, it does not matter which of the three semantics each one is).
- $A_0 = \{a_1, \quad a_2, \quad a_4, \quad a_5, \quad a_8, \quad a_9, \quad a_{10}, \quad a_{12}, \quad a_{13}, \quad a_{15}, \quad a_{16}\}$.
- $\mathsf{hs}((a_2, a_9, a_4)) = \{(a_{10}, a_5, a_{11})\}, \qquad \mathsf{hs}((a_3, a_9, a_4)) = \{(a_{10}, a_5, a_{11})\},$
  $\mathsf{hs}((a_{10}, a_5, a_{11})) = \{(a_2, a_9, a_4), (a_3, a_9, a_4)\}, \; \mathsf{hs}((a_{13}, a_9, a_{15})) = \{(a_{10}, a_{16}, a_{11})\},$

$\mathsf{hs}((a_{10}, a_{16}, a_{11})) = \{(a_{13}, a_9, a_{15}), (a_{14}, a_9, a_{15})\}, \quad \mathsf{hs}((a_{14}, a_9, a_{15})) = \{(a_{10}, a_{16}, a_{11})\},$
$\mathsf{hs}((a_{13}, a_4, a_{15})) = \{(a_6, a_{16}, a_5)\}, \qquad\qquad \mathsf{hs}((a_6, a_{16}, a_5)) = \{(a_{13}, a_4, a_{15})\}.$

- $\Rightarrow$ is as per Sect. 3.7.
- $\mathsf{n}_0^a(a_4) = 300, \mathsf{n}_0^a(a_5) = 1, \mathsf{n}_0^a(a_9) = 650, \mathsf{n}_0^a(a_{11}) = 0, \mathsf{n}_0^a(a_{15}) = 300, \mathsf{n}_0^a(a_{16}) = 1.$
  n_0^a is not defined for the other arguments.
- $\mathsf{n}^r((a_2, a_9, a_4)) = 400, \qquad \mathsf{n}^r((a_3, a_9, a_4)) = \star a_9, \qquad \mathsf{n}^r((a_{10}, a_5, a_{11})) = 1,$
  $\mathsf{n}^r((a_{13}, a_9, a_{15})) = 300, \qquad \mathsf{n}^r((a_{14}, a_9, a_{15})) = \star a_9, \qquad \mathsf{n}^r((a_{10}, a_{16}, a_{11})) = 1,$
  $\mathsf{n}^r((a_{13}, a_4, a_{15})) = 300, \qquad \mathsf{n}^r((a_6, a_{16}, a_5)) = 1.$
  n^r is not defined for any other members of R_p.
- $\mathsf{cst}((a_1, a_7)) = \{\star a_9 < 300\}.$
  $\mathsf{cst}((a_8, a_2, a_3)) = \mathsf{Nums}_2 = \{\star a_9 < \star(a_2, a_9, a_4), \star(a_2, a_9, a_4) < \star(a_{13}, a_9, a_{15})\}.$
  $\mathsf{cst}((a_8, a_{13}, a_{14})) = \mathsf{Nums}_4 = \{\star a_9 < \star(a_{13}, a_9, a_{15}), \star(a_{13}, a_9, a_{15}) < \star(a_2, a_9, a_4)\}.$
  $\mathsf{cst}((a_{11}, a_{10})) = \{1 < \star a_{11}\}.$
  $\mathsf{cst}((a_8, \epsilon, a_7)) = \mathsf{Nums}_1 = \{\star a_9 < \star(a_{13}, a_9, a_{15}), \star a_9 < \star(a_2, a_9, a_4)\}.$

Preference as Quantities and Numerical Constraints. Both e_1 and e_3 are trying to sell 1 Nintendo Switch console that they each have to e_2, see $(a_{13}, a_9, a_{15}) \in R_p$ in $\boxed{C}$ for e_1-e_2 negotiation and $(a_2, a_9, a_4) \in R_p$ in $\boxed{B}$ for e_3-e_2 negotiation. According to the preference spelled out in Sect. 1 (on the second page), e_2 chooses the cheapest offer. The preference is enforced in the constraint on the attack $a_8 \rightarrow a_{13}$, i.e. Nums_4 ($\boxed{C}$), and that on the attack $a_8 \rightarrow a_2$, i.e. Nums_2 ($\boxed{B}$). Specifically, $\star(a_2, a_9, a_4) < \star(a_{13}, a_9, a_{15})$ in Nums_2 dictates that e_2 complains at e_1 of her ask price and does not consider the deal if e_3's ask price is lower. Similarly, $\star(a_{13}, a_9, a_{15}) < \star(a_2, a_9, a_4)$ in Nums_4 dictates that e_2 complains at e_3 of his ask price and does not consider the deal if e_1's ask price is lower.

Non-deterministic Dynamic Transitions for Concurrent Multi-Agent Negotiations. As in the steps indicated in $\boxed{A}$, in this state, either e_2 or e_3, but not both of them, may obtain a Switch from e_1 (see $\boxed{C}$ for e_1-e_2 negotiation, and $\boxed{D}$ for e_1-e_3 negotiation). The reason that they cannot both obtain a Switch from e_1 is due to (**Resource-safety**) of Definition 14, since $\mathcal{I}^t((a_{10}, a_{16}, a_{11}), \mathsf{n}_0^a) + \mathcal{I}^t((a_6, a_{16}, a_5), \mathsf{n}_0^a) = 2$ which is strictly greater than $\mathsf{n}_0^a(a_{16}) = 1$. However, otherwise, either (a_{10}, a_{16}, a_{11}) and (a_{13}, a_9, a_{15}) or else (a_6, a_{16}, a_5) and (a_{13}, a_4, a_{15}) may be considered together for a dynamic transition in $F(A_0, \mathsf{n}_0^a)$. To wit, observe:

- $\mathsf{S}(A_0, \mathsf{n}_0^a, e_1) = \{\{a_{12}, a_{13}, a_{15}, a_{16}\}\} \equiv \{A_x\}.$
  $\mathsf{S}(A_0, \mathsf{n}_0^a, e_2) = \{\{a_8, a_9, a_{10}\}\} \equiv \{A_y\}.$
  $\mathsf{S}(A_0, \mathsf{n}_0^a, e_3) = \{\{a_1, a_2, a_4, a_5, a_6\}\} \equiv \{A_z\}.$
- $\Gamma_{F(A_0, \mathsf{n}_0^a)}^{A_i} = \{(a_{13}, a_4, a_{15}), (a_6, a_{16}, a_5), (a_{13}, a_9, a_{15}), (a_{10}, a_{16}, a_{11}), (a_2, a_9, a_4),$
  $(a_{10}, a_5, a_{11})\}$ for $i \in \{x, y, z\}.$
- $A_x \cup A_y \cup A_z \equiv A_d$ is the multi-agent union set in $F(A_0, \mathsf{n}_0^a).$
- $\Lambda_{F(A_0, \mathsf{n}_0^a)}^{A_d} = \{(a_{13}, a_4, a_{15}), (a_6, a_{16}, a_5), (a_{13}, a_9, a_{15}), (a_{10}, a_{16}, a_{11}), (a_2, a_9, a_4),$
  $(a_{10}, a_5, a_{11})\}.$

(a_{10}, a_{16}, a_{11}) and (a_{13}, a_9, a_{15}), as well as (a_6, a_{16}, a_5) and (a_{13}, a_4, a_{15}), satisfy (**Handshake-compatibility**) and (**Resource-safety**).

Haggling and Concession. Let us think of a scenario where e_2 gets a Switch console from e_1 before e_3 does. The negotiation state $F(A_0, n_0^a)$ transitions to the next state $F(A_1, n_1^a)$, for which we have graphical representation of $\boxed{B'}$, $\boxed{C'}$, and $\boxed{D'}$ from $\boxed{B}$, $\boxed{C}$, and $\boxed{D}$. A_1 denotes $\{a_{1-2,4-6,8-11,12-13,15}\}$ with $a_{1,2,\dots}$ abbreviating $a_1, a_2, \dots$ and a_{i-j} abbreviating $a_i, a_{i+1}, \dots, a_j$. Meanwhile, n_1^a is such that $n_1^a(a_9) = 350$ (reduced from 650 by e_2 paying 300 to e_1), that $n_1^a(a_{11}) = 1$ (increased from 0 by e_2 obtaining 1 Switch from e_1), that $n_1^a(a_{15}) = 600$ (increased from 300 by e_1 obtaining 300 from e_2), and that $n_1^a(a_{16}) = 0$ (reduced from 1 by e_1 selling 1 Switch to e_2), while all the other values are unchanged from those with n_0^a.

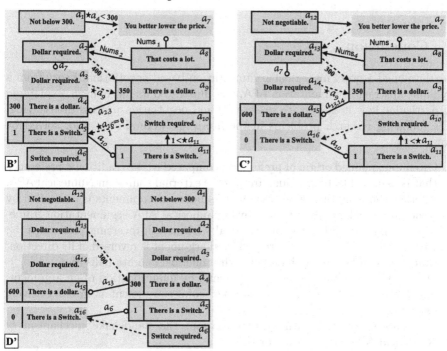

At this point, e_2 may only obtain a Switch from e_3. The ask price of a Switch, however, is 400 dollars from e_3, and e_2 only has 350 dollars. See $\boxed{B'}$ for e_3-e_2 bilateral negotiation. According to e_2's preference (find it on the second page), e_2 asks e_3 to lower the ask price to 350 dollars. That e_2 decides to negotiate over the price with e_3 is characterised in $a_8 \overset{Nums_1}{\multimap} a_7 \dashrightarrow a_2 \overset{a_7}{\multimap} a_3$, and by the facts that $n^r((a_3, a_9, a_4)) = \star a_9$, and that $\mathcal{I}^t(\star a_9, n_1^a) = 350$.

Since a_8 is visible in $F(A_1, \mathsf{n}_1^a)$, $\mathsf{sat}(\mathsf{Nums}_1, \mathsf{n}_1^a)$ (i.e. $350 < 400$), and no $a \in A_1$ attacks a_8 in $F(a_1, \mathsf{n}_1^a)$, there is a transition from $F(A_1, \mathsf{n}_1^a)$ into $F(A_2, \mathsf{n}_1^a)$ with $A_2 = A_1 \cup \{a_7\}$. In this state, e_2 is trying to convert e_3's a_2 with $\mathsf{n}^r((a_2, a_9, a_4)) = 400$ into a_3 with $\mathsf{n}^r((a_3, a_9, a_4)) = \star a_9$ which is basically 350 in $F(A_2, \mathsf{n}_1^a)$, since $\mathcal{I}^t(\star a_9, \mathsf{n}_1^a) = 350$.

Now, the conversion is not automatic in all states, because of $a_1 \xrightarrow{\star a_4 < 300} a_7$. As per e_3's preference (find it on the second page), in case e_2 tries to lower the price below 300 dollars, e_3 simply refuses the request. In $F(A_2, \mathsf{n}_1^a)$, however, $\mathcal{I}^t(\star a_4, \mathsf{n}_1^a) = 350$, thus e_3 agrees to lower the ask price of a Switch from 400 dollars to 350 dollars, which results in another transition from $F(A_2, \mathsf{n}_1^a)$ into $F((A_2 \backslash \{a_2\}) \cup \{a_3\}, \mathsf{n}_1^a)$.

5   Conclusion

We developed a novel numerical argumentation-based negotiation theory from a dynamic abstract argumentation APA, and illustrated its mechanism, explaining in particular how it deals with preference and negotiation process interleaving. The following research problems in the literature were alleviated or solved by our theory.

1. Often unexplained origin of preference: compared to the traditional preference that is assumed to be provided from some external source, in Numerical APA, whether there are or are not any attacks between arguments is controlled by some numerical values within a given Numerical APA argumentation framework. While we did not explicitly deal with attack-reversing preference [5], with which an attack on a more preferred argument is reversed of its direction, that, too, can be readily handled with numerical conditionalisation.
2. Difficulty in handling resource arguments: by quantification of an argument, any potentially diminishing (or strengthening) argument is now intuitively expressed.
3. Difficulty in dealing with synchronisation: the handshake mechanism of Numerical APA can be used for this issue.
4. Difficulty in handling interleaved negotiations: Numerical APA is an extension of APA which can handle concurrency. Further, resource allocation is an inferable, instead of hard-coded, information in Numerical APA, which adapts well to modelling concurrent negotiations.

As immediate future work, we have two agendas. First, the ability to reason about game-theoretical properties in agent-negotiation is desirable. While agents' preferences about the conditions under which to permit a resource reallocation may be expressed by means of numerical information, an inference system will be required for judging whether a certain specific resource allocation optimal to a group of agents is reachable. To this end, we consider embedding of this theory into ATL [1], in a similar manner to CTL embedding shown in [7]. Second, we consider relaxation of some assumptions made about Numerical APA. For instance, collaboration among agents may be permitted. It should be interesting to see how different types of agent interactions can influence the overall negotiation outcomes. Also, while in this work we did not take into account defence from k-step eliminations for an arbitrary k, any positive value for k reflects agent's foresight to grasp steps ahead in negotiation, which should influence its decision-making.

References

1. Alur, R., Henzinger, T.A., Kupferman, O.: Alternating-time temporal logic. J. ACM **49**(5), 672–713 (2002)
2. Amgoud, L., Cayrol, C.: Inferring from inconsistency in preference-based argumentation frameworks. Int. J. Approximate Reason. **29**(2), 125–169 (2002)
3. Amgoud, L., Dimopoulos, Y., Moraitis, P.: A unified and general framework for argumentation-based negotiation. In: AAMAS, pp. 158:1–158:8 (2007)
4. Amgoud, L., Vesic, S.: A formal analysis of the role of argumentation in negotiation dialogues. J. Logic Comput. **5**, 957–978 (2011)
5. Amgoud, L., Vesic, S.: Rich preference-based argumentation frameworks. Int. J. Approx. Reason. **55**(2), 586–606 (2014)
6. Arisaka, R.: Turing-Completeness of Dynamics in Abstract Persuasion Argumentation. CoRR abs/1903.07837 (2019)
7. Arisaka, R., Satoh, K.: Abstract Argumentation / Persuasion / Dynamics. In: PRIMA, pp. 331–343 (2018)
8. Bench-Capon, T.J.M.: Persuasion in practial argument using value-based argumentation frameworks. J. Logic Comput. **13**(3), 429–448 (2003)
9. Bonzon, E., Dimopoulos, Y., Moraitis, P.: Knowing each other in argumentation-based negotiation (extended abstract). In: AAMAS, pp. 1413–1414 (2012)
10. Dung, P.M.: On the acceptability of arguments and its fundamental role in non-monotonic reasoning, logic programming, and n-person games. Artif. Intell. **77**(2), 321–357 (1995)
11. Dung, P.M.: Assumption-based argumentation. In: Simari, G., Rahwan, I. (eds.) Argumentation in AI, pp. 25–44. Springer, Boston (2009). https://doi.org/10.1007/978-0-387-98197-0_10
12. Dung, P.M., Thang, P.M., Toni, F.: Towards argumentation-based contract negotiation. In: COMMA, pp. 134–146 (2008)
13. Haddi, N., Dimopoulos, Y., Moraitis, P.: Argumentative alternating offers. In: AAMAS, pp. 441–448 (2010)
14. Kakas, A., Moraitis, P.: Adaptive agent negotiation via argumentation. In: AAMAS, pp. 384–391 (2006)
15. Kim, J., Segev, A.: A framework for dynamic ebusiness negotiation processes. In: CEC, pp. 84–91 (2003)
16. Niu, L., Zhang, F., Zhang, M.: Feasible negotiation procedures for multiple interdependent negotiations. In: AAMAS, pp. 641–649 (2018)
17. Rahwan, I., Pasquier, P., Sonenberg, L., Dignum, F.: On the benefits of exploiting underlying goals in argument-based negotiation. In: AAAI, pp. 116–121 (2007)
18. Rahwan, I., Ramchurn, S.D., Jennings, N.R., Mcburney, P., Parsons, S., Sonenberg, L.: Argumentation-based negotiation. Knowl. Eng. Rev. **18**(4), 343–375 (2003)
19. Sim, K.M.: Complex and concurrent negotiations for multiple interrelated e-Markets. IEEE Trans. Cybern. **43**(1), 230–245 (2013)
20. Zhang, J., Zhang, M., Ren, F.: A dynamic resource allocation approach for concurrent emergency events in metropolitan regions (Extended Abstract). In: AAMAS, pp. 1775–1777 (2017)

Deep Learning for Human Activity Recognition

Deep Learning for Human Activity Recognition

Zhenghua Chen

Institute for Infocomm Research, Agency for Science, Technology and Research (ASTAR)
chen_zhenghua@i2r.a-star.edu.sg

1 Workshop Overview and Goals

Human activity recognition (HAR) can be used for a number of applications, such as health-care services and smart home applications. Many sensors have been utilized for human activity recognition, such as wearable sensors, smartphones, radio frequency (RF) sensors (WiFi, RFID), LED light sensors, cameras, etc. Owing to the rapid development of wireless sensor network, a large amount of data has been collected for the recognition of human activities with different kind of sensors. Conventional shallow learning algorithms, such as support vector machine and random forest, require to manually extract some representative features from large and noisy sensory data. However, manual feature engineering requires export knowledge and will inevitably miss implicit features.

Recently, deep learning has achieved great success in many challenging research areas, such as image recognition and natural language processing. The key merit of deep learning is to automatically learn representative features from massive data. This technology can be a good candidate for human activity recognition. Some initial attempts can be found in the literature. However, many challenging research problems in terms of accuracy, device heterogeneous, environment changes, etc. remain unsolved.

This workshop intends to prompt state-of-the-art approaches on deep learning for human activity recognition. The organizers invite researchers to participate and submit their research papers in the Deep Learning for Human Activity Recognition Workshop.

2 Workshop Content and Highlights

During the workshop, six papers have been presented. The first paper deals with fall detection via pose motion estimator. They first use a CNN to extract the pose motion feature from a sequence of the 2D RGB video frames. Then a MLP or LSTM is trained for multi-level fall prediction. This pipeline is able to work on the simulated and real-life scenarios.

The second paper is presented by Dr. Zhang Le. It handles action recognition by using hierarchically aggregated deep convolutional neural networks (HACNN). HACNN is able to process the video in a hierarchical manner. Input to HACNN consists of multiple disjoint snippets from an action video. At each level, the input video snippets or feature maps are processed via multiple parallel subConvNets (deep ConvNets that share the same parameters) followed by an aggregation and regularization function (G&R). This produces feature maps for the next level of hierarchy. The output of our HACNN is a C dimensional vector of scores indicating the probability of belonging to a particular action class.

The third paper presents a semi-supervised learning approach based on manifold regularization dynamic graph convolutional networks (MRDGCN). The MRDGCN can automatically update the structure information by manifold regularization until model fitting. In particular, they build an optimization convolution layer formulation to acquire the optimal structure information. Thus, MRDGCN can automatically learn high-level sample features to improve the performance of data representation learning.

The fourth paper proposes a LSTM-CNN based human activity recognition system using WiFi CSI data. They use LSTM as the encoder and CNN as the decoder. The output of LSTM is the input of CNN with three convolutional layers which can extract features spaces. And then, the features space via log softmax-based activation function achieves probability value. They accomplish human activity recognition according to the above probability value.

The fifth paper deals with semi-supervised learning for action recognition by using co-trained deep convolutional neural networks. Their co-training method starts with two base classifiers (spatial ConvNet and temporal ConvNet) trained using labeled data. Given an unlabeled dataset, both the ConvNets label a preset number of samples (U1 and U2 based on their confidence) and add it to the training set of the other ConvNet, which includes the initial labeled data. The two ConvNets are then re-trained on the newly augmented dataset. This process is continued until the ConvNets show no further improvement or a predetermined number of iterations are reached. We chose this paper to be included in the volume due to its effectiveness in improving existing vision based activity recognition in a semi-supervised fashion.

The last paper intends to improve human activity recognition performance with data sources integration. They model the respective importance of data sources as well as their low-level interactions through the analysis of the induced neural architectures space. They further leverage obtained importance and interaction models with a model of activity transitions in the perspective of intelligent data sampling. Qualitative analysis that is conducted with a series of runs give promising results and some aspects remain to be investigated concerning, in particular, the confidence of the learning process and the ways they could optimize this aspect in order to reduce transition periods and the number of trials.

3 Concluding Remarks and Insights for Future Research

Some valuable research directions are identified during this workshop. They include but are not limited to: 1) more advanced network architecture for HAR. 2) Fusion of vision and non-vision sensors for HAR. 3) Federated learning for HAR.

Action Recognition Using Co-trained Deep Convolutional Neural Networks

Le Zhang[1]([⊠]), Jagannadan Varadarajan[2], and Yong Pei[3]

[1] I2R, A*STAR, Singapore, Singapore
zhangleuetsc@gmail.com
[2] Grab, Singapore, Singapore
vjagan@gmail.com
[3] Webank, Shenzhen, People's Republic of China
pei.yong@adsc.com.sg,
https://zhangleuestc.github.io/,
https://sites.google.com/site/vjagan/,
http://publish.illinois.edu/multimodalvisualanalytics/people/

Abstract. Deep convolutional networks have become ubiquitous in computer vision owing to their success in visual recognition task on still images. However, their adaptations to video classification have not clearly established their superiority over conventional hand crafted features. Existing CNN methods for action recognition typically train multiple streams to independently deal with spatial and temporal information and then combine their prediction scores. But relatively little is known about the benefits of combining these modalities during the training process. In this work, we propose a novel semi-supervised learning approach that allows multiple streams to supervise each other in a co-training strategy, thus making the training simultaneous in the two modalities. We show that transferring information between the networks by predicting labels on an unlabeled set outperforms state-of-the-art methods. Furthermore, we also show that performance of our approach is comparable to existing methods but while using less data. We demonstrate the effectiveness of our approach through extensive experiments on the UCF 101 and HMDB datasets.

1   Introduction

Human action recognition is an active research topic in computer vision due to its wide ranging applications in domains including visual surveillance, human behavior analysis, human machine interaction, health care and robotics. Since the earliest methods for automated analysis of human actions, several visual features [1–5] and learning methods [6–8] have consistently improved the recognition performance leading the research community to address more challenging scenarios and complex datasets [9,10]. However, significant hurdles due to variations in appearance, view point, illumination and speed of execution come in the way of solving the problem.

© Springer Nature Switzerland AG 2020
A. El Fallah Seghrouchni and D. Sarne (Eds.): IJCAI 2019 Workshops, LNAI 12158, pp. 155–172, 2020.
https://doi.org/10.1007/978-3-030-56150-5_8

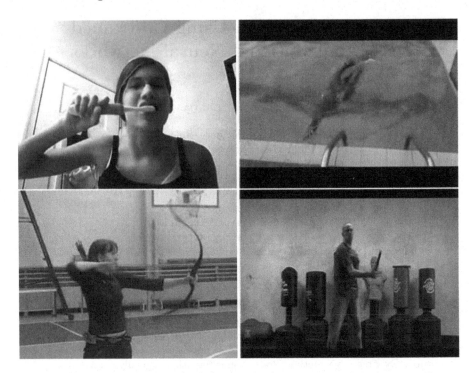

Fig. 1. Example classes demonstrating the strengths of RGB (spatial) and Flow (temporal) networks. Top row: classes *Brushing teeth* (prediction confidence from [24] RGB: 0.05, Flow: 0.68) and *Front crawl* (RGB: 0.20, Flow: 0.58) have relatively high prediction scores from the spatial stream than the flow stream. Bottom row: classes *Archery* (RGB: 0.28, Flow: 0.65) and *Nunchucks* (RGB: 0.3, Flow: 0.54) have high prediction scores from flow stream than the spatial stream.

Recently, deep convolutional neural network (ConvNets) based methods have made vast inroads into computer vision due to their commendable performance in several vision tasks including image classification [11–14], crowd counting [15,16], segmentation [17,18], affective computing [19], visual tracking [20–22] and face recognition [23], where (near) human performance is achieved. Inspired by this, several ConvNet models were proposed for video based action recognition too. Typically, these methods process videos by training two parallel networks (also called streams), where one stream (called the spatial stream) focuses on learning spatial features from RGB input images and the other temporal stream processes motion information from optical flow. The final classification scores are obtained using some weighted combination of the individual network scores.

However, unlike other still image based applications, action recognition is yet to witness such vast improvements due to ConvNet models. In fact, it is interesting to note that most of the ConvNet methods for action recognition still prefer to incorporate Fisher vector encodings of hand crafted features such as HOG, HOF from improved dense trajectories (iDT) [5]. One of the main reasons for this lag in performance is the lack of large scale annotated datasets for action recognition, which ConvNets require to reach an optimum and stable solution. Nonetheless, due to difficulties in data collection and annotation, publicly available action recognition datasets (*e.g.*, UCF101, HMDB51) remain quite limited in both size and variety. As a side effect, from our experience in training several two stream models on these action recognition (from scratch) datasets, we observe that the training error typically reduces to zero while the validation error still remains high indicating a high risk of over fitting.

Next, we observe that the two streams have their own strengths in classifying certain classes better than the other. For instance, from our experiments with the [24] model we observe that certain actions such as *Archery* and *Nunchucks* (see Fig. 1) have high classification accuracy from the temporal stream due to their unique motion patterns and relatively low accuracy from the spatial stream. On the other hand, actions such as *Brushing teeth* and *Front crawl* are classified more accurately by the spatial stream. We posit that exchanging information between the two streams through confidently predicted (informative) samples can greatly improve the performance of the individual networks. However, existing methods do not exploit this fact and train the two streams independently [24–26].

This motivates us to study two problems: i) How to develop methods that can deal with both existing labeled datasets as well as the more easily available unlabeled data with less risk of over-fitting; ii) how to improve existing two streams (or even multiple streams) so as to exploit the strengths of the other stream more effectively. To address this, we propose a **semi-supervised learning** (SSL) process which exploits both labeled and unlabeled data effectively by combining deep ConvNets with **co-training**. Co-training is a multi-view semi-supervised learning method where two learners are trained from the same set of examples, ideally using two independent set of features. During co-training, each learner iteratively labels several unlabeled examples with highest confidence value from its point of view, and these newly labeled examples are added to the labeled training set of the other learner. Iteratively, each learner improves the labeled training set of the other as well as its own performance. Co-training has been shown to be useful for various applications including text classification and object detection [27–30]. However, it has not been explored in the context of deep ConvNets so far.

Co-training requires that the different views are sufficient and conditionally independent given the class labels [31]. However, in practice, given strong learners on each view, co-training has been shown to improve performance even when the aforementioned assumptions are relaxed. In this paper, we hypothesize that spatial stream dealing with appearance and temporal stream dealing with motion information are two strong learners dealing with different aspects of an action and therefore can be co-trained using unlabeled data[1]. The key idea is that some examples which would have been confidently labeled by the spatial stream would

---

[1] Since we consider the spatial and temporal aspects as two views of the data, we use the terms *streams* and *views* interchangeably.

be misclassified by the temporal stream and vice-versa. Letting each stream focus on those informative samples improves overall performance as detailed in Sect. 5.

The main contributions of this work are as follows: We propose a novel co-training based learning process that can exploit both labeled and unlabeled data for the problem of action recognition. We present exhaustive experimental results on the challenging UCF-101 and HMDB datasets using different proportions of labeled and unlabeled data and show competitive results with less labeled data. We further exploit additional *more challenging unlabeled data* from the THUMOS15 challenge and improve existing state-of-the-art results.

2   Related Work

Below we review previous works that are closely related to ours which fall in two categories: (1) Action recognition using convolutional neural networks, and (2) Semi-supervised learning and co-training.

Action Recognition using ConvNets. One of the first attempts to perform action recognition using ConvNets was proposed in [32] to recognize actions from real-life scenes, where 3D convolutions were applied on frame sequences to obtain both appearance and motion information. Following this, Karpathy *et al.* [33] released a large scale video dataset and investigated several aspects of CNN architectures including early fusion, late fusion, 3D CNN on classification performance. A notable development in ConvNets for action recognition was made by Simonyan et al. [24], where a two stream ConvNet architecture (inspired by the object centric ventral stream and motion centric dorsal stream of the human visual cortex) was proposed. Here, the spatial ConvNet (also called a stream) processes the RGB channels and the temporal stream processes several channels of images that encode optical flow in the horizontal and vertical directions. The outputs from the two *independent* streams are then fused to obtain the final confidence scores for an input video.

Following this, several approaches modifying the network architecture [34,35] and (or) the input features [25,26] were proposed. In the C3D method [36], 3D convolutions on limited temporal support of 16 frames with $3 \times 3 \times 3$ kernels were proposed to extract generic features for video analysis tasks. Long range temporal dependencies were learned using dynamic models such as recurrent neural networks on sequence of features in [37]. More recently, Wang *et al.* [35] proposed a network model that takes score consensus from sparse temporal segments and showed improved performance on the UCF101 and HMDB datasets.

Most of the above mentioned methods suffer from two main drawbacks: i) they train the spatial and temporal streams independently without exchanging any information between them and simply combine the individual scores by some weighted averaging; ii) they rely heavily on labeled data which is obtained through a laborious and time consuming process. More recently proposed methods [38,39] address by allowing multiplicative interactions between the spatial and temporal feature maps. However, they end up handcrafting the features

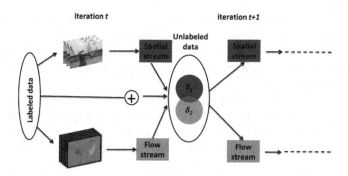

Fig. 2. Co-training two stream models. Our co-training method starts with two base classifiers (spatial ConvNet and temporal ConvNet) trained using labeled data. Given an unlabeled dataset, both the ConvNets label a preset number of samples (U_1 and U_2 based on their confidence) and add it to the training set of the other ConvNet, which includes the initial labeled data. The two ConvNets are then re-trained on the newly augmented dataset. This process is continued until the ConvNets show no further improvement or a predetermined number of iterations are reached.

maps of one network using the output of the other. Moreover, it remains unclear on how the two streams can interact with each other to boost the final performance.

While considerable progress has been made by aggressively exploring deeper architectures together with novel regularization techniques under the standard "convolution + pooling" recipe as we mentioned above, we contribute from a different view, for the first time, by combining the merits of deep ConvNets with a semi-supervised training process that can make use of both labeled and unlabeled data. Our method exploits the strengths of multiple streams by exchanging information through the most confident samples obtained from each stream on an unlabeled pool of samples.

Semi-supervised Learning and Co-training. With the rapid growing of online and personal media archives, we are generating, storing and consuming very large collections of videos. In this big data era, unlabeled training data are usually easy to obtain than labeled training data in many practical applications. Therefore, SSL methods which exploit unlabeled data to improve the performance of classifiers trained using limited training data has attracted much research attention in the past [27–30].

Co-training, initially proposed in [40], is a SSL method that trains two classifiers separately on two sufficient but independent views, and lets the two classifiers label some unlabeled instances for each other. This process has been shown to improve the classification performance in many applications such as web-page classification [41] and object detection [42]. Co-training assumes view sufficiency, *i.e.*, each view is sufficient to predict the class label and conditional independence. Since in many practical applications sufficient and independent views do not exist, variants of co-training to address this issue have been proposed.

For instance, a heteroscedastic Bayesian co-training for multi-view object recognition and audio visual classification was proposed in [43]. Other solutions include using two different data sources (text, images and videos) [31], different supervised learning algorithms [44], different parameter configurations of the same base learner [45].

We observe that SSL methods have not been studied earlier in the context of deep ConvNets and video classification. Therefore, our approach to combine co-training with deep ConvNets will be one of the first attempts, which we believe is pertinent due to increasing need for more data to learn powerful ConvNet models.

3   Approach

In this section, we firstly review the basics of co-training and provide detailed description of how it is applied using a two stream architecture for action recognition.

As stated earlier, our objectives are twofold: i) to train the two streams by using their strengths more effectively, and ii) use more easily available unlabeled data along with existing labeled data. To tackle this, we propose a co-training based learning framework which considers the spatial and temporal streams as two different views and iteratively refines each view using additional unsupervised data.

More precisely, as illustrated in Fig. 2, given a dataset $\mathcal{D} = \mathcal{S} \cup \mathcal{U}$, where $\mathcal{S} = \{(x_k^m, x_k^s, y_k)\}_{k=1}^{l}$ is a labeled dataset and $\mathcal{U} = \{(x_k^m, x_k^s)\}_{k=l}^{l+n}$ is an unlabeled data set, we assume that each sample is endowed with two views, $i.e.$, $x_k^s \in \mathcal{X}^s$ corresponding to the raw RGB input which will be handled by the spatial stream and $x_k^m \in \mathcal{X}^m$ corresponding to optical flow used by the temporal stream. $y_k \in \mathcal{Y} \subset \{0,1\}^C$ is the label for the kth instance given as a C dimensional binary vector, where C is the number of classes. Let $f^s : \mathcal{X}^s \to \mathcal{Y}$ and $f^m : \mathcal{X}^m \to \mathcal{Y}$ be the classifier representing the spatial and temporal ConvNets respectively. Our goal in co-training is to infer the parameters of f^s and f^m by minimizing the following loss given $\mathcal{S}$ and $\mathcal{U}$:

$$
\begin{aligned}
\min \quad & \mathcal{L}_s(f^s; \mathcal{S}) + \mathcal{L}_s(f^m; \mathcal{S}) + \lambda \mathcal{L}_u(f^s, f^m; \mathcal{U}) \\
\text{s.t.} \quad & f^s \in \mathcal{F}^s, f^m \in \mathcal{F}^m,
\end{aligned}
\tag{1}
$$

where $\mathcal{F}^\diamond$ is the space of classifiers($\diamond \in \{s, m\}$). The first two loss terms penalize the classifiers with respect to annotated dataset $\mathcal{S}$. Typically, the classifiers are obtained by minimizing a loss function (over mini-batches), where the loss is given by the standard categorical cross-entropy loss function:

$$
\mathcal{L}_s(f^\diamond; \mathcal{S}) = \sum_{k=1}^{l} \sum_{i=1}^{C} y_i \left(f^\diamond(x_k)_i - \log \sum_{j=1}^{C} \exp f^\diamond(x_k)_j \right)
\tag{2}
$$

Here y_i and $f(x)_i$ indicate the ith component of x's ground truth and the estimated label $f^\diamond(x)$, $\diamond \in \{s, m\}$. The loss in the third term of Eq. 1 is calculated in the same way as in Eq. 2:

$$\mathcal{L}_u(f^\diamond, \tilde{f}^\diamond; \mathcal{U}) = \sum_{k=l+1}^{l+n} \sum_{i=1}^{C} y_i^\star \left(f^\diamond(x_k)_i - \log \sum_{j=1}^{C} \exp f^\diamond(x_k)_j \right) \tag{3}$$

where the *pseudo-ground-truth* $y^\star$ is obtained from the other network $\tilde{f}^\diamond$, which represents the complementary stream for $f^\diamond$ (in our case $\tilde{f}^\diamond = f^m$ *iff* $f^\diamond = f^s$ and vice-versa). This term penalizes the two classifiers jointly by measuring their disagreement on the unlabeled dataset $\mathcal{U}$. Finally, λ is a weight parameter associated with the third term which is set to be 1 in this study.

Objective function of this form can be seen in co-regularization [46] formulations, where two-view consensus is built based on simultaneously learning of multiple classifiers. Here, the third term in the objective function can also be seen as a regularization term that penalizes a high level of disagreement between the two views.

Solving the above objective function in Eq. 1 directly is difficult. Instead, we adopt an alternating optimization procedure similar to Co-EM [46] that optimizes one view at a time. More specifically, we follow the iterative process as detailed below:

– train base classifiers f_0^s and f_0^s (corresponding to iteration $t = 0$) using supervised data $\mathcal{S}$.
– loop until a preset number of iterations $\{t = 1, \ldots, N\}$.

- compute predictions and confidence of f_t^s and f_t^m for all the unlabeled instances.
- f_t^s selects the top u unlabelled instances from $\mathcal{U}$ based on its confidence score and adds these newly labeled examples into data δ_1 which contains $\mathcal{S}$
- f_t^m selects the top u unlabelled instances from $\mathcal{U}$ based on its confidence score and adds these newly labeled examples into data δ_2 which contains $\mathcal{S}$
- refine f_t^s and f_t^s using δ_2 and δ_1 respectively to obtain f_{t+1}^s and f_{t+1}^m.

It is important to note that in each iteration, one view considers the labels provided by the other view as the ground truth and therefore tries to minimize only a portion of the objective function in Eq. 1. More precisely, at each iteration the spatial stream minimizes $\mathcal{L}_s(f_t^s; \mathcal{S}) + \mathcal{L}_u(f_t^s, f_t^m; \mathcal{U})$ by treating the scores from f_t^m as constant, whereas the temporal stream minimizes $\mathcal{L}_s(f^m; \mathcal{S}) + \mathcal{L}_u(f^s, f^m; \mathcal{U})$, keeping f_t^s fixed.

Intuitively, each stream, with different biases will have different confidences in labeling different instances from the unlabeled dataset, the higher confidence ones of which can be more informative to the other stream. Forcing each stream to focus on these informative instances (labeled confidently by the other stream) results in significantly improved classifiers at the end (see Sect. 5). This also promotes consensus between the two classifiers as co-training process proceeds.

Note that this learning process is significantly different from existing two stream methods which are mostly trained one stream at a time, in an opaque manner. More precisely, each stream minimizes only $\mathcal{L}_s(f^\circ; \mathcal{S})$ without any opportunity to exchange or focus on informative examples.

In summary, we first train a spatial and temporal network using labeled data (as detailed in Sect. 5). Confidence scores for samples from the unlabeled data are then obtained using the two networks. For each network, samples are sorted based on their confidence scores and the top 50% of the samples are selected for labeling. The samples and their predicted *pseudo-labels* are then added to the training set of the other network. Both networks are then retrained on the newly available data. We let the networks co-train for a maximum of 6 iterations. In practice, we observe little improvement in the prediction accuracy after 4 iterations, as shown in Fig. 3. Note that the labels obtained could be noisy depending upon the classification accuracy of the model, hence the name *pseudo-label*. Finally, labels corresponding to test samples are predicted by combining the scores obtained from the two co-trained networks using a weighted average. The weights corresponding to the spatial and temporal networks are set to 1 and 1.5 respectively.

Combined Scoring. It is widely accepted that combining two streams of networks leads to higher overall classification accuracy. Therefore, instead of using only the spatial or temporal network to create new labeled data from the unlabeled dataset, we use the combined model ($\lambda_1 f^s + \lambda_2 f^m$) to predict the class labels on the unlabeled dataset. Since the combined model is better than the individual ones, we can expect to have a cleaner labeled data for retraining the two streams at the next iteration. In principle, it can be argued that this results in the same pool of newly labeled data for both the networks to retrain, however, the impact of the other network (complementary view) in generating the labels is non-negligible and hence does not violate the idea of co-training. In practice, this leads to cleaner newly labeled data and some improvements in overall classification performance. λ_1 and λ_2 is also set to be 1 and 1.5, respectively. We denote this approach "**Co-train combo**" in our experiments. Unless explicitly stated, we use the conventional co-training procedure in reporting our experimental results.

4   Datasets

We conduct experiments on two commonly used action datasets, namely HMDB51 [10] and UCF101 [9]. The UCF101 dataset consists of 13320 video clips from 101 classes. We follow the evaluation scheme of the THUMOS13 challenge and adopt the three training/testing splits for evaluation.

We demonstrate our co-training experiments by splitting the training data within split 1 of UCF-101 into different proportions ($\rho = \{50\%, 70\%, 90\%\}$) of labeled and unlabeled datasets. We ignore the labels to create the unlabeled dataset. However, we also conduct experiments using a more challenging unlabeled data collection obtained from the validation set of THUMOS15 challenge [47]. This data contains 2104 untrimmed video sequences from the same classes as UCF 101 data. Since these videos are long (average duration of $\approx$2–3 min), we applied a simple pre-processing step (shot detection) to obtain a short clip containing a maximum of 500 frames. We use only one such clip from each video sequence. It is important to note that this dataset is significantly more challenging than UCF101 due to the presence of large intra-class variations, more complex background and large camera motions [47].

The HMDB51 dataset is a large collection of realistic videos from various sources, such as movies and web videos. The dataset is composed of 6,766 video clips from 51 action categories with large human motion from various sources such as movies and web videos. Similar to UCF-101, we use different proportions of labeled training data from split 1 and consider the remaining portion of the data as unlabeled.

5   Experiments

We adopt the commonly used two-stream approach which incorporates spatial and temporal networks. The spatial network receives RGB images extracted from videos to learn a discriminative ConvNet to model what makes the action whereas the temporal network operates on optical flow channels to represent how the action proceeds over time. A late fusion by weighted average of the scores from two networks are employed to predict the category of each video data.

In this work, we choose the Inception with Batch Normalization (BN-Inception) [48] model as our building block as it is more efficient and accurate than the commonly used VGG-like networks [48,49]. More specifically, we employ the state-of-the-art *Temporal Segment Networks* (TSN) framework [48] and model a sequence of snippets as follows:

$$f^\diamond = G(f^\diamond_{base}(T_1^\diamond, \theta^\diamond), f^\diamond_{base}(T_2^\diamond, \theta^\diamond), ..., f^\diamond_{base}(T_K^\diamond, \theta^\diamond)), \tag{4}$$

here $\diamond \in \{s, m\}$ indicates the input modality. The TSN learns a pool of base models f_{base} where each of them share the same parameter $\theta^\diamond$. G is a consensus function which combines the outputs from multiple short snippets to obtain a consensus of class hypothesis among them. We use the same pipeline as [48], where the temporal stream receives a stack 5 optical frames as input and the spatial stream receives three (red, green and blue) color channels as input. K is set to be 3 and G is a simple averaging function.

Training. Stochastic gradient descent is adopted to minimize the loss function in Eq. 2 where f is defined as in Eq. 4. We set the mini-batch size to be 16 and the momentum to 0.9. The spatial network is initialized with pre-trained models from ImagNet [50]. We use the same strategy to initialize the temporal model from [51] where the filters of first layer is averaged firstly across the channel and the filters of the first layer of temporal model is set to be the averaged results for each channel. The learning rate for the spatial stream is set to a conservatively small value, *i.e.*, 0.001. We further reduce the learning rate by a factor of 0.1 for every 2000 iteration until reaching a maximum of 4500 iterations. For the temporal stream, the learning rate is set to a slightly larger value, *i.e.*, 0.005, so as to cope up with the new input modality coming from optical flow. We reduce the learning rate by a factor of 0.1 at 12000-th iteration. The maximum number of iterations is set to 18000. For data augmentation, location and scale jittering, horizontal flipping, corner cropping are used [48,51]. In corner cropping, we extract regions randomly from the corners and the center of the input image (either raw RGB and optical flow). For scale jittering, the input is firstly resized into 256×340. The width and the height of the cropped region are then randomly selected from a set of values $\{256, 224, 192, 168\}$ to insert arbitrary variations in the aspect ratio. Finally, we resize the cropped regions to 224×224 and feed them into ConvNets. We use the TVL1 optical flow algorithm [52] in OpenCV with CUDA to extract the optical flows for the temporal stream. We further employ a data-parallel strategy with two TitanX GPUs in a customized version of Caffe [53] and OpenMPI[2]. The training time of 1 iteration takes around 3 h in our platform.

Testing. For fair comparison with established results in the literature, we follow the testing scheme introduced in [24,35]. During the evaluation phase, 25 frame images or optical flow fields are selected for testing of spatial and temporal nets, respectively. From each input frame, we derive 10 inputs from the five different crops (from the four corners and center) and their horizontally flipped versions. The final prediction score is obtained by averaging across the sampled frames and their cropped regions. For the fusion of spatial and temporal ConvNets, we use a weighted linear combination of their prediction scores, where the weight is set as 1.5 for temporal net and 1 for spatial net.

5.1   Experiments on UCF-101 and HMDB Datasets

In this section, we focus on the study of our co-training based framework. We first study the effect of co-training using split 1 of UCF101 dataset and split 1 of HMDB dataset. For this, we first split the training data of UCF101 into two parts and consider one part as training or labeled data and the rest as unlabeled data. Although we have labels for the entire split, we ignore the labels corresponding to the unlabeled portion for our co-training purposes. We consider three different proportions, $(50\%, 50\%)$, $(70\%, 30\%)$ and $(90\%, 10\%)$ for the labeled and unlabeled data respectively. Note that the datasets are created by randomly selecting

---

[2] https://github.com/yjxiong/caffe.

the samples (without replacement) from each class according to the given proportions. The goal here is to study the effect of various proportions of labeled and unlabeled data on co-training.

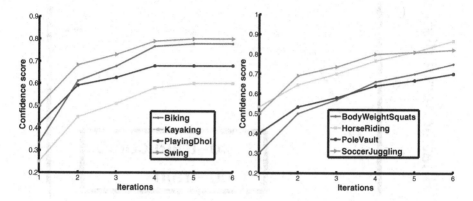

Fig. 3. Effect of co-training on prediction accuracy of the spatial and temporal networks. Four classes with the highest improvements over six co-training iterations are shown. (left) *Biking, Kayaking, PlayingDhol* and *Swing* are the four classes with maximum improvement from the spatial stream and (right) *BodyWeightSquats, HorseRiding, PoleVault* and *SoccerJuggling* are the four classes with maximum improvement from the temporal stream. The basic co-training (scoring) method is used here.

To start with, a basic model is trained using the labeled dataset. Co-training is then initiated using the labeled and unlabeled set. Finally, the co-trained model is evaluated on the validation data corresponding to split-1. Table 1 shows the results obtained from UCF101 (split 1) using various proportions of labeled and unlabeled data. We see that co-training improves the accuracy by around 2–5% in most cases. The method achieves significant improvement using only 50% of the training data, with the remaining 50% used as unlabeled data for co-training. In fact, this performance is better than several two-stream models [24,36,54,55] that were trained using the entire labeled data from the split.

It is also important to note that improvements in the individual networks does not always lead to a similar effect when the two models are combined. This could be due to the fact that the two networks are improved by building consensus over informative or challenging samples leaving their combination somewhat redundant.

Table 2 summarizes the results obtained on split-1 of HMDB dataset using different proportions of labeled and unlabeled data. Here again, we see that co-training helps in improving the individual networks' performance as well as the overall performance by about 1% (Table 3).

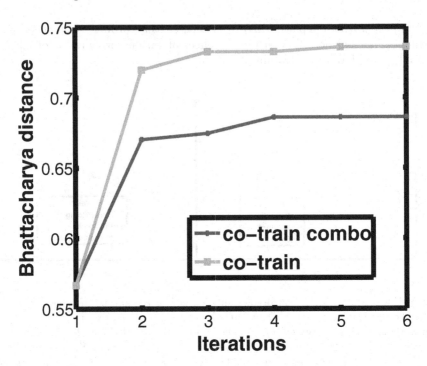

Fig. 4. Co-training promotes consensus between the two streams. We measure the similarity between the scores of the two models on the unlabeled data after each co-training iteration. The basic co-training (scoring) method is used here.

Table 1. Exploring the effect of Co-training using different proportions of labeled and unlabeled data on the UCF101 (split 1). First column refers to the amount of labeled and unlabeled data used. "Base" refers to the base model obtained by training the networks [35] using the given proportion of labeled data. We observe that co-training improves the individual classifiers as well as the overall score.

Label:unlabel	Model	Spatial	Temporal	Two-stream
50%:50%	Base	75.8%	75.0%	87.1%
	Co-train	**80.7%**	**81.7%**	**89.7%**
70%:30%	Base	78.8%	78.5%	88.8%
	Co-train	**81.4%**	**83.5%**	**89.2%**
90%:10%	Base	82.5%	84.3%	92.0%
	Co-train	**83.9%**	**87.1%**	**93.2%**

Table 2. Exploring the effect of co-training using different proportions of labeled and unlabeled data on the HMDB101 (split 1).

Label:unlabel	Model	Spatial	Temporal	Two-stream
50%:50%	Base	**48.1%**	53.1%	64.0%
	Co-train	47.7%	**54.9%**	**65.0%**
70%:30%	Base	50.8%	57.3%	66.1%
	Co-train	**52.0%**	**57.5%**	**66.9%**
90%:10%	Base	53.1%	58.8%	69.2%
	Co-train	**54.2%**	58.8%	**70.2%**

Table 3. Results from co-training on the UCF101 data. Detailed results from the three splits of UCF101 dataset and mean performance. Co-training the two views consistently improves performance in all the cases.

Split	Model	Spatial	Temporal	Two-stream
Split 1	Base model	85.7%	87.9%	93.5%
	Co-trained	86.2%	88.3%	93.7%
	Co-train-combo	**87.0%**	**88.3%**	**93.9%**
Split 2	Base model	84.9%	90.2%	94.3%
	Co-trained	**85.9%**	90.6%	94.4%
	Co-train-combo	**85.9%**	**91.1%**	**94.6%**
Split 3	Base model	84.5%	91.3%	94.2%
	Co-trained	**86.9%**	91.2%	**94.5%**
	Co-train-combo	86.1%	**91.5%**	94.3%
Mean	Base model	85.0%	89.8%	94.0%
	Co-trained	**86.3%**	90.0%	94.2%
	Co-train-combo	**86.3%**	**90.3%**	**94.3%**

5.2   Comparison with State-of-the-Art

After exploring the co-training approach on the two datasets and establishing the effectiveness of the approach we summarize the results obtained by our method and compare it with several state-of-the-art approaches. Table 4, presents a detailed analysis of various methods which includes traditional methods relying on iDT [5,56,57] and deep learning representations such as the 2 stream architecture [24,25], Recurrent neural networks [60] and 3D convolutions [36], Trajectory-pooled deep convolutional descriptors (TDD) [25] and the more recently proposed temporal segment networks (TSN) [35] and spatio-temporal Resnets (ST-ResNet) [34].

We report the accuracies obtained using two different scoring functions used in creating the pseudo-labels: The first approach uses only the other stream to label, whereas the second approach uses the combination of both the models to predict

Table 4. Comparison of our method with other state-of-the-art methods on UCF101 dataset.

Method	Accuracy
DT+MVSV [56]	83.5%
IDT+FV [57]	85.9%
IDT+HSV [58]	87.9%
MoFAP [59]	88.3%
Two stream [24]	88.0%
C3D (3 nets ensemble) [36]	85.2%
Two stream+LSTM [54]	88.6%
FSTCN (SCI fusion) [55]	88.1%
TDD+FV [25]	90.3%
LTC [60]	91.7%
KVMF [61]	93.1%
Two stream SR-CNN [35]	92.6%
TSN (two stream version) [48]	94.0%
TSN (3 modalities) [48]	94.2%
CNN-fusion [39]	89.1%
Conv-fusion (Two Stream Version) [38]	92.5%
Conv-fusion+IDT [38]	93.5%
ST-ResNet (two stream version) [34]	93.4%
ST-ResNet+IDT (two stream version) [34]	94.6%
Ours (co-trained)	**94.2%**
Ours (co-trained-combo)	**94.3%**

the labels. Our co-training approach achieves an accuracy of 94.2%, whereas co-training with the combination score improves this slightly to 94.3%. Note that we do not combine iDT features as done by several earlier methods [34,38].

5.3   Analysis of Co-training

In order to understand the effect of co-training on the classification performance, we analysed the classification accuracy of each class after every iteration of co-training. We observed that co-training indeed improves the accuracy of most of the classes. More precisely, classification accuracies for 85 of the 101 classes in UCF-101 improved, 10 remained almost the same, 5 reduced, although marginally. This small reduction could be due to noise introduced through the pseudo-labels. In the 85 classes that improved on their prediction accuracies, nearly 30 classes improved from below 0.5 to well beyond 0.5. Figure 3 shows the confidence scores obtained for four different action classes from the spatial and temporal networks after each iteration of co-training. These classes have the maximum improvement over the co-training iterations. From this we confirm that the co-training improves the classification accuracy by a good margin. Note that the classification accuracy saturates after 4 iterations of co-training.

Another measure to understand the working of co-training is to check if the models agree on the unlabeled samples as learning proceeds. Typically, as the learning proceeds, consensus between the two streams emerge leading to a greater similarity between their prediction scores. Note that, this also a result of the third penalty term in the objective function, where similarity between the two views is encouraged. For this, we computed the Bhattacharya similarity co-efficient between the two models' prediction scores on the unlabeled data. In Fig. 4, we show the Bhattacharya coefficients for the two methods, (i) basic co-training, and (ii) co-training with combo. We see that the similarity between the prediction scores of the two networks increases steeply during the second and third iteration and saturates thereafter. It is also interesting to note that the basic co-training promotes more consensus between the two networks.

6   Conclusion

In this paper, we proposed a new semi-supervised approach based on co-training to learn two stream models for action recognition. Our approach considers the appearance and motion aspects of video as two views and exploits their strengths on unlabeled data to improve the individual classifiers. Experiments on two large scale datasets done by varying the proportions of unlabeled data used for co-training confirms the fact that co-training indeed improves the performance of the individual streams and their combination. Furthermore, we also proposed to use a more challenging unsupervised dataset to further improve the state-of-the-art method. We observe that our approach significantly improves the individual networks and marginally improves the overall accuracy over a tough baseline model. We plan to further explore this approach using large scale unlabeled datasets in the future.

References

1. Brand, M., Kettnaker, V.: Discovery and segmentation of activities in video. IEEE Trans. Pattern Anal. Mach. Intell. **22**, 844–851 (2000)
2. Bobick, A.F., Davis, J.W.: The recognition of human movement using temporal templates. IEEE Trans. Pattern Anal. Mach. Intell. **23**(3), 257–267 (2001)
3. Efros, A.A., Berg, A.C., Mori, G., Malik, J.: Recognizing action at a distance, vol. 2003 (October 2003)
4. Laptev, I., Lindeberg, T.: Space-time interest points. Int. J. Comput. Vis. **64**(2–3), 107–123 (2005)
5. Wang, H., Kläser, A., Schmid, C., Liu, C.-L.: Action recognition by dense trajectories. In: CVPR (2011)
6. Niebles, J.C., Wang, H., Fei-Fei, L.: Unsupervised learning of human action categories using spatial-temporal words. Int. J. Comput. Vis. **79**(3), 299–318 (2008)

7. Brand, M., Oliver, N., Pentland, A.: Coupled hidden Markov models for complex action recognition. In: IEEE Conference on Computer Vision and Pattern Recognition (1997)
8. Turaga, P., Chellappa, R., Subrahmanian, V.S., Udrea, O.: Machine recognition of human activities: a survey. IEEE Trans. Circuits Syst. Video Technol. **18**, 1473–1488 (2008)
9. Soomro, K., Zamir, A.R., Shah, M.: Ucf101: a dataset of 101 human actions classes from videos in the wild. Crcv-tr-12-01, UCF (2012)
10. Kuehne, H., Jhuang, H., Garrote, E., Poggio, T., Serre, T.: HMDB: a large video database for human motion recognition. In: ICCV (2011)
11. Sutskever, I., Krizhevsky, A., Hinton, G.E.: Imagenet classification with deep convolutional neural networks. In: NIPS (2012)
12. Szegedy, C.: Going deeper with convolutions. In: CVPR (2015)
13. Simonyan, K., Zisserman, A.: Very deep convolutional networks for large-scale image recognition. In: ICLR (2014)
14. He, K., Zhang, X., Ren, S., Sun, J.: Deep residual learning for image recognition. arXiv preprint arXiv:1512.03385 (2015)
15. Zhang, L., et al.: Nonlinear regression via deep negative correlation learning. In: IEEE TPAMI (2019)
16. Shi, Z., et al.: Crowd counting with deep negative correlation learning. In: CVPR, pp. 5382–5390 (2018)
17. Long, J., Shelhamer, E., Darrell, T.: Fully convolutional networks for semantic segmentation. In: IEEE Conference on Computer Vision and Pattern Recognition, pp. 3431–3440 (2015)
18. Liu, Y., et al.: DEL: deep embedding learning for efficient image segmentation. In: IJCAI, vol. 864, p. 870 (2018)
19. Zhang, L., Peng, S., Winkler, S.: Persemon: a deep network for joint analysis of apparent personality, emotion and their relationship. IEEE Trans. Affect. Comput. (2019)
20. Zhang, L., Varadarajan, J., Nagaratnam Suganthan, P., Ahuja, N., Moulin, P.: Robust visual tracking using oblique random forests. In: CVPR, pp. 5589–5598 (2017)
21. Zhang, L., Suganthan, P.N.: Robust visual tracking via co-trained kernelized correlation filters. PR **69**, 82–93 (2017)
22. Zhang, L., Suganthan, P.N.: Visual tracking with convolutional random vector functional link network. IEEE Trans. Cybern. **47**(10), 3243–3253 (2016)
23. Schroff, F., Kalenichenko, D., Philbin, J.: Facenet: a unified embedding for face recognition and clustering. In: CVPR (2015)
24. Simonyan, K., Zisserman, A.: Two-stream convolutional networks for action recognition in videos. In: NIPS (2014)
25. Wang, L., Qiao, Y., Tang, X.: Action recognition with trajectory-pooled deep-convolutional descriptors. In: CVPR, pp. 4305–4314 (2015)
26. Zhang, B., Wang, L., Wang, Z., Qiao, Y., Wang, H.: Real-time action recognition with enhanced motion vector CNNs. In: CVPR, pp. 2718–2726 (2016)
27. Misra, I., Shrivastava, A., Hebert, M.: Watch and learn: semi-supervised learning of object detectors from videos. CoRR arxiv:1505.05769 (2015)
28. Dai, D., Van Gool, L.: Ensemble projection for semi-supervised image classification (2013)
29. Dai, D., Van Gool, L.: Unsupervised high-level feature learning by ensemble projection for semi-supervised image classification and image clustering. Technical report, ETH Zurich (2016)

30. Carbonetto, P., Dorkó, G., Schmid, C., Kück, H., de Freitas, N.: A semi-supervised learning approach to object recognition with spatial integration of local features and segmentation cues. In: Ponce, J., Hebert, M., Schmid, C., Zisserman, A. (eds.) Toward Category-Level Object Recognition. LNCS, vol. 4170, pp. 277–300. Springer, Heidelberg (2006). https://doi.org/10.1007/11957959_15
31. Gupta, S., Kim, J., Grauman, K., Mooney, R.: Watch, listen and learn: co-training on captioned images and videos. In: Daelemans, W., Goethals, B., Morik, K. (eds.) ECML PKDD 2008. LNCS (LNAI), vol. 5211, pp. 457–472. Springer, Heidelberg (2008). https://doi.org/10.1007/978-3-540-87479-9_48
32. Ji, S., Wei, X., Yang, M., Kai, Y.: 3D convolutional neural networks for human action recognition. IEEE Trans. Pattern Anal. Mach. Intell. **35**(1), 221–231 (2013)
33. Karpathy, A., Toderici, G., Shetty, S., Leung, T., Sukthankar, R., Fei-Fei, L.: Large-scale video classification with convolutional neural networks. In: CVPR (2014)
34. Feichtenhofer, C., Pinz, A., Wildes, R.P.: Spatiotemporal residual networks for video action recognition. In: NIPS (2016)
35. Wang, Y., Song, J., Wang, L., Van Gool, L., Hilliges, O.: Two-stream SR-CNNs for action recognition in videos. In: BMVC (2016)
36. Tran, D., Bourdev, L., Fergus, R., Torresani, L., Paluri, M.: Learning spatiotemporal features with 3D convolutional networks. In: ICCV (2015)
37. Donahue, J., et al.: Long-term recurrent convolutional networks for visual recognition and description. In: CVPR (2015)
38. Feichtenhofer, C., Pinz, A., Zisserman, A.: Convolutional two-stream network fusion for video action recognition. In: CVPR (2016)
39. Park, E., Han, X., Berg, T.L., Berg, A.C.: Combining multiple sources of knowledge in deep CNNs for action recognition. In: WACV (2016)
40. Blum, A., Mitchell, T.: Combining labeled and unlabeled data with co-training. In: COLT, pp. 92–100 (1998)
41. Nigam, K., Ghani, R.: Analyzing the effectiveness and applicability of co-training. In: CIKM (2000)
42. Levin, A., Viola, P.A., Freund, Y.: Unsupervised improvement of visual detectors using co-training. In: ICCV (2003)
43. Christoudias, C.M., Urtasun, R., Kapoorz, A., Darrell, T.: Co-training with noisy perceptual observations. In: CVPR, pp. 2844–2851 (2009)
44. Goldman, S.A., Zhou, Y.: Enhancing supervised learning with unlabeled data. In: ICML (2000)
45. Zhou, Z.-H., Li, M.: Semi-supervised regression with co-training. In: IJCAI (2005)
46. Yu, S., Krishnapuram, B., Steck, H., Rao, R.B., Rosales, R.: Bayesian co-training. In: JMLR, vol. 12 (November 2011)
47. Gorban, A., et al.: THUMOS challenge: action recognition with a large number of classes (2015). http://www.thumos.info/
48. Wang, L., et al.: Temporal segment networks: towards good practices for deep action recognition. In: Leibe, B., Matas, J., Sebe, N., Welling, M. (eds.) ECCV 2016. LNCS, vol. 9912, pp. 20–36. Springer, Cham (2016). https://doi.org/10.1007/978-3-319-46484-8_2
49. Ioffe, S., Szegedy, C.: Batch normalization: accelerating deep network training by reducing internal covariate shift. arXiv preprint arXiv:1502.03167 (2015)
50. Deng, J., Dong, W., Socher, R., Li, L.-J., Li, K., Fei-Fei, L.: Imagenet: a large-scale hierarchical image database. In: Computer Vision and Pattern Recognition, pp. 248–255. IEEE (2009)
51. Wang, L., Xiong, Y., Wang, Z., Qiao, Y.: Towards good practices for very deep two-stream convnets. arXiv preprint arXiv:1507.02159 (2015)

52. Zach, C., Pock, T., Bischof, H.: A duality based approach for realtime TV-L^1 optical flow. In: Hamprecht, F.A., Schnörr, C., Jähne, B. (eds.) DAGM 2007. LNCS, vol. 4713, pp. 214–223. Springer, Heidelberg (2007). https://doi.org/10.1007/978-3-540-74936-3_22

53. Jia, Y., et al.: Caffe: convolutional architecture for fast feature embedding. arXiv preprint arXiv:1408.5093 (2014)

54. Yue-Hei Ng, J., Hausknecht, M., Vijayanarasimhan, S., Vinyals, O., Monga, R., Toderici, G.: Beyond short snippets: deep networks for video classification. In: IEEE Conference on Computer Vision and Pattern Recognition, pp. 4694–4702 (2015)

55. Sun, L., Jia, K., Yeung, D.-Y., Shi, B.E.: Human action recognition using factorized spatio-temporal convolutional networks. In: IEEE International Conference on Computer Vision, pp. 4597–4605 (2015)

56. Cai, Z., Wang, L., Peng, X., Qiao, Y.: Multi-view super vector for action recognition. In: IEEE conference on Computer Vision and Pattern Recognition, pp. 596–603 (2014)

57. Wang, H., Schmid, C.: Lear-Inria submission for the thumos workshop. In: ICCV Workshop on Action Recognition with a Large Number of Classes, vol. 2, p. 8 (2013)

58. Peng, X., Wang, L., Wang, X., Qiao, Y.: Bag of visual words and fusion methods for action recognition: comprehensive study and good practice. Comput. Vis. Image Underst. **150**, 109–125 (2016)

59. Wang, L., Qiao, Y., Tang, X.: MoFAP: a multi-level representation for action recognition. Int. J. Comput. Vis. **119**(3), 254–271 (2016)

60. Donahue, J., et al.: Long-term recurrent convolutional networks for visual recognition and description. In: IEEE Conference on Computer Vision and Pattern Recognition, pp. 2625–2634 (2015)

61. Zhu, W., Hu, J., Sun, G., Cao, X., Qiao, Y.: A key volume mining deep framework for action recognition. In: IEEE Conference on Computer Vision and Pattern Recognition, pp. 1991–1999 (2016)

Humanizing AI

Humanizing AI

Pushpak Bhattarcharya[1], Niranjan Nayak[2], Manoj Kumar Chinnakotla[3],
Puneet Agrawal[2], and Kedhar Nath Narahari[2]

[1] IIT Patna
pb@cse.iitb.ac.in
[2] Microsoft AI, India
{niranjan,punagr,kedharn}@microsoft.com
[3] Bing, USA
manojc@microsoft.com

1 Workshop Overview and Goals

To build a stronger partnership between humans and AI agents, it is vital to move away from a world where humans try to understand these agents to a world where the agents understand us, answer and behave in the way a human would do. However, what aspects will make these agents human-like and how can we develop algorithms and techniques to make progress in achieving human-like behavior are the questions we raise in this workshop.

The main goal of the workshop was to bring the researchers working in the related fields such as Conversational Understanding, Human-AI interactions, Cognitive Science, Empathy, Philosophy etc. together and share the learnings, discuss new directions and associated practical challenges to make further advancements in this field of Humanizing AI.

To that end, the workshop had invited talks across a diverse set of topics by some renowned researchers, lightning talks by young researchers who presented their work in the main conference and poster sessions of all the papers accepted by the workshop. The workshop saw a participation of over 70 researchers from the community.

2 Invited Talks

The workshop invited researchers pioneering diverse aspects of Humanizing AI to share their thoughts and experiences with the audience. Dr. Rui Yan talked about *Recent Advances and Challenges on Human-Computer Conversational Systems*. In another talk on *Building Intelligent and Visceral Machines: From Sensing to Synthesis*, Dr. Daniel McDuff introduced the concept of affective computing to the audience. Later, Dr. Rafal Rzepka in a related talk on *Humanizing Machines by Simulating Empathy and Understanding Human Needs* opined that Humanizing AI means making machines not violating our common sense. Dr. Virginia Dignum spoke on the topic of *Responsible AI* where she spoke about various characteristics of Responsible AI. The last talk of the day was given by Dr. Pascale Fung on *Towards a More Gender Equal World using AI*. Overall, the invited talks helped the researchers understand important aspects associated with the area of Humanizing AI which include being responsible, being cognizant of different implicit biases, practical challenges in addition to building algorithms.

3 Lightning Talks and Poster Session

The workshop had 7 lightning talks by young researchers who had acceptances in the main conference. The talks spanned problems like talking face generation, story ending prediction, code switched text, meta-learning in low resource setting, question-answering and other related fields. Lightning talks helped the attendees understand the breadth of umbrella of Humanizing AI and how that learning can be shared across disciplines. Further, a total of 8 posters and 3 demos were accepted in the workshop. The papers covered areas such as Conversational Understanding, Human Computer interaction and Machine Learning. Problems related to code mixing languages, emotion understanding, passage ranking, question generation, human computer interaction and other related areas were addressed by the authors. Overall, the poster sessions allowed researchers to gather early feedback on their work along with more ideas to improve the same.

4 Representative Workshop Paper

Based on the feedback received from the reviewers and the participants in the workshop, work done by Dahiya et. al. [1] was chosen as the representative paper of the workshop. The paper discusses the curriculum strategies that could be used to identify sentiment in code-mixed setup which is otherwise difficult for users not well versed with both the languages involved.

5 Concluding Remarks

Based on the submissions made to the workshop and the insights given by the invited speakers and the discussions thereafter, two main themes emerged as areas which require attention from AI community. First, Humanizing AI is a multi-disciplinary field which needs efforts across disciplines and that all of them should be applied coherently to make AI human-like. Second, we need to take a more holistic approach to building AI involving careful attention in all phases of development (purpose, planning, design and implementation) and further research is warranted in all these phases. We are thankful to all the speakers, participants of this workshop along with IJCAI'19 organizers.

Reference

1. Dahiya, A., Battan, N., Shrivastava, M., Sharma, D.M.: Curriculum learning strategies for hindi-english codemixed sentiment analysis. CoRR abs/1906.07382

Curriculum Learning Strategies for Hindi-English Code-Mixed Sentiment Analysis

Anirudh Dahiya[1(✉)], Neeraj Battan[2], Manish Shrivastava[1], and
Dipti Mishra Sharma[1]

[1] LTRC, IIIT Hyderabad, Hyderabad, India
anirudh.dahiya@research.iiit.ac.in,
{m.shrivastava,dipti}@iiit.ac.in
[2] CVIT, IIIT Hyderabad, Hyderabad, India
neeraj.battan@research.iiit.ac.in

Abstract. Sentiment Analysis and other semantic tasks are commonly used for social media textual analysis to gauge public opinion and make sense from the noise on social media. The language used on social media not only commonly diverges from the formal language, but is compounded by code-mixing between languages, especially in large multilingual societies like India.

Traditional methods for learning semantic NLP tasks have long relied on end to end task specific training, requiring expensive data creation process, even more so for deep learning methods. This challenge is even more severe for resource scarce texts like code-mixed language pairs, with lack of well learnt representations as model priors, and task specific datasets can be few and small in quantities to efficiently exploit recent deep learning approaches. To address above challenges, we introduce curriculum learning strategies for semantic tasks in code-mixed Hindi-English (Hi-En) texts, and investigate various training strategies for enhancing model performance. Our method outperforms the state of the art methods for Hi-En code-mixed sentiment analysis by 3.31% accuracy, and also shows better model robustness in terms of convergence, and variance in test performance.

Keywords: Code-mixed text processing · Curriculum learning · Social media analysis · Transfer learning · Sentiment analysis

1 Introduction

Code-mixing is the phenomenon of intermixing linguistic units from two or more languages in a single utterance, and is especially widespread in multilingual societies across the world Muysken et al. (2000). With increasing internet access to such large populations of multilingual speakers, there is active ongoing research on processing code-mixed texts on online social media communities such as Twitter and Facebook Singh et al. (2018a); Prabhu et al. (2016). Not only do these

© Springer Nature Switzerland AG 2020
A. El Fallah Seghrouchni and D. Sarne (Eds.): IJCAI 2019 Workshops, LNAI 12158, pp. 177–189, 2020.
https://doi.org/10.1007/978-3-030-56150-5_9

texts contain a diverse variety of language use spanning the formal and collo-
quial spectra, such texts also pose challenging problems such as out of vocabulary
words, slang, grammatical switching and structural inconsistencies.

Muysken et al. (2000) theorize the phenomenon of code-mixing as the culmi-
nation of several distinct processes at work:

- insertion of material (lexical items or entire constituents) from one language
  into a structure from the other language.
- alternation between structures from languages
- congruent lexicalization of material from different lexical inventories into a
  shared grammatical structure.

These three basic processes operate in different ways and to different extents
in various multilingual settings, based on the lexicon and structure of the languages and the discourse in operation.

Previously, various approaches Prabhu et al. (2016); Jhanwar and Das (2018);
Singh et al. (2018a,b) have focused on task specific datasets and learning architectures for syntactic and semantic processing for code-mixed texts. This has
facilitated development of various syntactic and semantic task specific datasets
and neural architectures, but has been limited by the expensive efforts towards
annotation. As a result, while these efforts have enabled processing of code-mixed
texts, they still suffer from data scarcity and poor representation learning, and
the small individual dataset sizes usually limiting the model performance.

Curriculum Learning, as introduced by Bengio et al. (2009) is "to start small,
learn easier aspects of the task or easier subtasks, and then gradually increase
the difficulty level". They also draw parallels with human learning curriculum
and education system, where different concepts are introduced in an order at
different times, and has led to advancement in research towards animal training Krueger and Dayan (2009). Previous experiments with tasks like language
modelling Bengio et al. (2009), Dependency Parsing, and entailment Hashimoto
et al. (2016) have shown faster convergence and performance gains by following
a curriculum training regimen in the order of increasingly complicated syntactic
and semantic tasks. Weinshall and Cohen (2018) also find theoretical and experimental evidence for curriculum learning by pretraining on another task leading
to faster convergence.

With this purview, we propose a syntactico-semantic curriculum training
strategy for Hi-En code-mixed twitter sentiment analysis. We explore various
pretraining strategies encompassing Language Identification, Part of Speech Tagging, and Language Modelling in different configurations. We investigate the role
of different transfer learning strategies by changing learning rates and gradient
freezing to prevent catastrophic forgetting and interference between source and
target tasks. We also propose a new model for code-mixed sentiment analysis
based on character trigram sequences and pooling over time for representation
learning. We investigate the convergence rate and model performance across
various learning strategies, and find faster model convergence and performance
gains on the test set.

2   Related Work

Research on semantic and syntactic processing of code-mixed texts has increasingly gained attention, and various approaches have been proposed over time to this end. Jamatia et al. (2015) proposed a feature based learning approach for Part of Speech Tagging for Facebook En-Hi Code-mixed texts. Sharma et al. (2016) released a dataset on English - Hindi code-mixed social media text. They also developed a Part of Speech tagger, a language identifier, a token normalizer and a shallow parser for the code-mixed texts. Their work also relies on feature identification for development of individual modules.

More recently, various end to end approaches have been proposed towards processing code mixed texts. While these approaches do not require manual feature identifications, they reply on learnt dense representations for word or subword units. Prabhu et al. (2016) released a dataset comprising user comments on Facebook pages, and proposed a convolutions over character embeddings approach towards sentiment analysis for Hi-En Code-mixed texts. Jhanwar and Das (2018) propose a character trigram approach coupled with an ensemble of an RNN and a Naive Bayes classifier towards sentiment analysis for code-mixed data.

More generally for monolingual sentiment analysis, RNNs and other sequential deep learning models have shown to be successful. Socher et al. (2012) obtained significant performance improvement by incorporating compositional vector representations over single vector representations. Zheng and Xia (2018) take a different approach by capturing the most important words on either side to perform targeted sentiment analysis. Their LSTM based model uses context2target attention to achieve better benchmark performance on three datasets. Singh et al. (2018b) developed a dataset for Hi-En code-mixed Part of Speech tagging, and proposed a CRF based approach towards the sequence tagging problem. Singh et al. (2018b) developed a dataset for Hindi English Code-mixed Language Identification and NER, and propose a CRF based approach with handcrafted features for Named Entity Recognition.

Bengio et al. (2009) introduced curriculum learning approaches rooting from a human and animal learning perspective. They hypothesize that introducing the training tasks and/or samples in a meaningful order can lead to advantages in speed of convergence and the quality of local minima obtained. They experiment with both vision and language related tasks, and show significant convergence and performance gains for language modelling task, thus highlighting curriculum training as a crucial development towards generalization.

Hashimoto et al. (2016) propose a hierarchical multitask neural architecture with the lower layers performing syntactic tasks, and the higher layers performing the more involved semantic tasks while using the lower layer predictions. Swayamdipta et al. (2018) also propose a syntactico semantic curriculum with chunking, semantic role labelling and co-reference resolution, and show performance gains over strong baselines. Like Hashimoto et al. (2016), they hypothesize the incorporation of simpler syntactic information into semantic tasks, and provide empirical evidence for the same.

3   Datasets

Prabhu et al. (2016) released a Hi-En code-mixed dataset for Sentiment Analysis, comprising 3879 Facebook comments on popular public pages of Salman Khan and Narendra Modi. Comments are annotated as positive, negative or neutral based on their sentiment polarity, and are distributed across the 3 classes as 15% negative, 50% neutral and 35% positive comments (Table 1 and Fig. 1).

Table 1. Examples of Hi-En Code Mixed Facebook Comments from dataset

Example	Meaning	Sentiment polarity
Aisa PM naa hua hai aur naa hee hoga	Such a PM has never existed nor will ever exist	Positive
abe kutte tere se kon baat karega	who will talk to you dog?	Negative
Trailer dhannnsu hai bhai	Trailer os awesome bro	Positive

The authors intentionally filter out plain English or non roman texts to highlight the phenomenon of code-mixing in the texts. Thus the comments in the dataset characterize typical nature of code-mixed texts with spelling variations due to phonetic change from Hindi to English because of romanization of texts.

```
TOKEN            LANG  POS
Lets             en    VERB
take             en    VERB
Pakistan         rest  PROPN
under            en    ADP
our              en    PRON
control          en    NOUN
.                rest  X
Na               hi    PART_NEG
rahega           hi    VERB
bass             hi    NOUN
na               hi    PART_NEG
rahegi           hi    VERB
basuri           hi    NOUN
.                rest  X
#Uriattack       rest  X
#Pakistan        rest  X
#India           rest  X
@PMOIndia        rest  X
@rajnathsingh    rest  X
@arunjaitley     rest  X
```

Fig. 1. A sample of data from the POS dataset

They also exhibit loss of grammatical and structural consistency, and report many short texts with no clear structure in the comments.

Singh et al. (2018a) released a twitter corpus for Part of Speech tagging for Hindi English code-mixed tweets about 5 incidents, and annotated 1489 tweets with the Part Of Speech tag for each token. Out of the 1489 tweets, 1077 (72.33%) are code-mixed, 343 (23.04%) are English, and 69 (4.63%) are Hindi. The dataset contains a high fraction of named entities with 1.84 named entities per tweet on an average. There is a high frequency of occurrence of interrogative pronouns (421 occurrences) which along with the '?' symbol signifies inquiries in the dataset. The code-mixed language exhibited in the dataset aligns closely with the Facebook Sentiment Analysis dataset described above. The POS tags exhibit fundamental linguistic lexical categories, and have shown to be useful features for many downstream semantic tasks. We thus use POS tagging as part of our curriculum training (Fig. 2).

```
I        en      0
liked    en      0
a        en      0
@YouTube         en      0
video    en      0
https:   en      0
Kabhi    hi      0
Palkon   hi      0
Pe       hi      0
Aasoon   hi      0
Hai-     hi      0
Kishore  hi      B-PERSON
Kumar    hi      I-PERSON
-Vocal   en      0
Cover    en      0
By       en      0
Stephen  en      B-PERSON
Qadir    rest    I-PERSON
```

Fig. 2. A sample of data from the NER dataset

Singh et al. (2018b) released a Hindi English code-mixed twitter corpus for Language Identification and Named Entities, where each token is annotated for its Language as English, Hindi or rest. Apart from this, they also annotate 2763 named entities in text, classified as Person, Location or Organization. Similar to the POS tagging dataset described above, the language aligns well with the characteristic code mixed texts in the Facebook sentiment dataset. The language tags have been long used as important features for various code mixed systems, and thus have been included as part of our proposed curriculum training regimen (Table 2).

Table 2. Symbol description

Symbol	Description
$h_{r_i}^{(j)}$	jth Layer's right directional hidden state at time i
$h_{l_i}^{(j)}$	jth Layer's left directional hidden state at time i
$H_i^{(j)}$	Left and right hidden state concatenation
$H_N^{(j)}$	Terminal H for layer j LSTM

4   Approach

In the following subsections, we introduce our proposed model architecture for processing the above tasks in a hierarchical manner, discuss the various curriculum strategies we experiment with, and finally discuss the transfer learning techniques we explore.

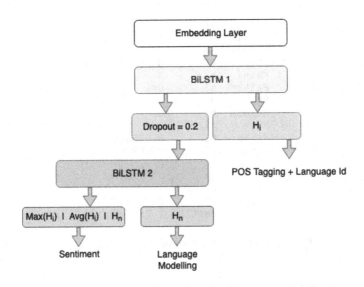

Fig. 3. Systematic overview of model architecture

4.1   Model

We case normalise the texts and mask user mentions and URLs with special characters. After tokenizing the texts, we append a token terminal "*" symbol to each token and further split each token into its constituent character trigrams. Thus, a token "girl" is split into "gir" + "l*#", where "#" is the padding symbol for character trigrams. Due to the high class imbalance in Sentiment Analysis data, we perform a mixture of oversampling and undersampling between classes than simply prune the samples of the larger classes.

As shown in Fig. 3, the model comprises of an Embedding layer followed by two layers of bidirectional LSTMs. The embedding layer serves as a lookup table for our character trigram dense representations, and a sequence of these representations are passed on to the LSTM stack for each input sample.

Layer 1 of the LSTM stack takes the sequence of character trigram embeddings as input, and is used to predict the corresponding POS tag and the Language tag at each time step. The concatenation of the left and right directional hidden states at each time step i is passed to a standard softmax classifier to output the probability distribution over the POS tags at that timestep. Similarly, another softmax classifier outputs the language tags at each timestep.

$$H_i^{(1)} = concat([h_{r_i}^{(1)}; h_{l_i}^{(1)}]) \tag{1}$$

$$y_{i_{pos}} = Softmax(W_{pos}H_i^{(1)} + b_{pos}) \tag{2}$$

$$y_{i_{lang}} = Softmax(W_{lang}H_i^{(1)} + b_{lang}) \tag{3}$$

The LSTM Layer 2 takes the concatenated bidirectional hidden states of Layer 1 $(H_i^{(1)})$ as input to learn the sequence representation as an abstraction over the layer 1 representations. This architecture allows the semantic task to consider both the character trigram dense representation as well as "POS" and "Language" aware bidirectional representations to perform more complex semantic tasks like language modelling and sentiment analysis.

For language modelling, the concatenated terminal hidden states from the right and left directional LSTM layer 2 is passed to a standard softmax classifier, which outputs the probability distribution over the character trigram vocabulary for the next trigram in the input sequence. For sentiment analysis, we concatenate the max pooling over time, avg pooling over time, and the terminal hidden states of the Layer 2 BiLSTM to form the representation. The max-pooling and avg-pooling over time representations circumvents the information loss in sequence terminal representations. This representation is passed to a standard softmax classifier to predict the sentiment polarity over the 3 classes.

$$H_i^{(2)} = concat([h_{r_i}^{(2)} h_{l_i}^{(2)}]) \tag{4}$$

$$y_{LM} = Softmax(W_{LM}H_N^{(2)} + b_{LM}) \tag{5}$$

$$H_S^{(2)} = concat([H_N^{(2)};$$
$$maxpool(H_i^{(2)}); \tag{6}$$
$$avgpool(H_i^{(2)})])$$

$$y_{sentiment} = Softmax(W_{sentiment}H_S^{(2)} + b_{sentiment}) \tag{7}$$

For each of the tasks described above, we train our model to optimize the cross entropy loss for the given prediction, formulated as:

$$L = -\sum_{y \in Y} y \log p + (1 - y)log(1 - p) \tag{8}$$

where y is the true label, and p is the predicted probability of that label by the model.

4.2   Curriculum Training

While our proposed model enables efficient transfer learning by progressive abstraction of representations for more complicated tasks, the highlight of the approach lies in the training regimen followed.

Curriculum learning can be seen as a sequence of training criteria Bengio et al. (2009), with increasing task or sample difficulty as the training progresses. It is also closely related with transfer learning by pretraining, especially in the case when the tasks form a logical hierarchy and contribute to the downstream tasks. With this purview, we propose a linguistic hierarchy of training tasks for code-mixed languages, with further layers abstracting over the previous ones to achieve increasingly complicated tasks. Considering the code-mixed nature of texts and linguistic hierarchy of information, we propose the tasks in the order of: Language Identification, Part of Speech Tagging, Language Modelling and further semantic tasks like sentiment analysis.

Since tokens in code-mixed texts have distinct semantic spaces based on their source language, Language Identification can incorporate this disparity among the learnt trigram representations. Following this, the Part of Speech Tagging groups the words based on their logical semantic categories, and encodes simpler word category information in a sequence. Also, as in Singh et al. (2018a); Sharma et al. (2016), Language Tag and Part of Speech Tag have previously been provided as manual handcrafted features for a range of downstream syntactic and semantic tasks.

In addition to the above tasks, Language Model pretraining has shown significant performance gains as reported by Howard and Ruder (2018). It captures various aspects of language such as long range dependencies Linzen et al. (2016), word categories, and sentiment Radford et al. (2017) (Table 3).

Conforming with the linguistic hierarchical information, we first train our model to predict the language labels for each character trigram as per its token. This is followed by further training the model to predict the Part of Speech tag for each of its character trigram as per its token. Subsequently, the model is trained on Language Modelling task, in process training the LSTM Layer 2 to build over the LSTM Layer 1 inputs to learn meaningful sequence representation. Lastly, the model is trained to predict the sentiment of the input text based on the LSTM Layer 2 representation (Table 5).

Table 3. Model hyperparameters

Hyperparameter	Value
Embedding dimension	64
LSTM cell dimension	64
Dropout	0.2
Learning rate	0.04
Batch size	4

Table 4. Character encoding experiments

Character encoding	Accuracy
Character unigram	62.57
Convolution over character unigrams	64.23
Character trigram	67.83
Byte Pair Encoding (BPE)	64.61

Table 5. Model comparison

Model	Accuracy	Precision	Recall	F1-score
SVM (Unigrams)	61.7%	0.579	0.551	0.565
SVM (Unigrams + Bigrams)	64.1%	0.609	0.537	0.566
MNB (Unigrams)	64.5%	0.748	0.485	0.588
MNB (Unigrams + Bigrams)	66.1%	0.698	0.540	0.609
SentiWordNet	51.5%	-	-	0.252
Char-trigram based LSTM Jhanwar and Das (2018)	65.2%	0.610	0.563	0.586
Vowel-consonant based	62.8%	0.652	0.522	0.580
Sub-word Prabhu et al. (2016)	69.2%	0.684	0.623	0.652
Our approach	72.51%	0.712	0.645	0.677

Table 6. Curriculum and finetuning experiments

Training	Accuracy
From scratch (no curriculum)	70.19
+ POS + LangId pretraining	68.83
+ LM pretraining	72.51
LM only pretraining	72.16
No gradual unfreezing	70.74
No discriminative finetuning	71.68

4.3 Transfer Learning

As noted in earlier efforts Howard and Ruder (2018) towards finetuning pre-trained models for NLP tasks, aggressive finetuning can cause catastrophic forgetting, thus causing the model to simply fit over the target task and forget any capabilities gained during the pretraining stage. On the other hand, too cautious finetuning can cause slow convergence and overfitting. To this end, we experiment with different strategies which can be broadly categorized as (Table 6):

Discriminative Finetuning: As also noted by Yosinski et al. (2014), different layers capture different types of information, and thus need to be optimised differently. In the context of our model, the embedding layer captures the individual character trigram information, the LSTM layer 1 is trained towards capturing the token level information such as Part of Speech and Language Tag, and the final LSTM Layer 2 is trained to capture the overall textual representation to perform Language Modelling and Sentiment Analysis. With this purview, similar to Howard and Ruder (2018), we propose optimizing different layers in our model to different extents, and keep lower step sizes for the deeper pretrained layers while finetuning on a downstream task. We thus split the parameters as $\{\theta_1, ..., \theta_l\}$, where θ_i corresponds to the parameters of layer i, and optimize them with separate learning rates $\{\eta_1, ..., \eta_l\}$. Also, when finetuning a pretrained layer for a downstream task, we keep $\eta_i < \eta_j; \forall i < j$.

Thus, while finetuning the POS + Lang Id pretrained model for Language Modeling, we propose to keep the learning rates for Embedding Layer and LSTM Layer 1 lower than the LSTM Layer 2 weights. Similarly, when finetuning the Language Model for Sentiment Analysis, we keep the learning rates of the deeper layers lower than that of the shallower ones.

Gradual Unfreezing: Similar to Howard and Ruder (2018), rather than updating all the layers together for finetuning, we explore gradual ordered unfreezing of layers. Thus, initially we freeze all the layers. Then starting from the last layer, we train the model for a certain number of epochs before unfreezing the layer below it. Thus for Sentiment Analysis finetuning, for the first epoch, only $\theta_{sentiment}$ receives the gradient updates, after which we unfreeze the θ_{lstm2}, and subsequently unfreeze the lower layers in a similar manner.

5 Experiments

The input to the LSTM stack is the sequence of character trigram dense representations, which we keep as 64 dimensional vectors. We also explore other token representations such as sequence of unigrams, convolution over unigrams Prabhu et al. (2016), and Byte Pair Encoding (BPE) Sennrich et al. (2015). Byte Pair Encoding (BPE) is a simple data compression technique that iteratively replaces the most frequent pair of characters or character sequences in a sentence with a single, word unit. It is an unsupervised approach towards subword decomposition, and has shown improvements in various applications such as Machine

Translation and Summarization. We train our model from scratch for Sentiment Analysis using the above mentioned character encodings, and report the results in Table 4.

Our LSTM stack consists of two layers of bidirectional LSTMs, with 64 hidden state dimensions. We add a dropout layer with the dropout rate set to 0.2 between the LSTM layers to prevent overfitting. We experiment with average pooling and max pooling concatenation over hidden states for semantic prediction, similar to Howard and Ruder (2018), and observe increase in model accuracy by 2.2% on sentiment analysis.

To evaluate our baseline for curriculum training experiments, we initially train the model from scratch on the single target task (Sentiment Analysis) for 25 epochs. We approach the evaluation of our curriculum by training the model sequentially for four subtasks - Language Identification, POS Tagging, Language Modelling and Sentiment Analysis. We evaluate the strategy of pretraining with only POS Tagging and Language Identification, and observe similar performance as no curriculum training. We hypothesize the potential reasons for this drop and find a significant divergence in character trigram occurrence between the Source Tasks (POS + Lang Id) and Target Task (Sentiment Analysis). This experiment highlights the importance of inclusion of language model pretraining for better token level representation learning, and provides a better model prior for sequence representation (LSTM Layer 2 output). We experiment with only Language Modelling as pretraining task, and observe significant gains over no curriculum strategy.

We note the convergence of our model with and without curriculum training, and observe that the curriculum training regimen causes faster convergence, as has been observed in previous works Bengio et al. (2009); Howard and Ruder (2018). This is expected as the model is pretrained on prior tasks already have a general purpose representation learning, and only needs to adapt to the idiosyncrasies of the target task, i.e. Sentiment Analysis in this case.

As discussed in Sect. 4.3, for our transfer learning optimization experiments, we segment the optimization of different parameters of our model with different learning rates, in order to limit catastrophic forgetting and interference among the tasks, as proposed by Howard and Ruder (2018). We segregate our model parameters in the following 4 groups:

- Emb Layer
- LSTM Layer 1
- LSTM Layer 2
- Sentiment Linear Map

We set the learning rate of the previous layer $\eta_{l-1} = \eta_l/2.0$. For our gradual unfreezing experiments, we unfreeze the lower layer after training the model for 1 epoch with the lower layer unfrozen.

6   Future Work

In future work, we would like to explore word normalization and multilingual embeddings in conjunction to learning representations from scratch. Another line of potential study could be investigation into why BPE is able to lead to performance gains as in monolingual domains, but fails in the code-mixed multilingual tasks in our experiments. We would also like to explore convolution over character embeddings as a method to further circumvent the out of vocabulary problem with code-mixed social media data.

We also plan to explore better representation learning for the semantic tasks. One particular direction we plan to explore attention over the LSTM layer 2 as a weighted peek into the intermediate hidden states for the semantic classification task.

In future, we would like to experiment with more syntactic tasks like dependency label predictions, and also study more semantic tasks like aggression detection. Code-mixed domains suffer from severe resource scarcity, and thus vocabulary divergence between various datasets proves as a roadblock to generalizable models, as observed in POS + Language Id pretraining experiments.

Acknowledgements. I am extremely grateful to the professors and colleagues at Language Technology Research Center, IIIT-Hyderabad, for their valuable suggestions for this work. I'm also thankful for the Humanizing Workshop, IJCAI, 2019, for providing travel grant to participate in the conference.

References

Bengio, Y., Louradour, J., Collobert, R., Weston, J.: Curriculum learning. In: Proceedings of the 26th Annual International Conference on Machine Learning, pp. 41–48. ACM (2009)

Hashimoto, K., Xiong, C., Tsuruoka, Y., Socher, R.: A joint many-task model: growing a neural network for multiple NLP tasks. CoRR abs/1611.01587 arxiv:1611.01587 (2016)

Howard, J., Ruder, S.: Universal language model fine-tuning for text classification. In: Association for Computational Linguistics, ACL (2018). http://arxiv.org/abs/1801.06146

Jamatia, A., Gambäck, B., Das, A.: Part-of-speech tagging for code-mixed English-Hindi Twitter and Facebook chat messages. In: Proceedings of the International Conference Recent Advances in Natural Language Processing, pp. 239–248 (2015)

Jhanwar, M.G., Das, A.: An ensemble model for sentiment analysis of Hindi-English code-mixed data. CoRR abs/1806.04450 arxiv:1806.04450 (2018)

Krueger, K.A., Dayan, P.: Flexible shaping: how learning in small steps helps. Cognition **110**(3), 380–394 (2009)

Linzen, T., Dupoux, E., Goldberg, Y.: Assessing the ability of LSTMs to learn syntax-sensitive dependencies. Trans. Assoc. Comput. Linguist. **4**, 521–535 (2016)

Muysken, P., Díaz, C.P., Muysken, P.C., et al.: Bilingual Speech: A Typology of Code-Mixing, vol. 11. Cambridge University Press, Cambridge (2000)

Prabhu, A., Joshi, A., Shrivastava, M., Varma, V.: Towards sub-word level composi-
tions for sentiment analysis of Hindi-English code mixed text. CoRR abs/1611.00472
arxiv:1611.00472 (2016)

Radford, A., Jozefowicz, R., Sutskever, I.: Learning to generate reviews and discovering
sentiment. arXiv preprint arXiv:170401444 (2017)

Sennrich, R., Haddow, B., Birch, A.: Neural machine translation of rare words with
subword units. arXiv preprint arXiv:150807909 (2015)

Sharma, A., et al.: Shallow parsing pipeline for Hindi-English code-mixed social media
text. arXiv preprint arXiv:160403136 (2016)

Singh, K., Sen, I., Kumaraguru, P.: A Twitter corpus for Hindi-English code mixed POS
tagging. In: Proceedings of the Sixth International Workshop on Natural Language
Processing for Social Media, Association for Computational Linguistics, Melbourne,
Australia, pp. 12–17 (2018a). https://www.aclweb.org/anthology/W18-3503

Singh, K., Sen, I., Kumaraguru, P.: A Twitter corpus for Hindi-English code mixed POS
tagging. In: Proceedings of the Sixth International Workshop on Natural Language
Processing for Social Media, pp. 12–17 (2018b)

Socher, R., Huval, B., Manning, C.D., Ng, A.Y.: Semantic compositionality through
recursive matrix-vector spaces. In: Proceedings of the 2012 Joint Conference on
Empirical Methods in Natural Language Processing and Computational Natural
Language Learning, Association for Computational Linguistics, Jeju Island, Korea,
pp. 1201–1211 (2012). https://www.aclweb.org/anthology/D12-1110

Swayamdipta, S., Thomson, S., Lee, K., Zettlemoyer, L., Dyer, C., Smith, N.A.: Syntactic scaffolds for semantic structures. CoRR abs/1808.10485 arxiv:1808.10485 (2018)

Weinshall, D., Cohen, G.: Curriculum learning by transfer learning: theory and experiments with deep networks. CoRR abs/1802.03796 arxiv:1802.03796 (2018)

Yosinski, J., Clune, J., Bengio, Y., Lipson, H.: How transferable are features in deep
neural networks? In: Advances in Neural Information Processing Systems, pp. 3320–
3328 (2014)

Zheng, S., Xia, R.: Left-center-right separated neural network for aspect-based sentiment analysis with rotatory attention. arxiv:1802.00892 (2018)

Language Sense on Computer

Language Sense on Computer

Akinori Abe[1] and Hiroki Fukushima[2]

[1] Faculty of Letters, Chiba University, Japan
ave@ultimaVI.arc.net.my, ave@chiba-u.jp
[2] Kyushu Women's University, Japan
fukushima@kwuc.ac.jp

1 Workshop Overview and Goals

This year the workshop's theme was "Language Sense on Computers: What is a Language Sense and how to express and deal with it on computers." In this workshop, we aimed to discuss several problems related to language sense on computers and applications dealing with language sense. As in our definition the "language sense" indicates affective or psychological aspects of language, our natural interests lay in communication tools and natural ways of conveying our thoughts. A language should correctly transfer speaker or writer's intention to listeners or readers. However, sometimes we intentionally omit pieces of information, we veil messages enveloping them in poetic words, we use metaphors and sophisticated examples to influence other person in a specific way. For example means for conveying humor as jokes, ésprits or puns are phenomena that are difficult to explain and algorithmically mimicked. In our definition we also include sensuous (as aesthetically pleasing, gratifying, rich, sumptuous, luxurious; sensory, sensorial) aspect to language sense by which we attempted to attract not only AI researchers but also cognitive scientists, linguists or psychologists who could shed a light on how to deal with such non-logical sides of such language functionality. In addition, we aimed to attract persons in industries.

2 Workshop Content and Highlights

Overall we had 9 papers presented in the workshop, with various topics discussed. For instance, researches on a story or dialogue telling and creation, and the feature of the expression of the taste were presented in this workshop. Individual papers dealt with how the external activate factor affects human creativity, especially the process of product planning in business field, new methods which can generate conversational response for open domain dialogues, artificial agents to support security export control specialists and researches who are not sure how sensitive their work might be, narrative generation using motifs, generation mechanisms for Commercial message (CM), the analysis of crossdisciplinary data networks using summarized information about the data given in natural languages (data jackets), aspects of "aesthetic concepts of the taste", and more.

Actually a story telling is not only for literary works but also for business matters. Even in the business field, recently "story" has become a very important factor. In

[Jansen, 1999], the importance of a story is mentioned. They are very important theme in our field. Of course, for AI, such researches must be considered to deal with emotion and expression. In a logic programming, such emotional factors will not be able to deal with. Our researches will give additional value to the logic-based AI.

3   The Paper Selected for this Volume

The paper selected for this volume is: Mateusz Babieno, Rafal Rzepka, and Kenji Araki: Comparing Conceptual Metaphor Theory-Related Features in Searching for Figurative Expressions in Japanese Literary Texts. In this paper the authors propose an approach towards identifying expressions used figuratively (metaphorically) in Japanese literary texts by means of the classification algorithm. Here, the ultimate task is to create a computational model to be able to discern expressions used figuratively from those used literally within Japanese texts.

The most important part of their study is, they paid more attention to the theoretical aspect of the problem viewing the computational model from the cognitive linguistics perspective. In the current experiment they have tried to predict whether the input sentence contains at least one figuratively used expression by the means of the classification algorithm. Actually since this research is on-going research, the precision are not particularly high, but the best balanced results seem to be achieved by the combination of emotions (EM), body parts (BP), wago (Japanese language) verbs (WV) and position indicators (PI). Thus based on the cognitive linguistics perspective, they developed a figurative expression search system. For our research field, a metaphor is very important. For instance, we use a metaphor to express a taste. We use a metaphor to express our complex thinking. We also use a metaphor to create a story. Accordingly such a challenging research is very important.

4   Concluding Remarks and Insights for Future Research

As shown above, in this workshop, we discussed 'language sense' from the various aspects. In fact, researches on a story or dialogue telling and creation, and the feature of the expression of the taste are presented in this workshop. Each researches seem to have relationships. We will be able to cooperate the other research fields, for instance, literary. In addition, we also have an intention to cooperate with industry.

In IJCAI2021, we would like to have a similar and extended workshop to discuss more topics.

Reference

[Jansen, 1999] Rolf Jensen: *The Dream Society: How the Coming Shift from Information to Imagination Will Transform Your Business*, Mcgraw Hill 1999.

Comparing Conceptual Metaphor Theory-Related Features Using Classification Algorithms in Searching for Expressions Used Figuratively Within Japanese Texts

Mateusz Babieno[1]([✉]), Rafal Rzepka[1,3], Kenji Araki[1], and Pawel Dybala[2]

[1] Graduate School of Information Science and Technology, Hokkaido University,
Kita-Ku, Kita 14, Nishi 9, Sapporo 060-0814, Japan
{mbabieno,rzepka,araki}@ist.hokudai.co.jp
[2] Institute of the Middle and Far East, Jagiellonian University, 2a Oleandry Street,
30-036 Kraków, Poland
dybala@uj.edu.pl
[3] RIKEN AIP, Tokyo, Japan

Abstract. In this work we propose an approach towards identifying expressions used figuratively in Japanese literary texts by means of the classification algorithm. Our considerations are inspired mostly by the epoch-making Conceptual Metaphor Theory which once presented by Lakoff and Johnson [13] has instantly become a central problem to address not only from the perspective of cognitive linguistics but also other domains of scholarship. In NLP-related research, approaches of this sort - although already present - seem to be rarely applied to models dedicated to Japanese language. In our preliminary approach to build a trustworthy model able to create a large corpus of figurative expressions, we compare efficiency of several features selected as possibly relevant in the task of detecting non-literal language use. Our algorithm does not require complex system of rules which was the case in some of the computational models presented by other authors so far.

Keywords: Figurative language · Metaphor processing · Classification task

1 Introduction

Since the last decades of 20th century figurative use of language has proven to be much more important for human communication than it was thought to be so far. Eventually, it has become a pivotal issue for cognitive scientists, linguists, psychologists, psychotherapists and philosophers. In no time addressing the problem from computational perspective proved to be an inevitable step towards improving many NLP-related solutions (i.e. machine translation or sentiment analysis).

For anyone even remotely acquainted with metaphor-related research it should be agreeable that defining figurativeness is no easy task. Terms *metaphorical* and *figurative* often seem to be used interchangeably and this way shall we treat them henceforth. What

© Springer Nature Switzerland AG 2020
A. El Fallah Seghrouchni and D. Sarne (Eds.): IJCAI 2019 Workshops, LNAI 12158, pp. 195–212, 2020.
https://doi.org/10.1007/978-3-030-56150-5_10

is slightly less problematic but still not absolutely free from controversy is to differentiate between what is figurative and what is literal. Oxford Advanced Learner's Dictionary [10] describes *figurative* as *used in a way that is different from the usual meaning, in order to create particular mental picture.* The dictionary provides users with the example of: *He exploded with rage* along with the explanatory note: *the example shows a figurative use of the verb 'explode'.* The supposition that *metaphorical* is indeed often equated with *figurative* can be supported by the definition found in Oxford Dictionary of English [18], which views *figurative* as *departing from a literal use of words; metaphorical*; this is also the definition we adopt in current research.

In conformity with the ODE's definition, as literal we treat *taking words in their usual or most basic sense without metaphor or exaggeration.* While highly concise and rather vague this definition points at something crucial, namely at that it is rather the use of words – as opposed to the words themselves - that should be interpreted as literal or figurative.

While aware of the differences existing between them, we decide to treat as *figurative* both live (creative) and dead (conventional; frozen) metaphors. Since the mechanism accompanying figurative use of language sometimes happens to be rather metonymical than metaphorical, we do not exclude metonymical expressions from the scope of our considerations. For the purpose of this research also tropes such as synecdoches, similes, personifications and their opposites, oxymorons and alike are regarded as belonging to the same non-literal category. Also idioms and proverbs should be considered the objects of our investigation.

The ultimate task of our research is to create a computational model able to discern expressions used figuratively (which class, as shown above, is highly heterogeneous) from those used literally within Japanese texts. While many of NLP-researchers seem to focus mostly on enhancing performance of their models modifying their already complex algorithms, for the time being we would like to pay more attention to the theoretical aspect of the problem viewing it from the cognitive linguistics perspective. This kind of approach will hopefully give us some new insights into the very nature of the figurative language and help to qualitatively improve achievements of our algorithms in the future.

In this paper Japanese words transcribed to alphabet are indicated with italics. Hepburn romanization is utilized.

2   Related Work

2.1   Natural Language Processing

Among NLP-related works dealing with supervised identification of linguistic metaphor one can point at this of Heintz et al. [6]. The authors use LDA Topic Modeling for the classification and do not resort to WordNet-like semantic databases. Their algorithm is designed with Conceptual Metaphor Theory (CMT henceforth) as its theoretical foundation. The authors assume that certain sentence's probability of including linguistic metaphor is positively correlated with presence of words related to both target and source concepts. They prepare large number of seed words semantically connected to such source concepts. Trying to apply the model to different languages, in most cases they use translations of the seed words they have originally come up with for American English. What do we find particularly appealing in their approach is that the authors do not fail to take into account cultural differences existing between the users of different languages. For example, they enlist words belonging to the semantic field of American football as potential constituents of linguistic metaphors in American English. For it is however unlikely that American football would be used as a source domain underlying the metaphorical expressions in Spanish, authors decide not to simply translate American football-related seed words but instead use different words associated with soccer which they assume to be more familiar to Spanish speakers. One of this model's shortcomings is relatively low F-1 score (59%) achieved and the fact that the authors search for linguistic metaphors within only one target domain, namely the one of *governance.*

Another related work worth mentioning is the one of Dunn [4]. The author reflects on the concept of abstractness, proposes its multi-dimensional definition and takes these dimensions (41 altogether) as the features of his model used for metaphor identification. Category of abstractness appears as fairly complex, but the author proves it to be also very useful when it comes to detecting metaphorical mappings known from the CMT. As for the model's shortcomings, highly complicated structure and relying on external databases and numerous ontologies can be addressed.

Among supervised approaches to metaphor classification, the research of Klebanov et al. [12] should also be listed. The authors limit object of their investigation to linguistic metaphors which include verbs. Their model relies on several existing knowledge bases and corpora (VerbNet and WordNet; British National Corpus and VU Amsterdam Metaphor Corpus). They utilize different classifiers (Logistic Regression, Random Forest, Linear Support Vector Classifier) and compare their performance using different features on data belonging to different genres (news, academic writing, fiction, conversation). Results they present are relatively good when their model is tested on the data belonging to academic writing (71–76% F1-score depending on the features used) but they get noticeably worse for the other genres (47–51% F1 for fiction, 43–45% F1 for conversation).

2.2 Cognitive Linguistics

CMT has influenced several cognitive linguists dealing with the analysis of Japanese texts. Masako K. Hiraga [8] describes conceptual metaphor underlying such Japanese words as *bushidō, sadō, kadō, shodō, kyūdō, kendō* [7] etc. As can be easily noticed, each of the compound words listed above includes morpheme *dō* 'way, road', what suggests that they are semantically interrelated.

Let us note briefly that Japanese is a multi-systemic language, which lexicon contains three (excluding hybrid words) types of vocabularies: 1) *wago* (indigenous, native Japanese words, usually written with *Hiragana* or *Hiragana* and *Kanji*), 2) *kango* (Sino-Japanese words originating in Chinese, usually written with *Kanji*) and 3) *gairaigo* (vocabulary originating in foreign languages other than Chinese, mostly English, usually written with *Katakana*) [11].

Above presented words including logographic character *dō* belong to the Sino-Japanese lexical subsystem *kango*. In these examples morpheme *dō* is being suffixed to another morpheme (or multiple morphemes as *bushi* in *bushidō*) what results in forming words used as the names of classical disciplines (*sadō* 'way of tea', lit. 'tea' + 'road'; *kadō* 'way of flowers', 'ikebana', lit. 'flower' + 'road'; *shodō* 'Japanese calligraphy', lit. 'pen' + 'road'), martial arts (*kyūdō* 'Japanese archery', 'way of bow', lit. 'bow' + 'road'; *kendō* 'kendo', 'way of sword', lit. 'sword' + 'road') and philosophical systems (*bushidō* 'bushido', 'way of warrior', lit. 'warrior' + 'road'). This kind of word structure rooted in Chinese grammatical system allows users of Japanese to easily conceptualize ideas denoted by the above words within the scope of the underlying LEARNING IS A JOURNEY (vel LEARNING IS FOLLOWING A PATH) metaphor proposed by Hiraga. In concordance with this hypothesis, it can be implied that adepts of such classical disciplines are being conceptualized as travelers assisted by their teachers - guides preventing them from going astray.

Roughly speaking, conceptual metaphor can be described as a mechanism employing so called cross-domain mappings between distinct concepts. In case of the compound words listed above we are dealing with theoretically unrelated concepts of respectively: traditional ceremonial activities & traveling (*sadō, kadō, shodō*), martial arts & traveling (*kyūdō, kendō*); philosophical systems & traveling (*bushidō*). According to CMT, as the result of connecting (mapping) elements of such conceptual networks together, language users think of one concept in terms normally belonging to the another.

Although it might be tempting to label languages utilizing pictographic and ideographic writing systems as *more metaphorical* than the ones using only phonetic scripts, such a bold claim would require complex investigation and vast amount of evidence. It is nonetheless rather safe to say that languages like Japanese or Chinese provide their users with opportunity to almost immediately *notice* presence of conceptual metaphors underlying their linguistic realizations.

Even though we are aware of existing criticism aimed the premises of CMT (cf. Pinker's standpoint in [16]), we still think it can serve as a tool helpful in identifying figurative use of language.

For it is not rare in case of cognitive linguistics-related theories to get opposed with the objections of lacking measurable evidence, we hope that our future findings will contribute in filling this gap.

2.3 Philosophy of Language

In his classical paper from 1954 [1] American philosopher Max Black gives his thoughts on the problem of metaphor. Here I will touch upon only some of his remarks, yet the article definitely deserves to be read in full.

In the introduction not free from the irony Black writes about how metaphor has been so far neglected by most of the philosophers seemingly treating it as something non-scientific and therefore unsuited for being used in serious philosophical discourse.

The author proposes three different approaches in conceptualizing metaphor and its analysis labeling them as respectively:

i)   substitution view,
ii) comparison view,
iii) interaction view.

He briefly describes what these views consists in.

On substitution view, given metaphorical expression is used as a substitute for some literal expression using which would convey the same meaning. What is important here is that this account implies that the meaning of any metaphorical expression could be expressed with some literal counterpart, its paraphrase. If it was true, why then would anyone strive to speak metaphorically? One justified reason for that would be to fill the lexical gap, when encountering entities not yet named in certain language. Here Black calls up the notion of catachresis otherwise known from rhetorics which consists in ascribing new senses to already existing words. One example of such case would be that of *the leg* of an angle, the expression known from mathematics. Other than that, writers would use metaphors to simply amuse their readers providing them with entertaining linguistic riddles. On this view, when not used as a tool for catachresis, metaphor is considered to be mere linguistic decoration.

Another view on metaphor proposed by Black is that which he calls the *comparison view*. This stance treats a metaphor as condensed, elliptic variant of simile. Sticking to example sentence given above, it can be said that *Richard is a lion* is a shortened version of *Richard is like a lion (in being brave)*. As noticed by Black, this view on metaphor is not very informative, since it does not explain the reason why things are being compared in certain respect and not some other. After all, lion can be not only brave (in reality do we genuinely think of it as brave?) but also big, scary, hungry, etc. Also, out of many possible candidates, why is it a lion that gets employed by the metaphor? Adopting this view, we get no answers, whatsoever.

The last perspective presented by Black - according to him completely free from the flaws of the aforementioned ones and thus the most appropriate - is what he calls the *interaction view*. This view consists in that metaphor use two different concepts (here the one of a *man* represented by Richard and the other of a *lion*) which in mind of a reader become *active together* and *interact* to produce a meaning that is a resultant of that interaction. What is of great importance here is that these concepts are said to be constructed not based on some normative descriptions of lexemes one can find in a standard dictionary but rather on what Black calls the *system of associated commonplaces* shared by all members of a certain cultural community. In our example it does not matter what kind of animal *lion* objectively is; what is important is the set of associations connected to the concept of a *lion* in the mind of a layman, an average member of some society. At the same time the metaphor evokes in reader's mind another set of associations related to *man*. Again, these characteristics does not have to be objectively true, no expert knowledge is said to be employed in the process. Traits of lions that are – at least to some degree – possible to be ascribed to humans (that are conceivable without resulting in utter nonsense) become rendered as prominent and others lose their importance in a given situation. In our example out of many characteristics of a lion possible to be used in describing Richard *brave* seems like plausible to be chosen.

Another great philosopher of language whose quite controversial remarks on metaphor have reverberated through the world of science is Donald Davidson. Here I would like to briefly comment on some of his reflections presented in the article from 1978 [2].

In some first sentences Davidson argues that *understanding a metaphor is as much a creative endeavour as making a metaphor, and as little guided by rules*. This can well serve as an argument against not only claims of other philosophers of language including Black but also numerous NLP-related approaches to metaphor processing which seem to strongly rely on implementing complex systems of rules. Davidson would probably agree with that since metaphor can elicit various associations depending on its receiver, it is not possible to create their finite list.

Perhaps the most important of Davidson's claims to be found in the article is that, according to him, a metaphor does not hold any special meaning differing from the literal meaning of words it includes. His proposition is that metaphors mean whatever it is assumed as their literal meaning. At the same time, he argues that metaphors are very often false in a logical sense (in contrast to similes which are always true since everything is similar to everything else, at least to a certain degree). In accordance with this theory it follows that *lion* from the sentence *Richard is a lion* does not mean anything else than *lion* in any other context. If it is not a wild cat named Richard which is being talked about, this sentence shall be classified as false. To Davidson in a metaphor there is no hidden meaning behind the words, no special cognitive content to be found, no linguistic riddle to be solved.

Although author disagrees with Black in regards to the point just explained, in the end of the article he admits that a metaphor can indeed be conceptualized as a kind of a filter which makes it easier for the reader to notice something about the outer world that he might have not been fully aware of before encountering it. But this is just the effect a metaphor has on its receivers and it should not be mixed up with some special meanings that words allegedly hold in secret. In this respect metaphors are similar to pieces of music or photographs. They are what they are and nothing more. It is true that they can put us in a special mood by bringing some analogies and similarities to our attention, by intimating something surprising, but it is not because of some secret set of meanings concealed by the words. According to Davidson, there are no such secret meanings.

Since metaphor does not stand for anything else and there is nothing *inside* of it to be further translated into *more literal* expression, what is often called a paraphrase of the metaphor should not be taken as an explanation of the meaning. It is rather a description of interpreter's feelings accompanying him in his encounter with a metaphor. Such a paraphrase is never objective, it may be different from person to person. In the closing remarks Davidson bluntly formulates his view on metaphor's paraphrase and its function: *The legitimate function of so-called paraphrase is to make the lazy or ignorant reader have a vision like that of the skilled critic.*

We agree with Davidson on that creating a finite list of associations evoked by concrete metaphors is impossible. At the same time, we believe that some differences between literal and figurative language do exist. Deciding whether such differences are to be ascribed to semantics or to pragmatics is not vital from the perspective of our current study. We think that in the lexicon of any given cultural community at any given time in the history some words tend to be used figuratively more often than the others. Among its several conceivable causes one is that their designates might play some important symbolic role in a certain culture.

We think that our theoretical views on metaphor sometimes get really close to what Davidson claims in his article. Although he never firmly declares it, we suppose that he would agree with us when we say that it is not words that should be considered metaphorical or literal: it is their usage. When it elicits in us some special sensations, evokes some unusual associations in a given context, there is a big chance that we are dealing with a metaphor.

3 Datasets and Annotation

3.1 Datasets

Our training data can be largely divided into two parts: one constructed from sentences comprising figurative expressions and the other including sentences very likely to be used in a literal sense.

First group was obtained from the abridged digitalized dictionary of figurative expressions [15] available for members of our laboratory thanks to the generosity and kindness of its author. The second was collected from Japanese Wikipedia dump [21], local assembly minutes [22] and articles from Livedoor News [23]. Each set comprises 25,947 sentences.

The test set includes 82 sentences retrieved partly from Japanese novels' texts available at Aozora Bunko digital library [24]. 50 sentences from Aozora Bunko have been annotated for the presence of expressions used figuratively. Only 9 of them have got labeled as being used in non-literal senses. In order to match up the number of figurative sentences with the one of literal ones (41:41) another 32 items have been taken from above-mentioned dictionary [15] and added to the figurative subset.

All of the sentences (from both train- and test- sets) have been preprocessed using JUMAN parser [25]; ASCII characters and punctuation marks have been removed if present.

3.2 Annotation

We have asked three Japanese native speakers to annotate 50 sentences taken randomly from *Aozora Bunko* digital library. They were instructed to not only decide whether the sentence have literal or nonliteral sense but also - in case of the latter - to mark the expression used - according to their intuition - figuratively. The motivation behind setting the number of annotators to an odd number lies in the need for limiting anticipated disagreement between them. It is nonetheless obvious that majority does not necessarily have to be right. It should also be noted that some of the longer sentences included multiple expressions used figuratively.

Let us consider following example: *Jikaku ga tsuyoku natta*, '(one) became more aware' (lit. 'Awareness became strong'). In our opinion it should have been classified otherwise: it is after all an example of personification. Our algorithm also tended to classify it as figurative, which consequently lowered the overall performance score, but we have decided not to interfere with evaluation made by the annotators.

Another example of quite vivid (as the presence of figurative use of language is highlighted by the simile marker *yō-na*) mislabels was that made by one of our annotators who classified *mune o utareru yō-na kōkei* 'a touching scene' (lit. 'sight as if a chest got hit by <sth>').

Also, the sentence *Haisha wa (...) yagate shiorete suwarimashita* 'After a while stomatologist got downcast and took a sit' (lit. 'After a while stomatologist withered and sat'), while apparently including expression used metaphorically (for people do not wither as plants), was labeled as literal by one of the annotators.

We have already stated that to us it is not words that should be called metaphorical or literal but their usage.

Some argue that it would be better to classify single words or phrases rather than whole sentences, but in our opinion such approach would inevitably lead to even bigger confusion. In real life we are often dealing with metaphors much more complex than relatively simple one underlying the sentence *Richard is a lion*. In the following one, also quoted in [1], telling which part is used figuratively appears as no easy task:

Light is but the Shadow of God
With this kind of, so to speak, highly sophisticated, imagery-packed metaphors it becomes much more troublesome to decide where should one set a border between parts of sentence used figuratively and literally. We have therefore decided that it is the whole sentence that should be taken as the elementary unit of our analysis.

In similar manner one could argue that it is sometimes impossible to decide whether a sentence is used metaphorically or literally without even larger context and this would be a fair point. We are thinking about using even bigger units of text in order to improve our model's performance.

4   Features

It appears as hardly possible to coin the definition of figurative use of language free of contradictions and sufficient enough to cover all of its possible manifestations. It therefore does not seem to be counterintuitive trying to search for non-literal usages, enumerating at least some of the features conceivable as nontrivial in their identification. Good deal of consideration led us to adopt 7 categories of words as features for the classification task.

First one comprises words naming body parts (BP). These are enlisted and can be viewed in Appendix 1. Notice that while most of them are written using both *Hiragana* and *Kanji*, we have decided that some of them - especially the short ones - should be written with *Kanji* only. The reason for doing so is that we wanted to avoid *catching* completely unrelated words including same mora as the name of body parts. As an example consider the result of including *te* as phonetic variant of 手'hand'. Our program would erroneously treat all of the words written in *Hiragana* and including this syllable (i.e. *soshite* 'also', *aete* 'dare to', grammatical topic marker *tte*) as belonging to the category of body parts. We are aware of possible decrease of recall resulting from this decision, but at the same time we consider it as the best of possible solutions. Complete list of BPs consists of 57 elements; 20 examples are provided in the Appendix 1.

Similes (SI) also belong to the wide category of figurative language. We have therefore decided to treat words indicating their presence as another feature for our classifier. The list consists of 24 elements all of which can be seen in the Appendix 2.

Among the most popular conceptual metaphors discovered, UP IS GOOD and DOWN IS BAD can be mentioned. We have utilized words indicating spatial positions and directions (PI) as another feature for our model. Complete 17 elements list of related words can be viewed in the Appendix 3.

As abstract notions are often metaphorically described using words for sensory impressions, we have decided to use names of colors (CO) as the next feature. We have used traditional Japanese colors names which can be found at Wikipedia. We have added some commonly used color names belonging to xenic subset of Japanese lexicon *gairaigo* and therefore not available in the aforementioned list (*pinku* 'pink', *orenji iro* 'orange' and *gurē* 'gray'). In this category we have gathered 242 elements; 20 examples are shown in the Appendix 4.

It is well known that metaphor is often employed as a means to describe feelings more elaborately. Conceptual metaphors such as LOVE IS A JOURNEY and ANGER IS A HOT FLUID IN A CONTAINER should suffice as the evidence. We have therefore construed a list of words likely to be emotionally motivated. 20 out of all 266 elements belonging to the category of words emotion-related (EM) are listed in the Appendix 5. This list is obviously not complete and different words might be added to it as well.

We have also prepared a list of the most frequent words (130 elements) found in the dictionary of figurative expressions. We have named them *frequently poetical* (FP) and used as another feature (FP). 20 of its elements may be viewed in Appendix 6.

As Uchiyama and Ishizaki [19] point out, it is often the case that Japanese compound verbs of V1–V2 form (in other words compounds of two native Japanese verbs, i.e. *yomi-naosu* 'reread', *kaki-ageru* 'finish writing/drawing', etc.) are used metaphorically. We have therefore construed a list of verbs belonging to lexical subsystem *wago* and used them as our last feature (WV). The list consists of 1044 elements 20 of which can be seen in Appendix 7.

In the appendices below we present only fragmentary versions of the feature lists (along with English translations of their constituents). Complete versions of appendices presented in this work are available to download at: http://arakilab.media.eng.hokudai.ac.jp/MetaAppendix.zip.

5 Classification Experiment

In the classification experiment results of which can be found below our task was to check how well different machine learning algorithms can deal with identifying figurative use of language. In order to get the test data well-balanced, all of the input sentences have been taken solely from the literary texts (either directly from some novel's text [24] or from the quotations collected by the dictionary's compiler [15]). All of the test sentences have been labeled as used either figuratively (1) or literally (0) by the odd number of native annotators. In case of disagreement, the answer chosen by the majority has been treated as correct.

We have measured and compared performance of following classification algorithms: Random Forest, Naïve Bayes, Logistic Regression, K-Nearest Neighbors, Linear Discriminant Analysis and Support Vector Machines. *Scikit-learn* [26] library for Python has been utilized.

Before conducting the experiment, each of 51,894 sentences has been transformed into an array comprising the sentence itself combined with 8 elements long feature vector (1 label for each of 7 feature groups + 1 *figurativeness* label). The system first checks whether any member (*seed word*) of the feature group being in use is present in the given input sentence. If this is the case, value of 1 (if not - 0) is assigned to the respective place in the feature vector. Last element of each vector is set depending on whether the sentence belongs to the figurative (1) or the non-figurative (0) group.

As mentioned, 7 features (namely *body parts* BP, *simile indicators* SI, *directions and spatial position indicators* PI, *colors* CO, *emotion-related* EM, *frequently poetical* FP & *wago verbs* WV) have been adopted as possible clues for figurative usage. We wanted to check the effectiveness of every arrangeable feature setting; there is 127 such combinations and thereby we have run the program this number of times.

Vector representations of all 82 test sentences have been passed to the classification algorithms. Depending on the number of features in use, each vector was comprised of up to 8 elements including the evaluation of (non-)figurativeness. The predictions of the classifier have been counted as correct only when they were the same as the ones made by the annotators.

6   Results and Considerations

Figures below allow for the comparison of the results (F1-score) achieved by different classifiers using different subsets of features (Fig. 3).

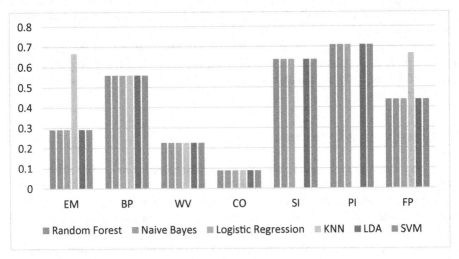

Fig. 1. Results (F1-score) for single features

Figure 1. shows that - when compared in isolation - out of all features it is *position indicators* (PI) which allow 5 of 6 classifiers achieve the highest score (70,9%). For some reason K-Nearest Neighbors outperforms other algorithms reaching level of 66,7% for

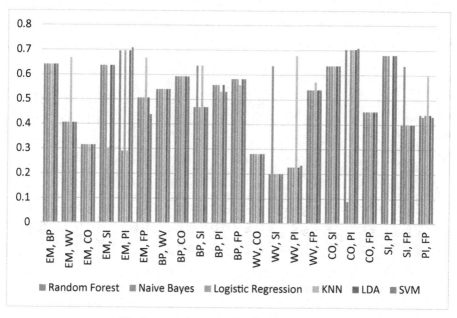

Fig. 2. Results (F1-score) for 2 given features

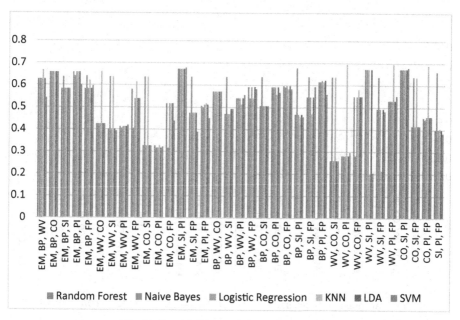

Fig. 3. Results (F1-score) for 3 given features

both *emotions* (EM) and *frequently poetical* (FP). At the same time other algorithms receive scores of 29,1% and 43,9% for EM and FP respectively.

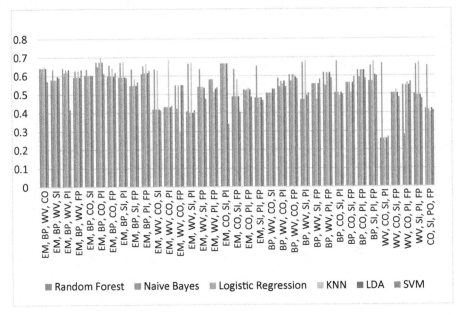

Fig. 4. Results (F1-score) for 4 given features

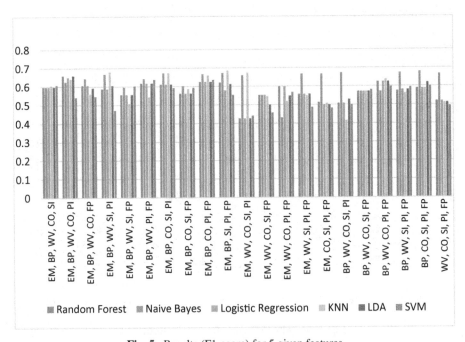

Fig. 5. Results (F1-score) for 5 given features

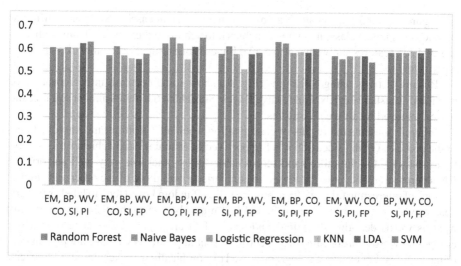

Fig. 6. Results (F1-score) for 6 given features

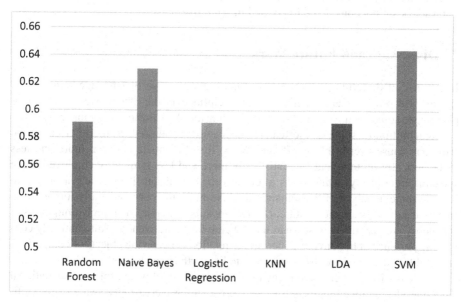

Fig. 7. Results (F1-score) for all available features (EM, BP, WV, CO, SI, PI, FP)

Trials conducted using different subsets of two features (cf. Figure 2.) confirm that KNN works visibly better than other algorithms in certain cases (WV + PI, PI + FP, BP + SI, EM + PI, EM + WV). Identifying the cause of such behavior is a part of our future work.

Figures 4 and 5 once again demonstrate that in certain cases KNN makes different decisions than most classifiers which enables it to achieve better scores. Trials with subsets of 4 & 5 features shows that also Naïve Bayes is often superior to other classification algorithms.

Results of trials using 6 features (Fig. 6.) show some decrease in performance of previously outstanding KNN and Naïve Bayes. Subsets of 6 features almost equalize the scores achieved by all the algorithms.

Figure 7 presents the results of classification when all 7 features are employed duri in the process. On this occasion it is Support Vector Machines that achieves the best F1 score (64,4%). On the other hand scores achieved by otherwise very well performing KNN surprisingly become the lowest in comparison with those of the other algorithms.

One of interesting thing we have noticed is that Random Forest tend to label as literary nearly every sentence in which it finds PI; it might be due to the fact that ideograms used as words denoting directions and spatial loci are highly frequent also in many compound words unrelated to the category of spatial positions we have adopted as one of the features. For example ideogram 中 used prototypically in senses 'middle', 'center', 'medium' appears also in compound words like Chūgoku 'China', chūko 'used', senaka 'back of the body' which - even if their structure was originally metaphorically motivated - nowadays are not considered to be used in figurative senses.

7 Discussion and Future Work

In the task of discerning figurative from non-figurative use of language some of the features we proposed are seemingly more helpful than the others. We are therefore planning to adjust their weights, hopefully leading the algorithm to work more efficiently.

Redefinition of some of the features appears to be needed; in their current shape they may cause overfitting (cf. PI and WV). To differentiate between more and less metaphorically prototypical (or statistically more and less frequently employed when speaking figuratively) *wago verb*s might also be significant. It may be reasonable to include some members of the semantic field Animals, the ones peculiarly important in Japanese culture as another feature. *Onomatopoeias* - category seemingly ubiquitous in Japanese - are also likely to serve as a good clue for figurativeness. Automatically confirming presence of hyponymy-hyperonymy relation between the objects of comparison is possible (i.e. using WordNet) and seem to be worth trying as well.

While not having yet tested many of the methods possibly helpful in computational detection of figurative language use, we are becoming increasingly aware of the difficulties impeding improvement of models dealing with the task. As it has been already emphasized in the previous chapters, it may be argued that there is no definition of figurativeness that would suffice to cover all of its possible linguistic manifestations and - to put it figuratively - it is very difficult to search for something without even knowing how does it really look.

Having that said we are nevertheless convinced that improving language-specific computational models of this kind can be considered as an effort of high value. Discussing the interconnection between culture and language Dobrovol'skij and Piirainen [3] argue that *Japanese is particularly well suited for researching the role of culture in figurative language.* Pointing at semantic similarities observed in the European languages (even in genetically highly idiosyncratic Finnish) they add that *Japanese, once completely isolated from Western cultural influences, serves as a contrast to the increasingly unified Euro-American languages. Japanese figurative language reveals its own original cultural components, rooted in the very different cultural traditions of Japan* ([3] p. 10).

While recognizing high level of the task's complexity, we hope that further trials of this kind will eventually lead us to create highly efficient computational model able to identify different kinds of linguistic expressions used figuratively in Japanese.

Acknowledgements. This work was supported by JSPS KAKENHI Grant Number 17K00295.
A section or subsection is not indented.

Appendices

Appendix 1 (Fragment): Body Parts (BP)

手て 'hand, arm, paw', 足・脚・あし'leg, foot', 指 ・ゆび 'finger, toe', 頭・あたま 'head', 体・からだ 'body', 身 'body', 全身・ぜんしん 'whole body', 顔・かお 'face', 髪・かみ 'hair', 毛 'hair', 眉・まゆ 'eyebrow, brow', まゆげ 'eyebrow', 目・眼 'eye', 耳・みみ 'ear', 鼻 ・はな 'nose', 口・くち 'mouth, maw', 唇・くちびる 'lips', 歯 'tooth', 舌・した 'tongue', 首 ・くび 'neck' (...)

Appendix 2: Simile Indicators (SI)

よう, みたい, っぽい, ごとく・如く, ごとし・ 如し, ごとき・如き, 位・くらい・ぐら い, まるで, さぞ・嘸, いかにも・如何にも, さも, あたかも・恰も・宛も, ほど, 宛ら・ さながら

Appendix 3: Directions and Spatial Position Indicators (PI)

中・なか 'interior, inside', 上・うえ 'upper side, top, upper part, surface', 下・もと 'bottom, bottom part, under' , 間・あいだ 'between, inbetween', 内・うち 'inside', 外・そと 'outside', 前・まえ 'front, frontal part, in front of'

Appendix 4 (Fragment): Colors (CO)

色 'color', 藍, 青・あお 'blue, green', 青竹・あおたけ 'bluish green, malachite green', 赤・あか 'red, crimson, scarlet', 茜色, あかね 'madder', 緋色・あけいろ・ひいろ 'scarlet, cardinal, crimson', 浅葱色・あさぎいろ 'pale greenish blue', 小豆色・あずきいろ 'reddish brown, russet', 亜麻色・あまいろ 'ecru, beige', 鶯色・うぐいすいろ 'brownish green, olive green', 鶯茶・うぐいすちゃ 'greenish brown', 鬱金色・うこんいろ 'bright yellow', 江戸紫・えどむらさき 'royal purple, bluish purple', 葡萄色・えびいろ 'reddish brown, maroon', 臙脂色・えんじいろ 'dark red, crimson', カーキ色 'khaki', 貝紫色・かいむらさきいろ 'Tyrian purple, royal purple', 柿色・かきいろ 'persimmon color, dark orange', 韓紅・唐紅・からくれない 'crimson', 黄・きいろ 'yellow' (...)

Appendix 5 (Fragment): Emotion-Related (EM)

安心・あんしん 'peace of mind, relief, sense of security, sense of safety', 不安・ふあん 'uneasiness, uncertainty, anxiety', 感謝・かんしゃ 'gratitude, gratefulness, appreciation', 驚愕・きょうがく 'astonishment, amazement, shock, fright', 興奮・こうふん 'excitement, arousal', 驚く・おどろく 'be surprised, be astonished, be amazed', 好奇心・こうきしん 'curiosity, inquisitiveness', 冷静・れいせい 'calm, cool, self-possessed', 焦る・あせる 'be hasty, act hastily, make (undue) haste', 不思議、・ふしぎ 'wonderful, wondrous, amazing, marvelous. strange', リラックス 'relax', 緊張・きんちょう 'tension, be tensed, nervous', 喜ぶ・悦ぶ・慶ぶ・歓ぶ・よろこぶ 'be glad, be happy, be pleased', 嬉しい・うれしい 'glad, joyful, delightful, happy', 幸せ・しあわせ 'happiness, happy, lucky, fortunate', 悲しい・かなしい 'sad, unhappy, sorrowful, depressed, depressing, tragic', 寂しい・淋しい・さみしい・さびしい 'lonely, lonesome, isolated', 怒り・いかり 'anger, rage, fury, wrath', 怒る・おこる 'be angry, be furious, be mad', 感動・かんどう 'deep emotion, strong impression, sensation' (...)

Appendix 6 (Fragment): Frequently Figuratively Used (FF)

声・こえ 'voice', 水・みず 'water', 音・おと 'sound, noise', 光・ひかり 'light, beam, ray', 空・そら 'sky, air', 風・かぜ 'wind, breeze', 花・はな 'flower, blossom', 波・なみ 'wave', 火 'fire, flame, blaze', 海・うみ 'sea', 底 'bottom, bed (of a river)', 女・おんな 'woman, female, lady', 言葉・ことば 'word, expression, language', 雨・あめ 'rain', 雲・くも 'cloud', 肌・はだ 'skin', 美しい・うつくしい 'beautiful, pretty, attractive, lovely, charming, picturesque, sweet', 葉・はっぱ 'leaf', 冷たい・つめたい 'cold, cool, icy, coldhearted, indifferent', 雪・ゆき 'snow', 影・かげ 'shade, shadow' (...)

Appendix 7 (Fragment): *Wago* **Verbs (WV)**

燃える・もえる 'burn, blaze, be in flames', 齧る・かじる 'bite, gnaw, nibble', あがる 'go up, rise, ascend', あく 'open, be opened', あしらう 'treat, handle', あてがう 'apply, fit', あてはまる 'apply, be applicable, be valid, fit', あてる 'put, place, apply', あなどる 'despise, disdain, scorn, look down on', あびる 'bathe in (sth), pour (sth) on oneself', あふれでる 'overflow', あふれる 'oveflow, spill over', いきれる 'get angry', いざなう 'invite', いじる 'play with, touch, tamper with', いらっしゃる 'come, visit, be', うっちゃる 'throw away, discard, abandon', うろたえる 'be flustered, be confused, be upset', おえる 'finish, complete, bring to an end', おきる 'get up, get out of bed', おののく 'shudder, tremble, shiver' (...)

References

1. Black, M.: Metaphor (1954)
2. Davidson, D.: What metaphors mean. Crit. Inq. **5**(1), 31–47 (1978)
3. Dobrovol'skij, D., Piirainen, E.: Figurative language: cross-cultural and cross-linguistic perspectives. Brill (2005)
4. Dunn, J.: Multi-dimensional abstractness in cross-domain mappings. In: Proceedings of the Second Workshop on Metaphor in NLP, pp. 27–32 (2014)
5. Gibbs Jr., R.W.: What do idioms really mean? J. Memory Lang. **31**(4), 485–506 (1992)
6. Heintz, I., et al.: Automatic extraction of linguistic metaphors with LDA topic modeling. In: Proceedings of the First Workshop on Metaphor in NLP, pp. 58–66 (2013)
7. Hiraga, M.K., Berendt, E.: Tao of learning: metaphors Japanese students live by. In: Metaphors of Learning, pp. 55–72 (2008)
8. Hiraga, M.K.: Metaphor and Iconicity: A Cognitive Approach to Analyzing Texts. Springer, London (2004). https://doi.org/10.1057/9780230510708
9. Hiraga, M.K.: Kanji: the visual metaphor. Style **40**(1–2), 133–147 (2006)
10. Hornby, A.: Oxford Advanced Learner's Dictionary. Oxford University Press, Oxford (2010)
11. Kageyama, T., Kishimoto, H. (eds.): Handbook of Japanese Lexicon and Word Formation. Walter de Gruyter GmbH & Co KG, Berlin (2016)
12. Klebanov, B.B., Leong, C.W., Gutierrez, E.D., Shutova, E., Flor, M.: Semantic classifications for detection of verb metaphors. In: Proceedings of the 54th Annual Meeting of the Association for Computational Linguistics, volume 2: Short Papers, pp. 101–106 (2016)
13. Lakoff, G., Johnson, M.: Metaphors we live by. University of Chicago Press, Chicago (1980)
14. Lyons, J.: Semantics, vol. 2. Cambridge University Press, Cambridge (1977)
15. Onai, H.: Great dictionary of 33800 Japanese metaphors and synonyms. Kodansha (2005). (in Japanese)
16. Pinker, S., Lakoff, G.: Does language frame politics? Public Policy Res. **14**(1), 59–71 (2007)
17. Ritchie, L.D.: Context and Connection in Metaphor. Palgrave Macmillan, Basingstoke (2006)
18. Soanes, C., Stevenson, A. (eds.): Oxford Dictionary of English, 2, revised edn. Oxford University Press, Oxford (2005)
19. Uchiyama, K., Ishizaki, S.: A disambiguation method for Japanese compound verbs. In Proceedings of the ACL 2003 Workshop on Multiword Expressions: Analysis, Acquisition and Treatment, vol. 18, pp. 81–88. Association for Computational Linguistics (2003)
20. Yamanashi, M.: Hiyu to rikai. Tōkyō Daigaku Shuppankai (1990)
21. Wikipedia dumps list. https://dumps.wikimedia.org/jawiki/latest
22. Japanese local assembly minutes corpus project. http://local-politics.jp

23. Livedoor news. http://news.livedoor.com
24. Aozora Bunko digital library. https://www.aozora.gr.jp
25. JUMAN (Morphological Analyzer for Japanese). http://nlp.ist.i.kyoto-u.ac.jp/EN/index.php? JUMAN
26. Scikit-learn. https://scikit-learn.org/stable/

Artificial Intelligence Safety

Artificial Intelligence Safety

Huáscar Espinoza[1], Han Yu[2], Xiaowei Huang[3], Freddy Lecue[4],
Cynthia Chen[5], José Hernández-Orallo[6], Seán Ó hÉigeartaigh[7],
and Richard Mallah[8]

[1] Commissariat à l'Energie Atomique, France
[2] Nanyang Technological University, Singapore
[3] University of Liverpool, UK
[4] Thales, Canada
[5] University of Hong Kong, China
[6] Universitat Politècnica de València, Spain
[7] University of Cambridge, UK
[8] Future of Life Institute, USA

1 Workshop Overview and Goals

The IJCAI-19 Workshop on Artificial Intelligence Safety (AISafety 2019) was held at
the 28th International Joint Conference on Artificial Intelligence (IJCAI) on August
11–12, 2019 in Macao, China.

In the last decade, there has been a growing concern on risks of Artificial Intelligence (AI). In particular, the technical foundations and assumptions on which traditional safety engineering principles are based, are inadequate for systems in which AI
algorithms, and in particular Machine Learning (ML) algorithms, are interacting with
people and/or the environment at increasingly higher levels of autonomy. We must also
consider the connection between the safety challenges posed by present-day AI systems, and more forward-looking research focused on more capable future AI systems,
up to and including Artificial General Intelligence (AGI).

The Workshop on Artificial Intelligence Safety (AISafety 2019) explored new ideas
on AI safety with particular focus on addressing the following questions:

- How can we engineer trustable AI and ML software architectures?
- What safety engineering considerations are required to develop safe human-
  machine interaction in automated decision-making systems?
- How can we characterize or evaluate AI systems according to their potential risks
  and vulnerabilities?
- How can we develop solid technical visions and paradigm shift about AI Safety?
- How do AI system feature for example ethics, explainability, transparency, and
  accountability relate to, or contribute to, its safety?

2   Workshop Content and Highlights

The AISafety 2019 programme on August 11 was organized in four thematic sessions, one keynote and two invited talks. The keynote, *Joel Lehman (Uber AI Labs, USA)*, gave a talk about AI Safety for evolutionary computation and evolutionary computation for AI Safety. The first session on *Safe Learning* included presentation about learning modular safe policies, and metric learning for value alignment. The second session was related to *Reinforcement Learning Safety* with presentations about the conservative agency, detecting spiky corruption in Markov decision processes, AGI safety, reachability, and causal influence modelling. An invited talk by *Shlomo Zilberstein (University of Massachusetts Amherst, USA)*, gave a presentation about AI Safety Based on Competency Models. The next session dealt with *Safe Autonomous Vehicles*, including presentations about DNN susceptibility to natural perturbations, uncertainty management and a framework for safety violation identification. Finally, a session on *AI Value Alignment, Ethics and Bias* discussed the glass box approach for verifying contextual adherence to values, ethical utility functions in value alignment, perception and moral decisions and bias in datasets using topological data analysis.

As part of this IJCAI workshop, we also started the AI Safety Landscape initiative. This initiative aims at defining an AI safety landscape providing a "view" of the current needs, challenges and state of the art and the practice of this field. AISafety 2019 was planned as a two-days' workshop with general AI Safety topics in the first day and AI Safety Landscape invited talks and discussions during the second day. The first session of the second day dealt with the *Challenge to Achieving Consensus* with Richard Mallah (Future of Life Institute) and John McDermid (University of York), as speakers and discussants. The second session focused on *The Need for Paradigm Change* in the AI Safety field, including talks and discussions by Gopal Sarma (Broad Institute of MIT and Harvard), Xiaowei Huang (University of Liverpool), and Joel Lehman (Uber AI Labs). A session *Towards More Human-Centered and Ethics-Aware Autonomous Systems* included talks and presentations by Virginia Dignum (University of Umeå, Sweden), Raja Chatila (Sorbonne University, France), and Jeff Cao (Tencent Research Institute, China). Finally, we wrapped up and proposed follow-up actions of the AI Safety Landscape.

3   Paper Selected for this Volume

We selected the paper "CPMETRIC: Deep Siamese Networks for Metric Learning on Structured Preferences" by Andrea Loreggia, Nicholas Mattei, Francesca Rossi and K. Brent Venable, because it is a solid paper technically, introducing methods that may be important in making preference aggregation and preference comparison systems practical, but also empirically strong through the testing on recovery of information.

4   Concluding Remarks and Insights for Future Research

One important ambition of this initiative is to align and synchronize the proposed activities and outcomes with other related initiatives. This AI Safety Landscape work will follow-up in future meetings and workshops.

Further information can be found at https://www.ai-safety.org/.

CPMetric: Deep Siamese Networks for Metric Learning on Structured Preferences

Andrea Loreggia[1,5]($\boxtimes$) [ID], Nicholas Mattei[2] [ID], Francesca Rossi[3] [ID],
and K. Brent Venable[4]

[1] Department of Mathematics, University of Padova, Padova, Italy
andrea.loreggia@gmail.com
[2] Department of Computer Science, Tulane University, New Orleans, LA, USA
nsmattei@gmail.com
[3] IBM Research, IBM T.J. Watson Research Center, Yorktown Heights, NY, USA
francesca.rossi2@ibm.com
[4] Institute for Human and Machine Cognition (IHMC), Pensacola, FL, USA
bvenable@ihmc.us
[5] European University Institute, Fiesole, Italy

Abstract. Preferences are central to decision making by both machines and humans. Representing, learning, and reasoning with preferences is an important area of study both within computer science and across the social sciences. When we give our preferences to an AI system we expect the system to make decisions or recommendations that are consistent with our preferences but the decisions should also adhere to certain norms, guidelines, and ethical principles. Hence, when working with preferences it is necessary to understand and compute a metric (distance) between preferences – especially if we encode both the user preferences and ethical systems in the same formalism. In this paper we investigate the use of CP-nets as a formalism for representing orderings over actions for AI systems. We leverage a recently proposed metric for CP-nets and propose a neural network architecture to learn an approximation of the metric, CPMetric. Using these two tools we look at how one can build a fast and flexible value alignment system (This is an expanded version of our paper, "Metric Learning for Value Alignment" [38]. In this version we have added the classification and regression results and significantly expanded the description of the CPMetric network.).

Keywords: Metric learning · Value alignment · Artificial intelligence · Ethics

1 Introduction

Preferences are central to individual and group decision making by both computer systems and humans. Due to this central role in decision making the study of representing [45], learning [21], and reasoning [18] with preferences is a focus

© Springer Nature Switzerland AG 2020
A. El Fallah Seghrouchni and D. Sarne (Eds.): IJCAI 2019 Workshops, LNAI 12158, pp. 217–234, 2020.
https://doi.org/10.1007/978-3-030-56150-5_11

of study within computer science and in many other disciplines including psychology and sociology [22]. Individuals express their preferences in many different ways: pairwise comparisons, rankings, approvals (likes), positive or negative examples, and many more examples are collected in various libraries and databases [7,39,40]. A core task in working with preferences is understanding the relationship *between* preferences. This often takes the form of a dominance query, i.e., which item is more or most preferred, or distance measures, i.e., which object is the closest to my stated preference. These types of reasoning are important in many domains including recommender systems [20], collective decision making [12], and value alignment systems [36,37,47].

Using a formal structure to model preferences, especially one that directly models dependency, can be useful for reasoning. For example, it can support reasoning based on inference and causality, and provide more transparency and explainability since the preferences are explicitly represented and hence scrutable [28]. A number of compact preference representation languages have been developed in the literature for representing and reasoning with preferences; see the work of Amor et al. [6] for a survey of compact graphical models; we specifically focus on conditional preference networks (CP-nets) [11].

CP-nets are a compact graphical model used to capture qualitative conditional preferences over features (variables) [11]. Qualitative preferences are important as there is experimental evidence that qualitative preferences may more accurately reflect humans' preferences in uncertain information settings [4,42]. CP-nets are a popular formalism for specifying preferences in the literature and have been used for a number of applications including recommender systems and product specification [20,43]. Consider a car that is described by values for all its possible features: make, model, color, and stereo options. A CP-net consists of a dependency graph and a set of statements of the form, *"all else being equal, I prefer x to y."* For example, in a CP-net one could say *"Given that the car is a Honda Civic, I prefer red to yellow."*, the condition sets the context for the preference over alternatives. These preferences are qualitative, i.e., there is no quantity expressing the degree of preference.

A CP-net induces an ordering over all possible *outcomes*, i.e., all complete assignments to the set of features. This is a partial order if the dependency graph of the CP-net is acyclic, i.e., the conditionality of the statements does not create a cycle, as is often assumed in work with CP-nets [23]. The size of the description of the CP-net may be exponentially smaller than the partial order it describes. Hence, CP-nets are called a *compact* representation and reasoning and learning on the compact structure, instead of the full order, is an important topic of research. Recent work proposes the first formal metric to describe the distance between CP-nets [35] and the related formalism of LP-trees [34] in a rigorous way. What is important is not the differences in the surface features of the CP-nets, e.g., a single statement or dependency, but rather the distance between their induced partial orders. Even a small difference in a CP-net could generate a very different partial order, depending on which feature is involved in the modification. While the metrics proposed by Loreggia et al. [35] are well grounded, they are computationally hard to compute, in general, and approximations must be used.

We envision the use of CP-nets to solve one part of the *value alignment* problem [36,37,47]. This is part of a broader research program we call *Ethically Bounded AI*, that seeks to understand how to harness the power of AI yet prevent these systems from making choices we do not consider ethical [46]. Most of the research in this line is focused on allowing an AI system to learn via either the rules driven top-down approach or the example driven bottoms-up approach [3,51]. Training systems to operate under constraints that come from ethical priorities, business rules, or social norms have been proposed for recommendation engines [1,8,9], reinforcement learning based teamwork engines [2], and even to play video games like PacMan [41]. In this work we envision using a distance metric to measure the difference between an individual agent's preferences over actions and another ordering given by, e.g., ethics, norms, or business values [36,37].

Following work in metric learning over structured representations [10], we wish to learn the distance between partial orders represented compactly as CP-nets. We do not want to work with the partial orders directly as they may be exponentially larger than the CP-net representation. Informally, given two CP-nets, we wish to estimate the distance between their induced partial orders using a neural network. The number of possible CP-nets grows extremely fast, from 481,776 for 4 binary features to over 5.24×10^{40} with 7 binary features [5]. However, the computation time of the approximation algorithm proposed by Loreggia et al. [35] scales linearly with the number of features, hence, new methods must be explored. Therefore, leveraging the inferential properties of neural networks may help us make CP-nets more useful as a preference reasoning formalism.

Contributions. We propose using metric learning as a tool to practically solve aspects of the value alignment problem. We propose to model both user preferences and ethical priorities over actions using the CP-net formalism and we demonstrate how one can use a state of the art neural network formulation, CPMETRIC, to quickly and accurately judge distances between preferred actions and ethical actions. We evaluate our models and metrics on generated CP-nets and show that CPMETRIC leads to a speed up in computation while still being accurate.

2   CP-Nets

Conditional Preference networks (CP-nets) are a graphical model for compactly representing conditional and qualitative preference relations [11]. CP-nets are comprised of sets of *ceteris paribus* preference statements (cp-statements). For instance, the cp-statement, *"I prefer red wine to white wine if meat is served,"* asserts that, given two meals that differ *only* in the kind of wine served *and* both containing meat, the meal with red wine is preferable to the meal with white

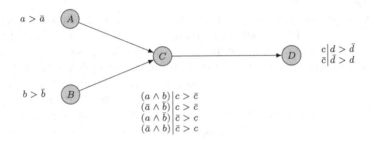

Fig. 1. An example of CP-net with $n = 4$ features. Next to each node there are examples of the correspondent CP-tables.

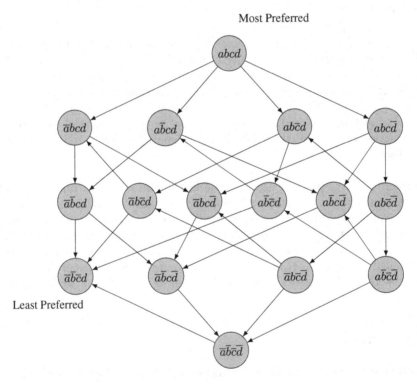

Fig. 2. The induced partial order of the CP-net reported in Fig. 1. Note that the partial order is over all $2^n = 16$ possible combinations and arrows denote the dominance relation. We have arranged the nodes so that each is one flip between the levels.

wine. CP-nets have been extensively used in the preference reasoning preference learning and social choice literature as a formalism for working with qualitative preferences [12,18,45]. CP-nets have even been used to compose web services [52] and other decision aid systems [43].

Formally, a CP-net has a set of features (or variables) $F = \{X_1, \ldots, X_n\}$ with finite domains $\mathcal{D}(X_1), \ldots, \mathcal{D}(X_n)$. For each feature X_i, we are given a set of *parent* features $Pa(X_i)$ that can affect the preferences over the values of X_i. This defines a *dependency graph* in which each node X_i has $Pa(X_i)$ as its immediate predecessors. An *acyclic* CP-net is one in which the dependency graph is acyclic. Given this structural information, one needs to specify the preference over the values of each variable X_i for *each complete assignment* to the parent variables, $Pa(X_i)$. This preference is assumed to take the form of a total or partial order over $\mathcal{D}(X_i)$. A cp-statement for some feature X_i that has parents $Pa(X_i) = \{x_1, \ldots, x_n\}$ and domain $\mathcal{D}(X_i) = \{a_1, \ldots, a_m\}$ is a total ordering over $\mathcal{D}(X_i)$ and has general form: $x_1 = v_1, x_2 = v_2, \ldots, x_n = v_n : a_1 \succ \ldots \succ a_m$, where for each $X_j \in Pa(X_i) : x_j = v_j$ is an assignment to a parent of X_i with $v_j \in \mathcal{D}(X_j)$. The set of cp-statements regarding a certain variable X_i is called the cp-table for X_i.

Consider the CP-net depicted graphically in Fig. 1 with features are A, B, C, and D. Figure 2 gives the full induced preference order for the CP-net. Each variable has binary domain containing f and $\overline{f}$ if F is the name of the feature. All cp-statements in the CP-net are: $a \succ \overline{a}$, $b \succ \overline{b}$, $(a \wedge b) : c \succ \overline{c}$, $(\overline{a} \wedge \overline{b}) : c \succ \overline{c}$, $(a \wedge \overline{b}) : \overline{c} \succ c$, $(\overline{a} \wedge b) : \overline{c} \succ c$, $c : d \succ \overline{d}$, $\overline{c} : \overline{d} \succ d$. Here, statement $a \succ \overline{a}$ represents the unconditional preference for $A = a$ over $A = \overline{a}$, while statement $c : d \succ \overline{d}$ states that $D = d$ is preferred to $D = \overline{d}$, given that $C = c$. The semantics of CP-nets depends on the notion of a *worsening flip*: a change in the value of a variable to a less preferred value according to the cp-statement for that variable. For example, in the CP-net above, passing from $abcd$ to $ab\overline{c}d$ is a worsening flip since c is better than $\overline{c}$ given a and b. One outcome α is *preferred to* or *dominates* another outcome β (written $\alpha \succ \beta$) if and only if there is a chain of worsening flips from α to β. This definition induces a preorder over the outcomes, which is a partial order if the CP-net is acyclic [11], as depicted in Fig. 2.

The complexity of dominance and consistency testing in CP-nets is an area of active study in preference reasoning [23,45]. Finding the optimal outcome of a CP-net is NP-hard [11] in general but can be found in polynomial time for acyclic CP-nets by assigning the most preferred value for each cp-table. Indeed, acyclic CP-nets induce a lattice over the outcomes as (partially) depicted in Fig. 2. The induced preference ordering, Fig. 2, can be exponentially larger than the CP-net Fig. 1, which motivates learning a metric using only the (more compact) CP-net.

3   Preferences and Ethical Priorities

In what follow we assume that we can describe a user's behavior through her preferences over the features of the domain. This can be modeled as a CP-net and it gives us an ordering over the actions the user would like to take. The example given in Loreggia et al. [37] concerns a driver of a vehicle: she may want to go as fast as possible and run over certain small animals. However, there may be some overall ethical or moral guidelines (priorities) the system must follow. In this case we want to evaluate the difference, or distance, between the individual user and the society. This idea of morality as ordering over actions was first proposed by Sen [48].

To operationalize this system we wish to describe both preferences and priorities using the CP-net formalism and using a notion of distance in the metric space of CP-nets. This enables us and the system to understand whether users' preferences are close enough to the moral principles or not. Eventually, when preferences deviate from the desired behavior, we can use CP-nets, since they induce an ordering, to find a trade-off so that the quality of the decision with respect to the subjective preferences does not significantly degrade when conforming to the ethical principles [36,37]. In this way we have bounded the behavior of the system to be *ethical* while still being responsive to the user preferences [46].

Traditional reasoning and learning approaches in AI provide different and complementary capabilities to an autonomous agent. Symbolic and logical reasoning allow these agents to manipulate symbols and perform inference, while machine learning techniques can learn and optimize many ill-defined problems from large amounts of data. As ongoing work, we intend to study the use of both kinds of approaches to model, learn, and reason with both preferences and ethical principles. Inspired by the System 1 and System 2 theory of Daniel Kahneman [27], we will define a dual-agent architecture that will provide autonomous agents with the ability to combine symbolic and accurate reasoning with data interpretation and learning, for both preferences and ethical principles. This will allow machines to be flexible and context-dependent in how they handle and combine these two sources of information for decision making [44,46].

The combined use of deep learning techniques and logical reasoning formalisms is an exciting research direction to find a principled ways to develop AI systems that are both accountable and able to explain themselves. We hope that these approaches will be able to overcome limitations of the "black-box paradigm" in the machine learning discipline [44].

4 Metric Learning on CP-Nets

Metric learning algorithms aim to learn a metric (or distance function) over a set of training points or samples [50]. The importance of metrics has grown in recent years with the use of these functions in many different domains: from clustering to information retrieval and from recommender systems to preference aggregation. For instance, many clustering algorithms like the k-Means or classification algorithm including k-Nearest Neighbor use a distance value between points.

Formally, a metric space is a pair (M, d) where M is a set of elements and d is a function $d : M \times M \to \mathbb{R}$ where d satisfies four criteria. Given any three elements $A, B, C \in M$, d must satisfy

1. $d(A, B) \geq 0$, there must be a value for all pairs;
2. $d(A, B) = d(B, A)$, d must be symmetric;
3. $d(A, B) \leq d(A, C) + d(C, B)$; d must satisfy the triangle inequality; and
4. $d(A, B) = 0$ if and only if $A = B$; d can be zero if and only if the two elements are the same.

Xing et al. [54] first formalized the problem of metric learning, i.e., learning the metric directly from samples rather than formally specifying the function d. This approach requires training data, meaning that we have some oracle that is able to give the value of the metric for each pair. The success of deep learning in many different domains [32] has lead many researchers to apply these approaches to the field of metric learning, resulting in a number of important results [10].

In this work we focus on metric spaces (M, d) where M is a set of CP-nets. Given this, we want to learn the distance d which best approximates the Kendall tau distance (KTD) [29] between the induced partial orders. Informally, the Kendall tau distance between two orderings is the number of pairs that are *discordant*, i.e., not ordered in the same way, in both orderings. This distance metric extended to partial orders (Definition 1) was shown to be a metric on the space of CP-nets by Loreggia et al. [35]. To extend the classic KTD to CP-nets, a penalty parameter p defined for partial rankings [19] was extended to the case of partial orders. Loreggia et al. [35] assume that all CP-nets are acyclic and in minimal (non-degenerate) form, i.e., all arcs in the dependency graph have a real dependency expressed in the cp-statements, a standard assumption in the CP-net literature (see e.g., [5,11]).

Definition 1. *Given two CP-nets A and B inducing partial orders P and Q over the same unordered set of outcomes U, we can define:*

$$KTD(A, B) = KT(P, Q) = \sum_{\forall i, j \in U, i \neq j} K_{i,j}^p(P, Q)$$

where i and j are two outcomes with $i \neq j$ (i.e., iterate over all unique pairs), we have:

1. *$K_{i,j}^p(P, Q) = 0$ if i, j are ordered in the same way or are incomparable in P and Q;*
2. *$K_{i,j}^p(P, Q) = 1$ if i, j are ordered inversely in P and Q;*
3. *$K_{i,j}^p(P, Q) = p$, $0.5 \leq p < 1$ if i, j are ordered in P and incomparable in Q (resp. Q, P).*

To make this distance scale invariant, i.e., a value in $[0, 1]$, it is divided by $|U|$.

CP-nets present two important challenges when used for metric learning. The first is that we are attempting to learn a metric via a compact representation of a partial order. We are not learning over the partial orders induced by the CP-nets directly, as they could be exponentially larger than the CP-nets. The second challenge is the encoding of the graphical structure itself. Graph learning with neural networks is still an active and open area of research; Goyal and Ferrara [24] give a complete survey of recent work as well as a Python library of implementations for many of these techniques. Most of these works focus on finding good embeddings for the nodes of the network and then using collections of these learned embeddings to represent the graph for, e.g., particular segmentation or link prediction tasks. None of these techniques have been applied to embedding graphs for metric learning.

5   Structure of CPMETRIC

The architecture of CPMETRIC is depicted in Fig. 3. In this section we will discuss the encoding used for the CP-nets and the design of our autoencoders, depicted in Fig. 4, that are used for transfer learning in this domain. We would like to leverage transfer learning in this domain since training examples become prohibitively expensive to compute at higher values of n as computing KTD requires exponential time in the size of the CP-net. Hence, if we can learn a good encoding for CP-nets it may be possible to train a network for small n and use it for problems with larger CP-nets.

In our task the metric space is (M, d) where M is a set of compact, graphical preferences that induce a partial order and our goal is to learn the metric d *only* from the compact, graphical representation. The key challenge is the need to find a vector representation of not only the graph but the cp-statement. We represent a CP-net I over m using two matrices. First is the adjacency matrix adj_I which represents the dependency graph of the CP-net and is a $m \times m$ matrix of 0s and 1s. The second matrix represents the list of cp-statements cpt_I, which is a $m \times 2^{m-1}$ matrix, where each row represents a variable $X_i \in F$ and each column represents a complete assignment for each of the variables in $F \setminus X_i$. The list is built following a topological ordering of variables in the CP-net. Each cell $cpt_I(i, j)$ stores the preference value for the ith variable given the jth assignment to variables in $F \setminus X_i$.

In graph learning, the central research question is how to redefine operators, such as convolution and pooling, so as to generalize convolutional neural network (CNN) to graphs [17,25]. The most promising research uses a spectral formulation of the problem [13,49]. The issue is that networks are sensitive to isomorphisms of the adjacency matrix, hence directly using an adjacency matrix would result in a siamese network that would not recognize isomorphic structures. We follow in the spirit of the work by Kipf and Welling [31] for GCN and use a simple convolutional network structure removing pooling layers from CPMETRIC, as we do not define any pooling operator over the graph structure. In graph spectral analysis, the Laplacian matrix is preferred as it has better properties for encoding, e.g., density, compared to just the adjacency matrix. The Laplacian matrix $L = D - A$, where D is the degree matrix, a diagonal matrix whose ith diagonal element d_i is equal to the sum of the weights of all the edges incident to vertex i, and A is the adjacency matrix representing the

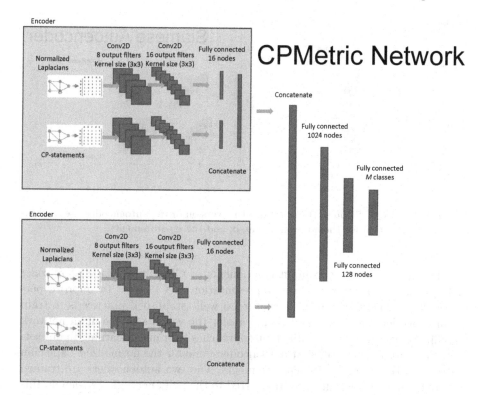

Fig. 3. Structure of CPMETRIC: CP-nets are provided to the encoder as a normalized Laplacian matrix and a list of cp-statements. The encoders output a compact representation of the CP-nets which is then concatenated and passed to the fully connected layers that connect to an m class classifier over $[0, 1]$ to predict KTD. For the regression task the network structure is the same except we change the output layer to be one node with a softmax activation layer.

graph. The normalized Laplacian $\mathcal{L} = I - D^{\frac{1}{2}} \times A \times D^{\frac{1}{2}}$ [49]. While the Laplacian matrix is still susceptible to exchanges of rows or columns, its spectrum (the vector of its eigenvalues) is an isomorphism invariant of a graph. The same graph can be represented using different structures (and this can be seen as a data augmentation technique) and we need all of these structures to learn the metric, so we cannot collapse to a single spectrum representation of the graph.

The set of training examples $X = \{x_1, \ldots, x_n\}$ is made up of pairs of CP-nets represented through their normalized Laplacians and the cp-statements. The set of corresponding labels $Y = \{y_1, \ldots, y_n\}^T$, where each $y_i \in Y, y_i \in [0, 1]$ is the normalized value of KTD between the CP-nets in x_i.

Each $x_i \in X$ is then a tuple $(\mathcal{L}_A, cpt_A, \mathcal{L}_B, cpt_B)$ representing a pair of CP-net (A, B) by their Laplacian, $\mathcal{L}_A$, and the encoding of their cp-statements, cpt_A.

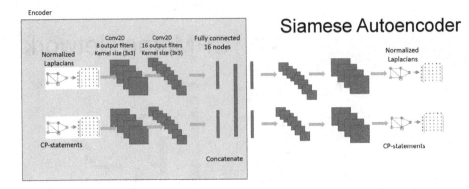

Fig. 4. Structure of *Siamese Autoencoder*: this version of the autoencoder uses a combined representation for the adjacency matrix and the cp-statements.

The purpose of the two input components of CPMETRIC, labeled *Encoder* in Fig. 3, is to output a compact representation of CP-nets. To improve performance with networks of this structure, a well-established practice is to train an autoencoder separately, and then transfer the weights to the main network [26,33]. We will evaluate two different approaches to transfer learning in our setting. First, we use two different autoencoders: one for the normalized Laplacian matrix and the other for the cp-statements. The two autoencoders are trained separately and then weights are transferred to the main network. We denote this approach as *Autoencoder* in subsequent experiments. In the second approach, shown in Fig. 4 and denoted as *Siam. Autoencoder*, we use a unique autoencoder designed to combine the two components of CP-nets. Informally, the output of two encoders are concatenated and then split into their respective components to be decoded. We conjecture that this combination should allow more information about the CP-net to be used.

6   Experiment

We train CPMETRIC to learn the KTD metric, varying the number of features of the CP-nets $n \in \{3, \dots, 7\}$ and using two different autoencoder designs. We evaluate our networks on both the regression and classification tasks and measure their performance against the current best approximation algorithm, I-CPD [35], for computing the KTD between two CP-nets. In the regression task the network computes the distance value exactly while in the classification task we divide the output in $m = 10$ intervals and the network must select the correct interval. CP-nets are represented by their normalized Laplacian and the list of the cp-statements in the CP-tables following a topological order of the variables. The encoder components of the network is composed by two CNNs [33]: one receives as input the normalized Laplacian matrices of the CP-net and the other the lists of cp-statements. The aim of the encoder is to output a compact representation of each CP-net. We will discuss data generation, training and mention challenges due to the unique properties of CP-nets.

6.1 Data Generation and Training

For each number of features $n \in \{3, \ldots, 7\}$ we generate 1000 CP-nets uniformly at random using the generators from Allen et al. [5]. This set of CP-nets is split into a training-generative-set (900 CP-nets) and test-generative-set (100 CP-nets) 10 different ways to give us 10 fold cross validation. For each fold we compute the training and test dataset comprised of all, e.g., $\binom{900}{2}$, possible pairs of CP-nets from the training-generative-set and test-generative-set, respectively, along with the value of KTD for that pair. While we generate the CP-nets themselves uniformly at random observe that this creates an unbalanced set of distances – it induces a normal distribution – and hence our sets are unbalanced. Figure 5 shows the distribution of CP-net pairs over 20 intervals for all CP-nets generated for $n \in \{3, \ldots, 7\}$. While our classification experiments are for $m = 10$ classes, dividing the interval into 20 classes provides a better visualization of the challenge of obtaining training samples at the edges of the distribution.

We ran a preliminary experiment on balancing our dataset by sub-sampling the training and test datasets. In these small experiments, performance was much worse than performance on the unbalanced dataset. Because we are learning a metric, for each CP-net A, there is only one CP-net B such $KTD(A, B) = 1$ and only one CP-net C such $KTD(A, C) = 0$. Consequently, attempting to balance or hold out CP-nets from test or train can lead to poor performance. We conjecture that in order to improve this task we should perform some kind of data augmentation, but this would introduce more subjective assumptions on how and where data should be augmented [53].

All training was done on a machine with $2 \times$ Intel(R) Xeon(R) CPU E5-2670 @ 2.60 GHz and one NVidia K20 128 GB GPU. We train CPMETRIC for 70 epochs using the Adam optimizer [30]. For each number of features of the CP-net n we use all $\binom{900}{2}$ pairs in the training-set. There are only 488 binary CP-nets with 3 features [5], hence, for $n = 3$ the training-set is 17K samples while for $n > 3$ the number of samples in the training-set is 800K. Both the *Autoencoder* and *Siamese Autoencoder* models are trained for 100 epochs using the Adam optimizer [30] using the same training-set. Model weights from the best performing epoch are saved and subsequently transferred to the deep neural network used to learn the distance function.

The training and validation loss for the autoencoder is shown in Fig. 6. Observe that the loss for the CPT representation approaches zero after only 3 epochs for both the training and validation phases. The same trend is true for the adjacency matrix, though the loss converges to ≈ 0.15.

6.2 Quantitative Performance: Classification and Regression

The first task for CPMETRIC is classifying the distance between two CP-nets, A and B, into the same one of $m = 10$ intervals of $[0, 1]$ where the value of

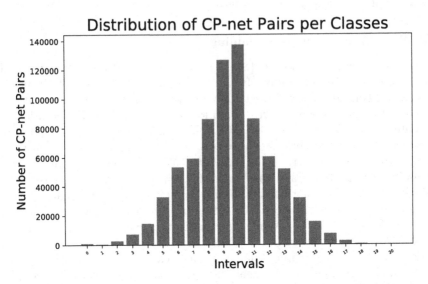

Fig. 5. Histogram of the number of CP-net pairs per interval across all experimental datasets. CP-nets pairs are not distributed uniformly in the class intervals.

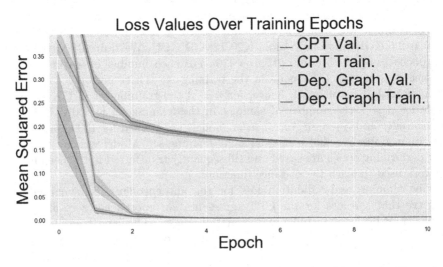

Fig. 6. Performance of the autoencoder on the validation and training set for 10 epochs.

KTD lies. Table 1 gives the F-score, Cohen's Kappa (Cohen-κ) [14], and mean absolute error (MAE) for the task with no autoencoder and each of the two autoencoder variants. Cohen's κ is a measure of inter-rater agreement where the two raters are the particular instance of CPMETRIC and the actual value of KTD. We measure mean absolute error as a value over the number of intervals between the value returned by CPMETRIC and KTD. For example, a MAE of 1.0 means that CPMETRIC is off by one interval, on average. In this setting, using a random classifier to guess the interval with $m = 10$ possible intervals and a normal distribution like the one seen in Fig. 5 would give an F-score ≈ 0.19 (Table 2).

Table 1. Performance of CPMETRIC on the classification task with and without the autoencoders. Numbers in parenthesis are standard deviations. Mean absolute error is computed as the number of intervals between the true and predicted values for the classification task.

N	No autoencoder			Autoencoder			Siam. autoencoder			I-CPD
	F-score	Cohen-κ	MAE	F-score	Cohen-κ	MAE	F-score	Cohen-κ	MAE	MAE
3	0.6643 (0.0275)	0.6113	0.3449	0.7051 (0.0306)	0.6578	0.2986	0.7295 (0.0501)	0.6860	**0.2734**	0.4235
4	0.7424 (0.0096)	0.6762	0.2582	0.7483 (0.0085)	0.6824	**0.2525**	0.7459 (0.0088)	0.6796	0.2548	0.4515
5	0.7074 (0.0111)	0.6146	0.3015	0.7271 (0.0084)	0.6385	0.2833	0.7278 (0.0077)	0.6393	**0.2831**	0.3875
6	0.6945 (0.0130)	0.5799	0.3194	0.7157 (0.0198)	0.6073	0.2971	0.7161 (0.0141)	0.6081	**0.2969**	0.3645
7	0.6887 (0.0227)	0.5571	0.3256	0.6497 (0.0892)	0.4957	0.3830	0.6884 (0.0274)	0.5549	**0.3266**	0.3340

Table 2. MAE of CPMETRIC on the regression task with and without the autoencoders. MAE is the mean over 10 folds and numbers in parenthesis are the standard deviations.

	No autoencoder	Autoencoder	Siam. autoencoder	I-CPD
3	0.0470	0.0426	**0.0421**	0.0576
4	0.0248 (0.0008)	**0.0242 (0.0005)**	0.0243 (0.0007)	0.0526
5	0.0269 (0.0006)	**0.0261 (0.0008)**	0.0262 (0.0008)	0.0463
6	0.0257 (0.0007)	**0.0255 (0.0007)**	0.0256 (0.0006)	0.0405
7	0.0257 (0.0008)	0.0257 (0.0022)	**0.0252 (0.0015)**	0.0373

Looking at Table 1 we see that CPMETRIC outperforms the I-CPD approximation algorithm across the test instances. The overall accuracy, measured as F-score, is above 70% across all CP-net sizes and we see that on average it is off by less than 0.5 intervals as measured by the MAE. The values for Cohen's κ indicate good agreement between the two methods and this is borne out by high accuracy numbers. The most interesting overall effect in Table 1 is that the performance does not decay much as we increase the number of features. Indeed, the F-score remains very stable across the range. We interpret this to mean that CPMETRIC is learning a good generalization of the distance function even when the solution space is exponentially larger than the number of training examples.

Table 3. Performance of the various network architectures on the qualitative comparison task as well as performance of *I*-CPD. While our networks do not achieve the best performance on this task they are competitive with the more costly approximation algorithm *I*-CPD.

N	No autoencoder	Autoencoder	Siam. autoencoder	*I*-CPD
	Accuracy on triples	Accuracy on triples	Accuracy on triples	Accuracy on triples
3	85.01% (2.01%)	85.76% (2.29%)	85.47% (2.32%)	91.80%
4	91.17% (0.92%)	91.38% (1.10%)	91.78% (1.13%)	92.90%
5	88.40% (0.91%)	89.36% (1.08%)	89.18% (1.08%)	90.80%
6	87.33% (0.80%)	87.17% (1.33%)	86.79% (1.84%)	90.10%
7	84.79% (1.16%)	84.57% (1.14%)	85.12% (0.86%)	89.90%

6.3 Comparison Task Performance

For many applications we are not concerned with the true value of the distance but rather deciding which of two preferences is closer to a reference point. For example, in product recommendation we may want to display the closer of two objects and not care about computing the values [43]. Formally, the qualitative comparison takes a set of CP-nets triples (A, B, C), where A is a reference CP-net and the task is to decide which other CP-net B or C is *closer* to A.

We generate uniformly at random 1000 triples of CP-nets for each $n \in \{3, \ldots, 7\}$. For each triple (A, B, C) we compute both $\text{KTD}(A, B)$ and $\text{KTD}(A, C)$ to establish ground truth and use our regression networks to predict the distance between (A, B) and (A, C). Table 3 displays the accuracy, as a percentage out of 1000 trials, of our three CPMETRIC architectures versus *I*-CPD for this task; Table 4 gives the average runtime per pair, averaged over all 1000 trials. The standard deviations in Table 3 are across the 10 folds of the training/test set. For all of our networks we obtain an accuracy above 85% and all the networks perform about the same on this task ($\pm 2.0\%$) and the trend for accuracy is flat across the size of the CP-nets. It is interesting to note that on this task neither of the autoencoders were able to significantly improve performance as they did for the quantitative comparison tasks. While the results are inconclusive, as all instances of CPMETRIC performed about the same, it will be interesting to see if there are autoencoder architectures that are more suited to the comparison task.

A positive take away is that, as Table 4 shows, we achieve a sub-linear increase in inference time for our model. *I*-CPD scales linearly with the description size of the CP-net so the neural network does, after training, offer the ability to, in a practical amount of time, compare CP-nets of larger sizes. This gives us hope

Table 4. Comparison of the mean runtime for a single triple over 1000 trials on the qualitative comparison task of the neural network and I-CPD.

N	I-CPD	Autoencoder Neural network
3	0.69 (0.48) ms	0.087 (0.004) ms
4	1.09 (0.33) ms	0.098 (0.004) ms
5	1.85 (0.49) ms	0.100 (0.005) ms
6	3.16 (0.74) ms	0.114 (0.003) ms
7	4.65 (0.86) ms	0.138 (0.001) ms

that while the metric itself is NP-hard to compute in a direct way, we can use the power of deep learning to enable systems that could be practically deployed.

Unfortunately the trend for accuracy is negative when the number of features increases. However, this is also the case for the I-CPD approximation and both metrics seem to be losing accuracy at about the same rate. The loss in accuracy for the neural network models could be caused by the unbalanced nature of the training and testing datasets. Again, as shown in Fig. 5, generating the CP-nets themselves uniformly at random does not give us a uniform distribution over distances and correcting this may give better performance.

Our conjecture for the slight disadvantage for CPMetric over I-CPD has to do with the directionality of the errors. When training the network we are optimizing for accuracy on the regression task. However, when using this metric it does not matter if CPMetric overestimates by a small amount or underestimates by some small amount. However, when looking at the comparison task, it may matter a lot if the direction of our errors is random. An important direction for future work is to try different optimization objectives when training the network to see if this bias is the reason for the underperformance.

7   Conclusion

In this paper we have discussed how to use CPMetric, a novel neural network model to learn a metric (distance) function between partial orders induced from a CP-net, a compact, structured preference representation, to enable practical value alignment systems. To our knowledge this is the first use of neural networks to learn and measure preferences for the value alignment problem. We feel that this is an interesting and fruitful direction for research in the AI Safety domain as we must develop practical and efficient tools that can be used to effectively harness the power of AI systems.

Important directions for future work include integrating novel graph learning techniques to our networks and extending our work to other formalisms including, e.g., PCP-nets [15] and LP-trees [34]. PCP-nets are a particularly interesting direction as they have been proposed as an efficient way to model uncertainty over the preferences of a single or multiple agents [16]. Another important extension involves setting contexts for different preference and ethical priority encodings. CP-nets and many other preference formalisms model a particular domain but do not give us any insight into when we may need to pass between one context and another.

References

1. Abdollahpouri, H., Burke, R.: Multi-stakeholder recommendation and its connection to multi-sided fairness. arXiv preprint arXiv:1907.13158 (2019)
2. Alkoby, S., Rath, A., Stone, P.: Teaching social behavior through human reinforcement for ad hoc teamwork-the star framework. In: Proceedings of 18th AAMAS, pp. 1773–1775 (2019)
3. Allen, C., Smit, I., Wallach, W.: Artificial morality: top-down, bottom-up, and hybrid approaches. Ethics Inf. Technol. **7**(3), 149–155 (2005)
4. Allen, T.E., et al.: Beyond theory and data in preference modeling: bringing humans into the loop. In: Walsh, T. (ed.) ADT 2015. LNCS (LNAI), vol. 9346, pp. 3–18. Springer, Cham (2015). https://doi.org/10.1007/978-3-319-23114-3_1
5. Allen, T.E., Goldsmith, J., Justice, H.E., Mattei, N., Raines, K.: Uniform random generation and dominance testing for CP-nets. JAIR **59**, 771–813 (2017)
6. Amor, N.B., Dubois, D., Gouider, H., Prade, H.: Graphical models for preference representation: an overview. In: Schockaert, S., Senellart, P. (eds.) SUM 2016. LNCS (LNAI), vol. 9858, pp. 96–111. Springer, Cham (2016). https://doi.org/10.1007/978-3-319-45856-4_7
7. Bache, K., Lichman, M.: UCI machine learning repository. University of California, Irvine, School of Information and Computer Sciences (2013). http://archive.ics.uci.edu/ml
8. Balakrishnan, A., Bouneffouf, D., Mattei, N., Rossi, F.: Using contextual bandits with behavioral constraints for constrained online movie recommendation. In: Proceedings of the 27th IJCAI (2018)
9. Balakrishnan, A., Bouneffouf, D., Mattei, N., Rossi, F.: Incorporating behavioral constraints in online AI systems. In: Proceedings of the 33rd AAAI (2019)
10. Bellet, A., Habrard, A., Sebban, M.: Metric Learning. Synthesis Lectures on Artificial Intelligence and Machine Learning. Morgan & Claypool Publishers, San Rafael (2015)
11. Boutilier, C., Brafman, R., Domshlak, C., Hoos, H., Poole, D.: CP-nets: a tool for representing and reasoning with conditional ceteris paribus preference statements. J. Artif. Intell. Res. **21**, 135–191 (2004)
12. Brandt, F., Conitzer, V., Endriss, U., Lang, J., Procaccia, A.D. (eds.): Handbook of Computational Social Choice. Cambridge University Press, Cambridge (2016)
13. Bruna, J., Zaremba, W., Szlam, A., LeCun, Y.: Spectral networks and locally connected networks on graphs. arXiv abs/1312.6203 (2013)
14. Cohen, P.R.: Empirical Methods for Artificial Intelligence. MIT Press, Cambridge (1995)
15. Cornelio, C., Goldsmith, J., Mattei, N., Rossi, F., Venable, K.B.: Updates and uncertainty in CP-Nets. In: Cranefield, S., Nayak, A. (eds.) AI 2013. LNCS (LNAI), vol. 8272, pp. 301–312. Springer, Cham (2013). https://doi.org/10.1007/978-3-319-03680-9_32
16. Cornelio, C., Grandi, U., Goldsmith, J., Mattei, N., Rossi, F., Venable, K.: Reasoning with PCP-nets in a multi-agent context. In: Proceedings of the 14th AAMAS (2015)

17. Defferrard, M., Bresson, X., Vandergheynst, P.: Convolutional neural networks on graphs with fast localized spectral filtering. In: Proceedings of the 30th NeurIPS, pp. 3837–3845 (2016)
18. Domshlak, C., Hüllermeier, E., Kaci, S., Prade, H.: Preferences in AI: an overview. AI **175**(7), 1037–1052 (2011)
19. Fagin, R., Kumar, R., Mahdian, M., Sivakumar, D., Vee, E.: Comparing partial rankings. SIAM J. Discret. Math. **20**(3), 628–648 (2006). https://doi.org/10.1137/05063088X
20. Fattah, S.M.M., Bouguettaya, A., Mistry, S.: A CP-net based qualitative composition approach for an IaaS provider. In: Hacid, H., Cellary, W., Wang, H., Paik, H.-Y., Zhou, R. (eds.) WISE 2018. LNCS, vol. 11234, pp. 151–166. Springer, Cham (2018). https://doi.org/10.1007/978-3-030-02925-8_11
21. Fürnkranz, J., Hüllermeier, E.: Preference learning. In: Sammut, C., Webb, G.I. (eds.) Encyclopedia of Machine Learning. Springer, Boston (2010). https://doi.org/10.1007/978-0-387-30164-8
22. Goldsmith, J., Junker, U.: Preference handling for artificial intelligence. AI Mag. **29**(4), 9 (2009)
23. Goldsmith, J., Lang, J., Truszczyński, M., Wilson, N.: The computational complexity of dominance and consistency in CP-nets. J. Artif. Intell. Res. **33**(1), 403–432 (2008)
24. Goyal, P., Ferrara, E.: Graph embedding techniques, applications, and performance: a survey. CoRR abs/1705.02801 (2017)
25. Henaff, M., Bruna, J., LeCun, Y.: Deep convolutional networks on graph-structured data. arXiv abs/1506.05163 (2015)
26. Hinton, G.E., Salakhutdinov, R.R.: Reducing the dimensionality of data with neural networks. Science **313**(5786), 504–507 (2006)
27. Kahneman, D.: Thinking, Fast and Slow. Farrar, Straus and Giroux, New York (2011)
28. Kambhampati, S.: Synthesizing explainable behavior for human-AI collaboration. In: Proceedings of the 18th AAMAS (2019)
29. Kendall, M.G.: A new measure of rank correlation. Biometrika **30**(1/2), 81–93 (1938)
30. Kingma, D.P., Ba, J.: Adam: a method for stochastic optimization. arXiv:1412.6980 (2014)
31. Kipf, T.N., Welling, M.: Semi-supervised classification with graph convolutional networks. arXiv abs/1609.02907 (2016)
32. Krizhevsky, A., Sutskever, I., Hinton, G.E.: ImageNet classification with deep convolutional neural networks. In: Proceedings of the Advances in Neural and Information Processing Systems (NeurIPS), pp. 1097–1105 (2012)
33. Lecun, Y., Bengio, Y.: Convolutional Networks for Images, Speech and Time Series, pp. 255–258. The MIT Press, Cambridge (1995)
34. Li, M., Kazimipour, B.: An efficient algorithm to compute distance between lexicographic preference trees. In: Proceedings of 27th IJCAI, pp. 1898–1904 (2018)
35. Loreggia, A., Mattei, N., Rossi, F., Venable, K.B.: On the distance between CP-nets. In: Proceedings of the 17th AAMAS (2018)
36. Loreggia, A., Mattei, N., Rossi, F., Venable, K.B.: Preferences and ethical principles in decision making. In: Proceedings of the 1st AAAI/ACM Conference on AI, Ethics, and Society (AIES) (2018)
37. Loreggia, A., Mattei, N., Rossi, F., Venable, K.B.: Value alignment via tractable preference distance. In: Yampolskiy, R.V. (ed.) Artificial Intelligence Safety and Security. CRC Press, Boca Raton (2018)

38. Loreggia, A., Mattei, N., Rossi, F., Venable, K.B.: Metric learning for value alignment. In: Proceedings of the Workshop on Artificial Intelligence Safety 2019 held at IJCAI 2019. CEUR Workshop Proceedings, vol. 2419. CEUR-WS.org (2019)

39. Mattei, N., Walsh, T.: PrefLib: a library for preferences. In: Proceedings of the 3rd ADT (2013). http://www.preflib.org

40. Mattei, N., Walsh, T.: A PrefLib.Org Retrospective: Lessons Learned and New Directions. In: Endriss, U. (ed.) Trends in Computational Social Choice, pp. 289–309. AI Access Foundation (2017)

41. Noothigattu, R., et al.: Teaching AI agents ethical values using reinforcement learning and policy orchestration. In: Proceedings of the 28th IJCAI (2019)

42. Popova, A., Regenwetter, M., Mattei, N.: A behavioral perspective on social choice. AMAI **68**(1–3), 135–160 (2013). https://doi.org/10.1007/s10472-012-9326-6

43. Pu, P., Faltings, B., Chen, L., Zhang, J., Viappiani, P.: Usability guidelines for product recommenders based on example critiquing research. In: Ricci, F., Rokach, L., Shapira, B., Kantor, P.B. (eds.) Recommender Systems Handbook, pp. 511–545. Springer, Boston (2011). https://doi.org/10.1007/978-0-387-85820-3_16

44. Rossi, F., Loreggia, A.: Preferences and ethical priorities: thinking fast and slow in AI. In: Proceedings of the 18th AAMAS, pp. 3–4 (2019)

45. Rossi, F., Venable, K., Walsh, T.: A Short Introduction to Preferences: Between Artificial Intelligence and Social Choice. Morgan and Claypool, San Rafael (2011)

46. Rossi, F., Mattei, N.: Building ethically bounded AI. In: Proceedings of the 33rd AAAI (2019)

47. Russell, S., Dewey, D., Tegmark, M.: Research priorities for robust and beneficial artificial intelligence. AI Mag. **36**(4), 105–114 (2015)

48. Sen, A.: Choice, Ordering, and Morality. Blackwell, Oxford (1974)

49. Shuman, D.I., Narang, S.K., Frossard, P., Ortega, A., Vandergheynst, P.: The emerging field of signal processing on graphs: extending high-dimensional data analysis to networks and other irregular domains. IEEE Signal Process. Mag. **30**(3), 83–98 (2013)

50. Sohn, K.: Improved deep metric learning with multi-class n-pair loss objective. In: Advances in Neural Information Processing Systems (NeruIPS), pp. 1857–1865 (2016)

51. Wallach, W., Allen, C.: Moral Machines: Teaching Robots Right From Wrong. Oxford University Press, Oxford (2008)

52. Wang, H., Shao, S., Zhou, X., Wan, C., Bouguettaya, A.: Web service selection with incomplete or inconsistent user preferences. In: Baresi, L., Chi, C.-H., Suzuki, J. (eds.) ICSOC/ServiceWave -2009. LNCS, vol. 5900, pp. 83–98. Springer, Heidelberg (2009). https://doi.org/10.1007/978-3-642-10383-4_6

53. Wong, S.C., Gatt, A., Stamatescu, V., McDonnell, M.D.: Understanding data augmentation for classification: When to warp? In: Proceedings of the 2016 International Conference on Digital Image Computing: Techniques and Applications (DICTA), pp. 1–6 (2016)

54. Xing, E.P., Ng, A.Y., Jordan, M.I., Russell, S.J.: Distance metric learning with application to clustering with side-information. In: Proceedings of the 15th NeurIPS, pp. 505–512 (2002)

Declarative Learning Based Programming

Declarative Learning Based Programming

Parisa Kordjamshidi[1], Kristian Kersting[2], Quan Guo[1],
Nikolaos Vasiloglou II[3], Hannaneh Hajishirazi[4], and Dan Roth[5]

[1] Michigan State University, USA
{kordjams,guoquan}@msu.edu
[2] TU Darmstadt, Germany
kersting@cs.tu-darmstadt.de
[3] RelationalAI, USA
nvasil@gmail.com
[4] University of Washington, USA
hannaneh@washington.edu
[5] University of Pennsylvania, USA
danroth@seas.upenn.edu

Abstract. This workshop was the fourth round of the Declarative Learning based Programming Workshop which was held in conjunction with the IJCAI conference, Macao, China, 2019. The goal of the workshop was to highlight the importance of Declarative Learning based Programming (DeLBP) as a new research area. DeLBP aims at investigating the challenges of programming for designing intelligent real-world applications that require the interaction of various learning and reasoning components. It investigates the new abstractions that can facilitate programming as well as combine and connect various formalisms and computational models for learning and reasoning.

1 Goals and Motivation

Currently, to solve real-world problems in many areas such as cognitive sciences, biology, finance, social sciences, scientists think about data-driven solutions. However, current technologies offer cumbersome solutions along multiple dimensions. Some of these include: Interaction with raw data; Necessity for extensive programming; Necessity of exploiting various learning techniques; and Extensive experimental exploration for appropriate models. DeLBP investigates how one can facilitate and simplify the design and the development of intelligent real-world applications that consider learning from data and reasoning based on knowledge. It highlights the challenges in making machine learning accessible to various domain experts and application programmers. Conventional programming languages have not been primarily designed to offer help for the above-mentioned challenges. To achieve the goals

---

Thanks to Office of NAVAL Research grant N00014-19-1-2308 for partially supporting the organization of this workshop.

of DeLBP, there is a need to go beyond classic machine learning and AI tools. We need new innovative abstractions to enrich the existing solutions and frameworks.

Over the past years, the research community has tried to address these problems from multiple perspectives, most notably approaches based on Probabilistic (Logical) programming, Constrained Conditional models (CCM) and Statistical relational learning. Moreover, Deep Learning community has created easy to use abstractions for programming deep neural architectures. We aim at motivating the need for further research toward a unified framework based on the aforementioned key existing paradigms. We investigate the required type of languages, representations and computational models to support an ideal DeLBP paradigm.

2 Workshop Program

The workshop[2] brought together researchers from various areas related to relational learning, probabilistic logic programming and neuro-symbolic learning. The workshop hosted two invited speakers and seven oral paper presentations. Four papers were original to the workshop and three of them were selected among accepted papers in IJCAI-2019 and UAI-2019. During the workshop, Parisa Kordjamshidi -as an organizer- provided a brief overview of the aims and the challenges of the DeLBP paradigm in the opening remarks. Guy van Den Broeck, from the University of California Los Angeles, presented an invited talk on their new framework for probabilistic programming. Brendan Juba from Washington University in St. Louis presented their paper in collaboration with Viashak Belle on learning to reason. Taisuke Sato presented his joint paper with Ryosuke Kojima on logical inference as cost minimization in vector spaces. Quan Guo presented his joint paper with Parisa Kordjamshidi and Andrzej Uszok on generating learning-based programs from OWL ontologies. Sebastian Dumancic presented their accepted paper at IJCAI main conference in the workshop, on auto-encoding logic programs. Paolo Morretin presented the research of his colleagues at UCLA, Zeng, and Van den Broeck, on Weighted Model Integration. Our afternoon session started with an invited talk presented by Loera Morgenstern from Systems & Technology Research. She explained her work on machine reading from both semi-structured and unstructured documents. Then Juba presented his work on query-driven pack learning for reasoning. The last presented paper was an IJCAI accepted paper on Formal languages for goal specification in reinforcement learning, presented by Alberto Camacho from the University of Toronto. Among the presented papers, originally submitted to the DeLBP workshop, we selected two best papers: 1) Implicitly Learning to Reason in First-Order Logic; Vaishak Belle and Brendan Juba, 2) *Logical inference as cost minimization in vector spaces; Taisuke Sato and Ryosuke Kojima.* The first paper is accepted to be published in NeurIPS-2019 and the second will be our representative paper for the IJCAI workshop's best selection. Our selected DeLBP paper proposes a novel differentiable framework for scalable inference over logical programs. We had a discussion session with the audience to conclude the

---

http://delbp.github.io.

workshop and discuss the next possible venues in collaboration with both statistical relational learning and programming languages community, it seems there is a lot of interest to highlight the challenges of programming for machine learning models in the next venues in collaboration with researches from programming languages and formal methods community.

Logical Inference as Cost Minimization in Vector Spaces

Taisuke Sato[1](✉)(iD) and Ryosuke Kojima[2](iD)

[1] AI research center AIST, Koto-ku, Japan
satou.taisuke@aist.go.jp
[2] Graduate School of Medicine, Kyoto University, Kyoto, Japan
kojima.ryosuke.8e@kyoto-u.ac.jp

Abstract. We propose a differentiable framework for logic program inference as a step toward realizing flexible and scalable logical inference. The basic idea is to replace symbolic search appearing in logical inference by the minimization of a cost function **J** in a continuous space. **J** is made up of matrix (tensor), Frobenius norm and non-linear functions just like neural networks and specifically designed for each task (relation abduction, answer set computation, etc) in such a way that $\mathbf{J}(\mathbf{X}) \geq 0$ and $\mathbf{J}(\mathbf{X}) = 0$ holds if-and-only-if **X** is a 0–1 tensor representing a solution for the task. We compute the minimizer X of **J** giving $\mathbf{J}(\mathbf{X}) = 0$ by gradient descent or Newton's method. Using artificial data and real data, we empirically show the potential of our approach by a variety of tasks including abduction, random SAT, rule refinement and probabilistic modeling based on answer set (supported model) sampling.

Keywords: Logical inference · Vector space · Minimization · Abduction · Supported model · Sampling

1 Introduction

We propose a differentiable framework for logic program inference as a step toward realizing flexible and scalable logical inference. The basic idea is to replace symbolic search by the minimization of a cost function **J** in a continuous space. We choose **J** specifically to each task and perform from abduction to probabilistic inference.

Consider the case of abduction where the task is to abduce a binary relation $r_2(Y, Z)$ satisfying $r_3(X, Z) \Leftrightarrow \exists Y r_1(X, Y) \land r_2(Y, Z)$ for given $r_3(X, Z)$ and $r_1(X, Y)$[1, 2]. **J** is chosen as

$$\mathbf{J}^{abd}(\mathbf{X}) = \frac{1}{2}\{\|\mathbf{R}_3 - \min_1(\mathbf{R}_1\mathbf{X})\|_F^2 + \ell \cdot \|\mathbf{X} \odot (\mathbb{1} - \mathbf{X})\|_F^2\}. \tag{1}$$

---

[1] We follow Prolog convention and logical variables begin with upper case letters.
[2] Stated another way, what we are doing here is "predicate invention" in inductive logic programming (ILP) in which $r_2(Y, Z)$ is invented.

© Springer Nature Switzerland AG 2020
A. El Fallah Seghrouchni and D. Sarne (Eds.): IJCAI 2019 Workshops, LNAI 12158, pp. 239–255, 2020.
https://doi.org/10.1007/978-3-030-56150-5_12

Here $\mathbf{R}_1$ and $\mathbf{R}_3$ are adjacency matrices (i.e. 0–1 matrices) representing $r_1(X, Y)$ and $r_3(X, Z)$ respectively. $\min_1(x)$ is a non-linear function defined by $\min_1(x) = \min(x, 1)$ (the lesser of x and 1)[3], $\odot$ denotes element-wise product, $\| \cdot \|_F$ Frobenius norm and $\mathbb{1}$ a matrix of all ones[4]. By construction, $\mathbf{J}^{abd}(\mathbf{X}) = 0$ holds if-and-only-if $\mathbf{X}$ is a 0–1 matrix[5] satisfying $\mathbf{R}_3 = \min_1(\mathbf{R}_1 \mathbf{X})$. The latter implies $\mathbf{X}$ is an adjacency matrix representing a binary relation $r_2(Y, Z)$ s.t. $r_3(X, Z) \Leftrightarrow \exists Y r_1(X, Y) \wedge r_2(Y, Z)$.

Note that our abductive setting of solving $\mathbf{R}_3 = \min_1(\mathbf{R}_1 \mathbf{X})$ is broad and includes SAT problem as a special case where $\mathbf{R}_3 = \mathbb{1}$ is a column vector with every element being one, $\mathbf{R}_1 = \mathbf{Q}_{CNF}$ is a 0–1 matrix encoding a CNF formula and $\mathbf{X}$ is a 0–1 column vector representing a truth-assignment (see Subsect. 3.3).

Also the problem of finding supported models (answer sets) [9, 19] is similarly formulated as a cost minimization problem of some $\mathbf{J}$ derived from normal logic programs.

In general, in our approach, $\mathbf{J}$ is constructed in such a way that $\mathbf{J}(\mathbf{X}) \geq 0$ and $\mathbf{J}(\mathbf{X}) = 0$ holds if-and-only-if $\mathbf{X}$ is a 0–1 tensor (multi-linear function, a generalization of vector and matrix) representing a solution such as relations and answer sets. Logical inference is therefore achieved either by minimizing $\mathbf{J}$ to zero or by root finding of $\mathbf{J}$[6]. We carry out the former by gradient descent (GD) and the latter by Newton's method. On the numerical side however, it is difficult and time-consuming to reduce $\mathbf{J}$ to completely zero. We therefore incorporate a "jumping to a solution" strategy which means while updating $\mathbf{X}$ by GD or by Newton's method, we threshold $\mathbf{X}$ into a 0–1 tensor using an appropriate thresholding value to see if the resulting $\mathbf{X}$ constitutes a solution. Although combining continuous relaxation of symbolic model search with thresholding is somewhat ad hoc, it works and opens a new way of logical inference using tensors.

One notable thing with $\mathbf{J}$ is that it enables random sampling of solutions (target relations and/or models). Consider for example the sampling of answer sets, or more specifically the sampling of supported models of a normal logic program DB [9, 19]. Usually DB has multiple supported models and which model is reached by minimizing $\mathbf{J}$ to zero depends on the initialization of $\mathbf{X}$ in GD or Newton's method. By uniformly sampling an initial point from $[0, 1]^n$, we can expect to perform (semi) uniform sampling of supported models as exemplified later by our experiments. Also by introducing a dynamic cost function that stochastically changes as sampling proceeds, "distribution-aware" sampling is realized and applied to probabilistic inference for supported models.

Performing logical inference or more generally symbolic reasoning in a continuous space is a rather old idea but the recent explosion of deep learning tech-

---

[3] For a matrix $\mathbf{A}$, $\min_1(\mathbf{A})$ indicates element-wise application of $\min_1(x)$ to $\mathbf{A}$.

[4] Throughout this paper, we implicitly assume vector, matrix dimensions are all compatible.

[5] $\| \mathbf{X} \odot (\mathbb{1} - \mathbf{X}) \|_F^2 = \sum_{ij} \mathbf{X}_{ij}^2 (1 - \mathbf{X}_{ij})^2 = 0$ implies $\mathbf{X}_{ij}(1 - \mathbf{X}_{ij}) = 0$ for all i, j where $\mathbf{X}_{ij}$ denotes the (i, j) element of $\mathbf{X}$.

[6] Be warned that this task can be extremely difficult because it includes solving SAT problem as we mentioned above.

nologies reignites interest in relating symbolic approaches to neural networks [4,17,18,23,31,33]. Our approach has a lot in common with these differentiable approaches in that we exploit the flexibility and scalability of linear algebraic operations combined with non-linear activity functions supported by modern computer technologies such as many cores and GPGPUs. We however differ in that we entirely reformulate logical inference as a simple cost minimization problem and are focused on logical/probabilistic inference, not on raw data processing such as image data and text data.

Our proposal may look rather broad, but when viewed from specific symbolic AI fields such as inductive logic programming (ILP) and probabilistic logic programming (PLP), it offers an entirely new approach to treat their problems, i.e. "predicate invention" in ILP and "probabilistic answer set programming" in PLP, in continuous spaces. Our work is at the crossroads of logic, linear algebra and machine learning and by formulating logical inference as minimization in a continuous space, we bridge them in a coherent and scalable way.

In what follows, after a preliminary section, we show how to perform exact abduction in a continuous space in Sect. 3. Then we apply this technique to random SAT problem and real data, i.e. rule discovery from knowledge graphs. Then we move on to the problem of sampling supported models (answer sets) [1,7,9] with constraints in Sect. 4 and apply it to probabilistic modeling by distribution-aware sampling in Sect. 5. Section 6 describes related work and Sect. 7 is conclusion. The reader is supposed to be familiar with the basics of logic programming.

2   Preliminaries

2.1   Tensorized Semantics

To perform logical inference in terms of vectors and matrices, we adopt a tensorized semantics introduced in [29]. For a syntactic object A, we use $[\![A]\!]$ to denote its interpretation (entities, relations, truth values). We assume a finite Herbrand domain $\{e_1, \ldots, e_n\}$ and each entity e_i $(1 \leq i \leq n)$ is represented by a one-hot column vector $\mathbf{e}_i = [0.., 1, 0..]^T$ which is a zero vector except the i-th element being 1. An m-ary predicate p/m is identified as an m-ary multi-linear mapping in the n-dimensional vector space and a proposition (ground atom) $p(e_{i_1}, \ldots, e_{i_m})$ takes a truth value 1 when true else 0, i.e, $[\![p(e_{i_1}, \ldots, e_{i_m})]\!] \in \{1, 0\}$. Note a unary predicate is computed by a dot product like $[\![p(e_i)]\!] = (\mathbf{p} \bullet \mathbf{e}_i)$ using a 0–1 vector $\mathbf{p}$ representing p. Likewise a binary predicate is computed as $[\![r(e_i, e_j)]\!] = \mathbf{e}_i^T \mathbf{R} \mathbf{e}_j = \mathbf{R}_{ij}$ using a 0–1 matrix $\mathbf{R}$ encoding r. Compound boolean formulas are inductively computed by $[\![\neg A]\!] = 1 - [\![A]\!]$, $[\![A \wedge B]\!] = [\![A]\!] \cdot [\![B]\!]$ and $[\![A \vee B]\!] = \min_1([\![A]\!] + [\![B]\!])$. Existential quantifiers are treated by grounding them to disjunctions. So we have $[\![\exists X p(X)]\!] = \min_1([\![p(e_1)]\!] + \cdots + [\![p(e_n)]\!])$. Fortunately however, oftentimes this grounding process is eliminable in particular in the case of existentially quantified conjunctions like

$$[\exists Y r_1(X, Y) \land r_2(Y, Z)] = \min_1\left(\sum_j \mathbf{x}^T \mathbf{R}_1 \mathbf{e}_j \mathbf{e}_j^T \mathbf{R}_2 \mathbf{z}\right)$$

$$= \mathbf{x}^T \min_1(\mathbf{R}_1 \mathbf{R}_2) \mathbf{z} \qquad (2)$$

where $\mathbf{x}$ and $\mathbf{z}$ are arbitrary entity vectors substituted for X and Z respectively.

Let $\mathbf{X}$ be a matrix. We use $|\mathbf{X}|$ to denote the number of nonzero elements of $\mathbf{X}$. So when $\mathbf{R}$ is a 0–1 matrix representing a binary relation, $|\mathbf{R}|$ coincides with the size of the relation.

2.2   Supported Model and Tensor Equation

Let DB be a ground normal logic program and consider clauses $\{h \Leftarrow B_1, \ldots, h \Leftarrow B_k\}$ about a ground atom h in DB. B_js are conjunctions of ground literals and can be empty (empty body is considered true). Denote the boolean formula $h \Leftrightarrow B_1 \lor \cdots \lor B_k$ by iff(h) and define iff(DB) = {iff(h) | h occurs in DB}. iff(DB) is said to be a *completion form* of DB.

A *model* of iff(DB), i.e., a truth assignment making every iff(h) $\in$ iff(DB) true is called a *supported model* of DB [1,7,9]. Supported models constitute a super class of stable models (answer sets) and when DB is tight, i.e. no looping dependency through positive atoms in DB, supported models and stable models coincide. In this paper, we assume programs are tight. When DB is non-ground, we always treat it as the set of all ground instantiations of the clauses in DB.

Now look at non-ground Datalog programs [6,10,15]. We show how tensor equations are derived from their supported models. Although more complex classes are possible to deal with, we concentrate on a simple class $\mathcal{C}$ of DB containing only binary predicates such that each clause of the form $r_0(X_0, X_m) \Leftarrow r_1(X_0, X_1) \land \cdots \land r_m(X_{m-1}, X_m)$. We furthermore assume that when DB is recursive, clauses have only one recursive goal in their clause body.

The following is a non-ground Datalog program (in the completion form) in $\mathcal{C}$ which takes the transitive closure $r_2(X, Y)$ of a base relation $r_1(X, Y)$.

$$r_2(X, Z) \Leftrightarrow r_1(X, Z) \lor \exists Y(r_1(X, Y) \land r_2(Y, Z)) \qquad (3)$$

In every supported model, both sides of (3) denote the same truth value for any instantiations of X, Z. Hence we have

$$[r_2(X, Z)] = [r_1(X, Z) \lor \exists Y(r_1(X, Y) \land r_2(Y, Z))].$$

By applying the interpretation mapping (2) to $\exists Y(r_1(X, Y) \land r_2(Y, Z))$, we obtain a matrix equation

$$\mathbf{R}_2 = \min_1(\mathbf{R}_1 + \mathbf{R}_1 \mathbf{R}_2) \qquad (4)$$

where $\mathbf{R}_1$ and $\mathbf{R}_2$ are 0–1 matrices respectively encoding $r_1(X, Z)$ and $r_2(X, Z)$ in a supported model. Since the derivation from (3) to (4) can go the other way around, computing supported models of (3) is equivalent to solving (4) using 0–1 matrices. By generalization, we see that supported models of a program in $\mathcal{C}$ are characterized as a solution of matrix equation derived from it (proof omitted).

3 Abducing Relations by Cost Minimization

In this section, we solve the abduction problem described in the beginning of Sect. 1: given $r_3(X, Z)$ and $r_1(X, Y)$, invent a binary relation $r_2(Y, Z)$ satisfying $r_3(X, Z) \Leftrightarrow \exists Y r_1(X, Y) \wedge r_2(Y, Z)$ by minimizing $\mathbf{J}^{abd}(\mathbf{X}) = \frac{1}{2}\{\|\mathbf{R}_3 - \min_1(\mathbf{R}_1\mathbf{X})\|_F^2 + \ell \cdot \|\mathbf{X} \odot (\mathbb{1} - \mathbf{X})\|_F^2\}$ w.r.t. $\mathbf{X}$ to zero. Here $\mathbf{R}_3$ and $\mathbf{R}_1$ are respectively 0–1 matrices representing $r_3(X, Z)$ and $r_1(X, Y)$.

3.1 Jacobian

To tackle this problem, we first derive a Jacobian $\partial \mathbf{J}^{abd}/\partial \mathbf{X}$[7]. For a matrix $\mathbf{A}$, write $\mathbf{A}_{\leq 1}$ to denote a 0–1 matrix defined by $(\mathbf{A}_{\leq 1})_{ij} = \begin{cases} 1 \text{ if } \mathbf{A}_{ij} \leq 1 \\ 0 \text{ otherwise} \end{cases}$. Then we can compute the Jacobian as follows[8].

$$
\begin{aligned}
\mathbf{J}_\mathbf{a}^{abd} &= \partial \mathbf{J}^{abd}/\partial \mathbf{X} \\
&= \mathbf{R}_1^T((\mathbf{R}_1\mathbf{X})_{\leq 1} \odot (\mathbf{R}_1\mathbf{X} - \mathbf{R}_3)) + \ell \cdot (\mathbf{X} \odot (\mathbb{1} - \mathbf{X}) \odot (\mathbb{1} - 2\mathbf{X})) \quad (5)
\end{aligned}
$$

Using this Jacobian, we update $\mathbf{X}$ by

$$\text{Gradient descent: } \mathbf{X}_{new} \leftarrow \mathbf{X} - \alpha \mathbf{J}_\mathbf{a}^{abd} \qquad \text{or} \qquad (6)$$

$$\text{Newton's method: } \mathbf{X}_{new} \leftarrow \mathbf{X} - (\mathbf{J}^{abd}/\|\mathbf{J}_\mathbf{a}^{abd}\|_F^2)\mathbf{J}_\mathbf{a}^{abd}. \qquad (7)$$

Here α in (6) is a learning rate. (7) is derived from the first order Taylor polynomial of $\mathbf{J}^{abd}$ and obtained by solving $\mathbf{J}^{abd} + (\mathbf{J}_\mathbf{a}^{abd} \bullet (\mathbf{X}_{new} - \mathbf{X})) = 0$[9].

Below is an abduction algorithm to search for a 0–1 matrix $\mathbf{R}_2$ representing $r_2(X, Y)$. It starts from an approximate solution (line 3) and then iteratively reduces $\mathbf{J}^{abd}$ toward zero while checking whether thresholding $\mathbf{X}$ gives an exact solution (line 5,6) in each iteration. We stop updating $\mathbf{X}$ when an exact solution is obtained (line 7) or i reaches max_itr.

The initial value of $\mathbf{X}$ (line 3) that minimizes the r.h.s. is given by $\mathbf{X} = (\lambda \mathbf{I} + \mathbf{R}_1^T \mathbf{R}_1)^{-1}(\mathbf{R}_1^T \mathbf{R}_3)$ where $\mathbf{I}$ is an identity matrix(derivation omitted). $\mathbf{X}_{>\theta}$ (line 5) denotes a 0–1 matrix computed by thresholding like $(\mathbf{X}_{>\theta})_{ij} = \begin{cases} 1 \text{ if } \mathbf{X}_{ij} > \theta \\ 0 \text{ otherwise} \end{cases}$. The best θ that minimizes $error$ is chosen by grid search between the minimum and maximum element of $\mathbf{X}$ divided into 50 levels.

---

[7] $\min_1(x)$ is differentiable except at one point $x = 1$ and hence $\partial \mathbf{J}^{abd}/\partial \mathbf{X}$ is almost everywhere differentiable.

[8] The derivation of $\mathbf{J}_\mathbf{a}^{abd}$ is described in **Appendix**.

[9] For matrices $\mathbf{X}, \mathbf{Y}$, $(\mathbf{X} \bullet \mathbf{Y}) = \sum_{ij} \mathbf{X}_{ij} \mathbf{Y}_{ij}$.

Algorithm 1: Relation abduction by matrix

---

1 **Input:** 0-1 matrices $\mathbf{R}_3(l \times n)$, $\mathbf{R}_1(l \times m)$

2 **Output:** 0-1 matrix $\mathbf{R}_2(m \times n)$ s.t. $\mathbf{R}_3 = \min_1(\mathbf{R}_1\mathbf{R}_2)$

3 $\mathbf{X} \leftarrow \min_{\mathbf{X}} \|\mathbf{R}_3 - \mathbf{R}_1\mathbf{X}\|_F^2 + \lambda\|\mathbf{X}\|_F^2$

4 **for** $i \leftarrow 1$ **to** *max_itr* **do**

5     $\mathbf{R}_2 \leftarrow \mathbf{X}_{>\theta}$ for some θ

6   *error* $\leftarrow |\mathbf{R}_3 - \min_1(\mathbf{R}_1\mathbf{R}_2)|$

7   **if** *error = 0* **then**
         └ **break**

8   Update $\mathbf{X}$ by (6) or by (7)

9 **return** $\mathbf{R}_2$

Table 1. Abducing relation $\mathbf{R}_2 : \mathbf{R}_3 = \min_1(\mathbf{R}_1\mathbf{R}_2)$

n	1000	2000	3000	4000	5000	6000	7000	8000	9000	10000
$|\mathbf{R}_3|$	1005.4	7985.2	27036.0	63582.0	125245.0	215527.0	343080.0	50777.0	730999.0	995653.0
ini_error	32.8	226.2	285.0	297.0	182.0	116.4	56.6	39.7	17.3	10.0
final_error	0.0	0.0	0.0	0.0	0.0	0.0	0.0	0.0	0.0	0.0
time(s)	2.6	73.8	661.8	1608.2	1920.0	1870.2	2300.6	2874.7	3306.7	4255.3

3.2 Experiment with Random Relations

To see the performance of our cost minimization approach, we conduct an experiment with relatively large relations, i.e., matrices[10]. Given n, we generate two $(n \times n)$ random 0–1 matrices $\mathbf{R}_1$ and $\mathbf{Y}$ s.t. an element is one with probability $p = 0.001$ and compute $\mathbf{R}_3 = \min_1(\mathbf{R}_1\mathbf{Y})$ as test data. Then we run the Algorithm 1 using Newton's method (7) with $\mathbf{R}_3$ and $\mathbf{R}_1$ as input to abduce $\mathbf{R}_2$ s.t. $\mathbf{R}_3 = \min_1(\mathbf{R}_1\mathbf{R}_2)$ and measure an *error* $= |\mathbf{R}_3 - \min_1(\mathbf{R}_1\mathbf{R}_2)|$. *max_itr* is set to 1,000. For n varying from 1,000 to 10,000, we repeat this process five times and abduce five solutions for $\mathbf{R}_2$ and compute averages of $|\mathbf{R}_3|$, *error* and execution time. The result is summarized in Table 1. Figures are averages over five trials. There "ini_error" is the error caused by an initial value of $\mathbf{X}$ (line 3) before iteration and "final_error" is the error by the returned $\mathbf{R}_2$.

According to Table 1, we have achieved zero error for every n and have successfully obtained an exact $\mathbf{R}_2$ that makes $\mathbf{R}_3 = \min_1(\mathbf{R}_1\mathbf{R}_2)$ true. Execution time looks rather linear w.r.t. n, which empirically supports the scalability of our approach. Note that the recursive case (4) of abducing a relation $\mathbf{R}_1$ (i.e. inventing a relation $r_1(X, Y)$) from $\mathbf{R}_2 = \min_1(\mathbf{R}_1 + \mathbf{R}_1\mathbf{R}_2) = \min_1(\mathbf{R}_1(\mathbf{I} + \mathbf{R}_2))$ is treated similarly by setting $\mathbf{R}_3 \leftarrow \mathbf{R}_2^T$, $\mathbf{R}_1 \leftarrow (\mathbf{I} + \mathbf{R}_2)^T$ and $\mathbf{R}_2 \leftarrow \mathbf{R}_1^T$.

---

[10] All experiments in this paper are carried out using GNU Octave 4.2.2 and Python 3.6.3 on a PC with Intel(R) Core(TM) i7-3770@3.40 GHz CPU, 28 GB memory.

3.3   3-SAT

Here we briefly show how to apply our approach to SAT problem. Consider a boolean formula in CNF: $(a \lor b \lor \bar{c}) \land (a \lor \bar{b})$. We encode this CNF as a 0–1 matrix $\mathbf{Q}_{CNF}$ by separately encoding positive literals and negative literal as follows where rows represent clauses.

$$\mathbf{Q}_{CNF} = \begin{matrix} a\ b\ c\ \bar{a}\ \bar{b}\ \bar{c} \\ \begin{bmatrix} 1\ 1\ 0\ 0\ 0\ 1 \\ 1\ 0\ 0\ 0\ 1\ 0 \end{bmatrix} \end{matrix}$$

As is obvious from this example, we can encode a SAT problem with n variables and m clauses by an $(m \times 2n)$ 0–1 matrix $\mathbf{Q}_{CNF}$. Let $\mathbf{u}$ be a 0–1 vector representing an assignment to n variables (1:true,0:false). Then a model (solution) of $\mathbf{Q}_{CNF}$ is represented by $(2n \times 1)$ 0–1 vector of the form $[\mathbf{u}; \mathbf{1}_n - \mathbf{u}]$ s.t. $\mathbf{1}_m = \min_1(\mathbf{Q}_{CNF}[\mathbf{u}; \mathbf{1}_n - \mathbf{u}])$. Here $\mathbf{1}_n$ is a vector of ones with length n. $[\mathbf{u}; \mathbf{v}]$ stands for a vertical concatenation of column vectors $\mathbf{u}$ and $\mathbf{v}$. Thus solving a SAT problem is considered as a form of abduction that abduces a 0–1 vector $\mathbf{u}$ satisfying $\mathbf{1}_m = \min_1(\mathbf{Q}_{CNF}[\mathbf{u}; \mathbf{1}_n - \mathbf{u}])$ for the given $\mathbf{Q}_{CNF}$.

Write $\mathbf{Q}_{CNF} = [\mathbf{Q}_1\ \mathbf{Q}_2]$ where $\mathbf{Q}_i(i = 1, 2)$ is an $(m \times n)$ matrix. Introduce a cost function $\mathbf{J}^{sat}$ and compute its Jacobian $\mathbf{J}_{\mathbf{a}}^{sat}$ as follows[11].

$$\mathbf{J}^{sat} = (\mathbf{1}_m \bullet \mathbf{1}_m - \min_1(\mathbf{Q}_{CNF}[\mathbf{u}; \mathbf{1}_n - \mathbf{u}]))$$
$$+ (\ell/2) \cdot \|\mathbf{u} \odot (\mathbf{1}_n - \mathbf{u})\|_F^2 \tag{8}$$
$$\mathbf{J}_{\mathbf{a}}^{sat} = (\mathbf{Q}_2 - \mathbf{Q}_1)^T (\mathbf{Q}_1 \mathbf{u} + \mathbf{Q}_2(\mathbf{1}_n - \mathbf{u}))_{\leq 1}$$
$$+ \ell \cdot (\mathbf{u} \odot (\mathbf{1}_n - \mathbf{u}) \odot (\mathbf{1}_n - 2\mathbf{u})) \tag{9}$$

It is easily proved that $\mathbf{J}^{sat} = 0$ if-and-only-if $\mathbf{u}$ is a 0–1 vector representing a satisfying assignment for the original SAT problem.

We preliminarily implement our approach as a matrix-based SAT solver Mat-Sat using GNU Octave 4.2.2 and conduct a random 3-SAT experiment comparing MatSat and MapleLCMDistChronoBT(MapleBT for short here) [12], the SAT Competition 2018 Main Track winner as follows. Given n, the number of boolean variables, we generate a satisfiable SAT instance by first randomly generating a "hidden" assignment $\mathbf{v}$ over n variables, and then randomly generating m clauses consisting of 3 literals satisfied by $\mathbf{v}$. We collect them as an $(m \times 2n)$ 0–1 matrix $\mathbf{Q}_{CNF}$ as a generated instance. We generate 100 such instances and we run the Algorithm 1 using Newton's method (7) with the Jacobian (9) where $\mathbf{R}_3 = \mathbf{1}_m$, $\mathbf{R}_1 = \mathbf{Q}_{CNF}$, $\mathbf{R}_2 = [\mathbf{u}; \mathbf{1}_n - \mathbf{u}]$. Also we initialize $\mathbf{u}$ (line 3) appropriately using a random 0–1 vector. Restart is allowed 100 times when failing to find a satisfying assignment. We repeat this process 10 times. Table 2 summarizes the average run time with std to solve all of 100 instances. On average, when $n = 100$, Mat-Sat runs 7 times slower than MapleBT but when $n = 500$, it runs 40 times faster than MapleBT (though MatSat is implemented in Octave).

---

[11] $\mathbf{J}_{\mathbf{a}}^{sat}$ is derived similarly to $\mathbf{J}_{\mathbf{a}}^{abd}$.

Table 2. Average run time(s) for solving 100 random 3-SAT instances

(n, m)	MatSat	MapleBT
$(100, 426)$	39.4(13.6)	5.91(0.17)
$(500, 2130)$	103.3(8.8)	4231.8(1465.3)

Why MatSat outperforms MapleBT for n = 500 which is the SAT Competition winner is not immediately clear but might be explained as follows. When updating the assignment for boolean variables, MatSat updates them little by little but simultaneously as a vector $\mathbf{u}$. So it globally and gracefully moves towards a satisfying assignment in a vector space, which is reflected on the fact that it solves the 100 instances in rather uniform time though they are randomly generated. On the other hand, MapleBT, a conflict-driven clause learning (CDCL) SAT solver, determines the truth value of each variable one by one (with backtracking) locally in a symbolic space. Unfortunately it has always been observed that some of the 100 random instances cause MapleBT to start extremely heavy backtracking.

Basically MapleBT implemented in C++ runs much faster than MatSat implemented in Octave, and so does for n = 100. However for n = 500, hard instances contained in the 100 instances cause MapleBT to take exponentially longer time on a larger scale compared to n = 100, and offset the superiority of mature implementation of MapleBT, resulting in much longer average execution time than MatSat as witnessed in Table 2.

This experiment reveals the potential of our approach to solution finding for random 3-SAT problems.

3.4 Rule Refinement for Knowledge Graph

Here we apply our relation abduction technique to refine rules extracted from a knowledge graph FB15k. FB15k is a well-known knowledge graph containing triples of the form (subject, relation, object) in RDF format for 1,345 binary relations and 14,951 entities [2]. Given two 0–1 matrices $\mathbf{R}_3$ and $\mathbf{R}_1$ representing two known relations $r_1(X, Y)$ and $r_3(X, Z)$ respectively in FB15k, it is possible to find a 0–1 matrix $\mathbf{R}_2$ representing a new relation $r_2(X, Y)$ which makes $r_3(X, Z) \Leftrightarrow \exists Y r_1(X, Y) \wedge r_2(Y, Z)$ *approximately* true in two steps. First compute $\mathbf{X} = (\lambda \mathbf{I} + \mathbf{R}_1^T \mathbf{R}_1)^{-1}(\mathbf{R}_1^T \mathbf{R}_3)$ which minimizes $\|\mathbf{R}_3 - \mathbf{R}_1 \mathbf{X}\|_F^2 + \lambda \|\mathbf{X}\|_F^2$ and then put $\mathbf{R}_2 = \mathbf{X}_{>\theta}$ for some θ that makes $error = |\mathbf{R}_3 - \min_1(\mathbf{R}_1 \mathbf{R}_2)|$ minimum. This way of new relation discovery is proposed in [30] and shown to give new rules such as

$$\text{language}(X, Z) \Leftarrow \text{genre}(X, Y) \wedge \textit{genre\_lang}(Y, Z) \tag{10}$$

which connects two existing relations, language/2 and genre/2 in the film domain of FB15k, by a new abduced relation genre_lang/2. The limitation is that this approach only provides approximation and there is no guarantee of exact abduction. Here we apply our abduction technique to reduce approximation error.

Let $\mathbf{R}_l$, $\mathbf{R}_g$ and $\mathbf{R}_{gl}$ be 0–1 matrices representing language(X, Z), genre(X, Y) and genre_lang(Y, Z) respectively. Put $\mathbf{A} = \mathbf{R}_l$ and $\mathbf{B} = \min_1(\mathbf{R}_g \mathbf{R}_{gl})$. To measure the quality of extracted rules containing abduced relations, we pretend that $\mathbf{A}$, the l.h.s. in the rule, is predicted by $\mathbf{B}$, the r.h.s. in the rule and measure the quality in terms of F-measure $F(\mathbf{A}, \mathbf{B}) = 2|\mathbf{A} \cap \mathbf{B}|/(|\mathbf{A}| + |\mathbf{B}|)$[12] and $error = |\mathbf{A} - \mathbf{B}|$.

Since Algorithm 1 contains the abduction procedure described in [30] as its initial part as lines from (line 3) to (line 6), it is expected to return better abduced relations than those found by [30]. We ran Algorithm 1 with $\mathbf{R}_l$ and $\mathbf{R}_g$ as input using Newton's method and have obtained an abduced relation $\mathbf{R}_{gl}$. We then compared the quality of the rule (10) between the one described in [30] and the other containing $\mathbf{R}_{gl}$ returned by Algorithm 1. We observed that while the former yields F-measure = 0.654 and $error = 1614$, the latter rule found by Algorithm 1 gives F-measure = 0.666 and $error = 1498$. That is, F-measure increased by 1.2% and $error$ decreased by 7.1%. We observed similar improvement with other rules such as nationality$(X, Z) \Leftarrow$ live_in$(X, Y) \wedge$ nationality_live_in(Y, Z) discovered by relation abduction.

4   Probabilistic Inference

4.1   Sampling Supported Models

In this section, we apply our cost minimization approach to a relatively unexplored area of probabilistic modeling by probabilistic normal logic programs. Our programs look like DB shown in Figure 1[13]. We assume DB consists of unit clauses labeled with probabilities and non-unit clauses without probability labels. To make matters simple, we also assume predicates are unary or binary and clauses have at most one recursive goal. Hereafter we focus on the 'Friends & Non-smokers' program for the sake of intuitiveness but generalization is not difficult.

$$0.3 :: \text{stress}(X)$$
$$0.2 :: \text{influences}(X, Y)$$
$$\text{smokes}(X) \Leftarrow \text{stress}(X)$$
$$\text{smokes}(X) \Leftarrow \text{friend}(X, Y) \wedge \text{influences}(Y, X) \wedge \neg\text{smokes}(Y)$$

Fig. 1. Friends & Non-smokers program

---

[12] We here consider $\mathbf{A}$ as a set $\{(i, j) \mid \mathbf{A}_{ij} = 1\}$ and use $|\mathbf{A}|$ as its cardinality.

[13] This is a variant of 'Friends & Smokers' program from ProbLog's tutorial (https://dtai.cs.kuleuven.be/problog/tutorial/basic/05_smokers.html).

Mathematically, DB is considered as a probabilistic program specifying a probability distribution over its supported models (distribution semantics [27]). Here we define a distribution by a sampling process; first we sample DB^{g14}, a ground instantiation of DB, by sampling ground unit clauses with probabilities specified by their labels together with all ground instantiations of non-unit clauses in DB. Then we sample uniformly one of the supported models of DB^g. By sampling repeatedly, we collect a set S of supported models $\mathbf{m}$ and compute various probabilities $P(A)$ of atoms A as a ratio (empirical probability) $|\{\mathbf{m} \mid \mathbf{m} \models A, \mathbf{m} \in S\}|/|S|$.

The point is that the latter sampling process can be carried out in a vector space. Recall that the equivalence (completion form):

$$\text{smokes}(X)$$
$$\Leftrightarrow \text{stress(X)} \vee$$
$$\exists Y \text{friend}(X,Y) \wedge \text{influences}(Y,X) \wedge \neg\text{smokes}(Y) \tag{11}$$

holds in any supported model of DB and vice versa [1,7,9]. Suppose there are n people. We rewrite the equivalence (11) to a tensor Eq. (12) as explained in Sect. 2 by introducing tensors representing relations in DB, i.e., $(n \times 1)$ vectors $\mathbf{S}_m$ and $\mathbf{S}_t$ for representing unary predicates smokes(X) and stress(X) respectively and $(n \times n)$ matrices $\mathbf{F}_r$ and $\mathbf{I}_n$ representing binary predicates friend(X,Y) and influences(X,Y) respectively.

$$\mathbf{S}_m = \min_1(\mathbf{S}_t + (\mathbf{F}_r \odot \mathbf{I}_n^T)(\mathbf{1}_n - \mathbf{S}_m)) \tag{12}$$

Here $\mathbf{F}_r \odot \mathbf{I}_n^T$ stands for friend$(X,Y) \wedge$ influences(Y,X) and $\mathbf{1}_n - \mathbf{S}_m$ for $\neg$smokes(Y). Since supported models of (11) and solutions of (12) have a one-to-one correspondence when stress/1, friend/2 and influences/2 are given, we can perform various types of sampling via (12) with the help of a cost function specifically designed for each purpose.

4.2   Posterior Computation

We conduct a small experiment of posterior computation as a proof of concept following [20]. We assume there are $n = 4$ people and a friend relation is given by {friend(1,2), friend(2,1), friend(2,4), friend(3,2), friend(4,2)}. Suppose we have observed that smokes(2) = true but influences(4, 2) = false. Under this condition, we would like to compute the posterior probability $P(\text{smokes}(1) \mid \text{smokes}(2))$, $P(\text{smokes}(3) \mid \text{smokes}(2))$ and $P(\text{smokes}(4) \mid \text{smokes}(2))$ by *constrained sampling*. So we introduce a cost function $\mathbf{J}^{samp}$:

$$\mathbf{J}^{samp}(\mathbf{S}_m)$$
$$= \frac{1}{2}\{\|\mathbf{S}_m - \min_1(\mathbf{S}_t + (\mathbf{F}_r \odot \mathbf{I}_n^T)(\mathbf{1}_n - \mathbf{S}_m))\|_F^2$$
$$+ \ell_1 \cdot \|\mathbf{S}_m \odot (\mathbf{1}_n - \mathbf{S}_m)\|_F^2 + \ell_2 \cdot (\mathbf{S}_m(2) - 1)^2\} \tag{13}$$

---

[14] We assume DB^g has supported models.

and perform the sampling of supported models satisfying the constraint { smokes(2) = true, influences(4, 2) = false} as follows. First sample a 0–1 ($n \times 1$) vector $\mathbf{S}_t$ where each element is one with probability 0.3. Similarly sample a 0–1 ($n \times n$) matrix $\mathbf{I}_n$ using probability 0.2 and put $\mathbf{I}_n(4,2) = 0$. After having sampled $\mathbf{S}_t$ and $\mathbf{I}_n$, sample $\mathbf{S}_m$ s.t. $\mathbf{J}^{samp}(\mathbf{S}_m) = 0$ by minimizing $\mathbf{J}^{samp}$ to zero with random initialization as described in the previous section. Put $\mathbf{C} = \mathbf{S}_t + (\mathbf{F}_r \odot \mathbf{I}_n^T)(\mathbf{1}_n - \mathbf{S}_m)$. The Jacobian $\mathbf{J}_{\mathbf{a}}^{samp} = \partial \mathbf{J}^{samp}/\partial \mathbf{S}_m$ used to minimize $\mathbf{J}^{samp}$ is given by (derivation omitted)

$$\mathbf{J}_{\mathbf{a}}^{samp} = (\mathbf{E} + \mathrm{diag}(\mathbf{C}_{\leq 1})(\mathbf{F}_r \odot \mathbf{I}_n^T))^T (\mathbf{S}_m - \min_1(\mathbf{C}))$$
$$+ \ell_1 \cdot \mathbf{S}_m \odot (\mathbf{1}_n - \mathbf{S}_m) \odot (\mathbf{1}_n - 2\mathbf{S}_m)$$
$$+ \ell_2 \cdot (\mathbf{S}_m(2) - 1)\mathbf{I}_2. \tag{14}$$

Here $\mathbf{E}$ is an $n \times n$ identity matrix, $\mathbf{I}_2$ is a zero vector except $\mathbf{I}_2(2) = 1$. $\mathrm{diag}(\mathbf{v})$ is the diagonalization of a vector $\mathbf{v}$ defined by $\mathrm{diag}(\mathbf{v})_{ij} = \begin{cases} \mathbf{v}(i) & \text{if } i = j \\ 0 & \text{otherwise} \end{cases}$.

Unfortunately sometimes sampling fails or returns a supported model not satisfying $\mathbf{S}_m(2) = 1$. So we try sampling 10^5 times with $max\_itr = 10$, collect "correct models", i.e. those that satisfy $\mathbf{S}_m = 1$ and compute the target posteriors using sampled correct models like rejection sampling. We run this process five times. The result is summarized as follows. On average, sampling is done in 41.2 s and we get 99,904 supported models including 38,842 correct ones. Inferred posteriors by the correct sampled models are shown in Table 3 (figures are averages over 5 runs) together with manually computed exact posteriors (derivation omitted). Seeing it, we may say that sampling by cost minimization fairly works well as long as the current example is concerned.

Table 3. Inferred and exact posteriors

$P(\cdot \mid \text{smokes}(2))$	smokes(1)	smokes(3)	smokes(4)
Inferred posterior	0.232	0.299	0.299
Exact posterior	0.231	0.300	0.300

4.3 Unconstrained Sampling

Here we examine the scalability of our approach using the 'Friends & Non-smokers' program in Fig. 1. We simply sample supported models of the program for various n without any constraint. We set $max\_itr = 10$, perform sampling 10^4 times and plot the execution time for each n up to 250. We also apply a quadratic fit to the plotted data. The result is shown in Fig. 2. The fitting curve seems to reflect the fact that the time complexity of computing $\mathbf{J}^{samp}$ and its Jacobian $\mathbf{J}_{\mathbf{a}}^{samp}$ is $O(n^2)$.

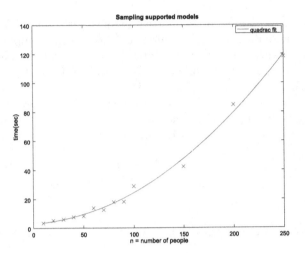

Fig. 2. Unconstrained sampling

5   Distribution-Aware Sampling

Now we deal with a more intricate problem of *distribution-aware sampling* [3,20]. By distribution-aware sampling, we mean the one to obtain a set of samples whose empirical distribution best matches the observed distribution of target random variables.

Suppose we have the 'Friends & Non-smokers' program in Figure 1 and observed $P(\text{smokes}(1)) = 0.2$ and $P(\text{smokes}(2)) = 0.8$ in a domain $\{1,\ldots,n\}$. Our task is to sample a set of supported models by distribution-aware sampling whose empirical distribution gives (approximately) these target probabilities. We implement distribution-aware sampling by cost minimization by using a cost function $\mathbf{J}^{dist}(\mathbf{S}_m)$:

$$\mathbf{J}^{dist}(\mathbf{S}_m) = \frac{1}{2}\{\|\mathbf{S}_m - \min_1(\mathbf{C})\|_F^2 + \ell_1 \cdot \|\mathbf{S}_m \odot (\mathbf{1} - \mathbf{S}_m)\|_F^2$$
$$+ \ell_2 \cdot \|\mathbf{t}_{\text{v\_ep}} - \mathbf{t}_{\text{v\_p}}\|_F^2\}. \tag{15}$$

Here $\mathbf{C} = \mathbf{S}_t + (\mathbf{F}_r \odot \mathbf{I}_n^T)(\mathbf{1}_n - \mathbf{S}_m)$. Let $\mathbf{t}_v$ be a list of target variables, $\mathbf{t}_{\text{v\_p}}$ their target probabilities and $\mathbf{t}_{\text{v\_ep}}$ an approximation to the empirical distribution by a set Δ of sampled $\mathbf{S}_m$s. Then $\ell_2 \cdot \|\mathbf{t}_{\text{v\_ep}} - \mathbf{t}_{\text{v\_p}}\|_F^2$ is a penalty term to force $\mathbf{t}_{\text{v\_ep}} \approx \mathbf{t}_{\text{v\_p}}$.

Let $\mathbf{t}_{\text{v\_fq}}$ be a list of frequencies of target variables in Δ. Suppose we are in the process of minimizing $\mathbf{J}^{dist}$ and currently $|\Delta| = N$. By an $N+1$-th sample $\mathbf{S}_m$, $\mathbf{t}_{\text{v\_ep}}$ is updated to $(\max(\min(\mathbf{S}_{m\_v},1),0)+\mathbf{t}_{\text{v\_fq}})/(N+1)$ where $\mathbf{S}_{m\_v}$ is a subvector of $\mathbf{S}_m$ for $\mathbf{t}_v$. Since $\mathbf{t}_{\text{v\_ep}}$ depends on the sampled $\mathbf{S}_m$s, the cost function $\mathbf{J}^{dist}$ *stochastically* changes during its minimization unlike $\mathbf{J}^{samp}$.

We conduct an experiment of distribution-aware sampling for target variables $\mathbf{t}_v = [\mathbf{S}_m(1)\ \mathbf{S}_m(2)]^T$ and their target probabilities $\mathbf{t}_{\text{v\_p}} = [0.2\ 0.8]^T$ by minimizing $\mathbf{J}^{dist}$ for sampled $\mathbf{S}_t$ and $\mathbf{I}_n$ using Algorithm 1 with necessary modifications.

Experimental parameters are $n = 100, \ell_1 = 1, \ell_2 = 1000, max\_itr = 300$. We try to sample $\mathbf{S}_m$ maximum $1,000$ times until 50 models are sampled (sometimes sampling fails). We then estimate the empirical probability of $\mathbf{t}_v$ using the sampled $\mathbf{S}_m$s.

We repeated sampling five times and estimated target probabilities as empirical probabilities computed from the sampled $\mathbf{S}_m$s. The result is shown in Table 4 (figures are averages). As seen from it, target probabilities are reasonably estimated, which demonstrates the viability of our proposal, i.e., distribution-aware sampling by cost minimization for probabilistic normal logic programs.

Table 4. Distribution-aware sampling

Target var.	$\mathbf{S}_m(1)$	$\mathbf{S}_m(2)$
Target prob.	0.200	0.800
Estimated prob.	0.222	0.785
#Sampled model	50.0 (all different)	

6   Related Work

As stated before, our proposal intersects several fields including logic, abduction, SAT, logic programming (LP), answer set programming (ASP)[15], probabilistic modeling, optimization and linear algebra (tensor). We mention not all but some of related topics in these fields.

Concerning logic and tensor, Grefenstette reformulated first-order logic in tensor spaces [11]. He rewrites logical formulas in terms of tensor and represents logical connectives (conjunction, disjunction, negation) as specific types of tensor but quantification is given a limited treatment. Tensorized first-order logic with full quantification was proposed by Sato in [29] in which disjunction is represented as $[\![A \vee B]\!] = \min_1([\![A]\!] + [\![B]\!])$ using a non-linear operation $\min_1(\cdot)$ unlike [11]. He showed how to evaluate closed sentences (formulas with no free variable) without a "grounding" process. Partial evaluation of logic programs has long been studied in LP as a general technique to prune search space before execution and Sakama et al. developed a methodology for partial evaluation with matrix encoding [26].

Our approach technically depends on the combination of linear algebraic operations on matrix (tensor) and nonlinear operations such as $\min_1(\cdot)$ and thresholding to deal with symbolic logic, and has a close relationship to recent trends of combining symbolic reasoning and neural networks [4,17,18,23,31,33]. When applied

---

[15] ASP is logic programming based on stable model semantics of logic programs and primarily applied to solve combinatorial problems.

to 3-SAT as a differentiable SAT solver MatSat, it outperforms a SAT Competition winner MapleLCMDistChronoBT [12] in some case, probably due to its global search nature in a continuous space as explained in Subsection 3.3. MatSat is not the only (purely) differentiable SAT solver. For example, NeuroSAT [31] operates on vectors embedding literals and clauses of a SAT problem and manipulates them through three multilayer perceptrons and two LSTMs. It predicts both of unsatisfiability and satisfiability but does not necessarily yield a solution even when it predicts satisfiability unlike MatSat. In a related context, Nickles proposed differentiable SAT/ASP [20] in which a differentiable cost function is incorporated into a symbolic reasoning system to choose a decision literal.

Abduction is a form of logical inference which infers a "best explanation" for the input data and has been explored in various fields, for example, [13,24,25] in NLP, [5,6,8,10,15] in (abductive/inductive) logic programming and [14,16,21,28,32] in probabilistic modeling. Traditionally abduction has been considered symbolic and formalized as such in a symbolic space, and hence little work has been done on tensorizing abduction. [30] seems the first to formalize abductive inference in terms of tensor and deal with real data to show the scalability of the proposed approach. The problem however is that the cost function there itself prevents exact abduction. As a result, it only performs approximate abduction. Contrastingly our formulation in this paper enables exact abduction (and deduction), and opens a way to sample exact supported models in vector spaces for probabilistic modeling by probabilistic normal logic programs, not possible by [30].

Probabilistic logic programming (PLP) provides methods of declarative high-level probabilistic modeling by first-order logic [22]. It started with probabilistic definite clause programs [21,22,27,28] but the use of probabilistic normal logic programs has been delayed primarily because of semantic difficulties. For example deciding the existence of stable model of a normal logic program is NP-complete. This is so even if we relax stable model to supported model. Nickles introduced a new approach to PLP by ASP (stable models) and combined SAT technologies with a differentiable cost function [20]. The main difference between our approach and Nickles's approach[16] is that although both use the derivatives of a cost function, our approach is entirely formulated as cost minimization in vector (tensor) spaces and implemented as such whereas his approach uses the derivatives to evaluate and select literals as part of SAT solving.

In the context of statistical relational learning (SRL) related to PLP, Roth et al. applied integer linear programming to infer named entities and their relations [24,25]. In their approach, relations are chosen from a fixed set by minimizing a cost function, not synthesized in a continuous space like our approach.

---

[16] Another difference is that Nickles [20] deals with stable models while we use supported models which are easier to compute than stable ones.

7 Conclusion

We have proposed to perform logical inference in vector spaces by minimizing a cost function, combined with thresholding, designed for each task. We demonstrated the effectiveness of our approach by several applications from relation abduction to random SAT in which we have achieved the state-of-the-art level performance, and also to rule discovery, to constrained sampling and distribution-aware sampling by probabilistic normal logic programs.

Acknowledgments. This paper is based on results obtained from a project commissioned by the New Energy and Industrial Technology Development Organization (NEDO).

Appendix

Here we describe how the Jacobian $\mathbf{J}_{\mathbf{a}}^{abd}$ in Sect. 1 is derived. Recall that our cost function (1) is

$$\mathbf{J}^{abd}(\mathbf{X}) = \frac{1}{2}\{\|\min_1(\mathbf{R}_1\mathbf{X}) - \mathbf{R}_3\|_F^2 + \ell \cdot \|\mathbf{X} \odot (\mathbb{1} - \mathbf{X})\|_F^2\}.$$

First we introduce a dot product for two matrices $\mathbf{X}$ and $\mathbf{Y}$ by $(\mathbf{X} \bullet \mathbf{Y}) = \sum_{ij} \mathbf{X}_{ij} \mathbf{Y}_{ij}$. Then $\|X\|_F^2 = (\mathbf{X} \bullet \mathbf{X})$ holds. Also $((\mathbf{XZ}) \bullet \mathbf{Y}) = (\mathbf{Z} \bullet (\mathbf{X}^T\mathbf{Y}))$ and $((\mathbf{X} \odot \mathbf{Z}) \bullet \mathbf{Y}) = (\mathbf{Z} \bullet (\mathbf{X} \odot \mathbf{Y}))$ hold. Let $\mathbf{X}_{pq}$ be the (p,q) element of a matrix $\mathbf{X}$ and $\mathbf{I}_{pq}$ a zero matrix except the (p,q) element which is one. We also put $\mathbf{C} = \mathbf{R}_1\mathbf{X}$, $\mathbf{B} = \min_1(\mathbf{C}) - \mathbf{R}_3$ and use the fact that $\mathbf{C}_{\leq 1} \odot \mathbf{B} = \mathbf{C}_{\leq 1} \odot (\mathbf{C} - \mathbf{R}_3)$ for simplification. Now we have

$$
\begin{aligned}
&\partial \mathbf{J}^{abd}/\partial \mathbf{X}_{pq} \\
&= ((\mathbf{C}_{\leq 1} \odot (\mathbf{R}_1\mathbf{I}_{pq})) \bullet \mathbf{B}) + \\
&\quad \ell \cdot ((\mathbf{I}_{pq} \bullet (\mathbf{X} \odot (\mathbb{1} - \mathbf{X}) \odot (\mathbb{1} - \mathbf{X}))) - (\mathbf{I}_{pq} \bullet (\mathbf{X} \odot \mathbf{X} \odot (\mathbb{1} - \mathbf{X})))) \\
&= ((\mathbf{R}_1\mathbf{I}_{pq}) \bullet (\mathbf{C}_{\leq 1} \odot \mathbf{B})) + (\mathbf{I}_{pq} \bullet \ell \cdot (\mathbf{X} \odot (\mathbb{1} - \mathbf{X}) \odot (\mathbb{1} - 2\mathbf{X}))) \\
&= (\mathbf{I}_{pq} \bullet (\mathbf{R}_1^T(\mathbf{C}_{\leq 1} \odot \mathbf{B}))) + (\mathbf{I}_{pq} \bullet \ell \cdot (\mathbf{X} \odot (\mathbb{1} - \mathbf{X}) \odot (\mathbb{1} - 2\mathbf{X}))) \\
&= (\mathbf{I}_{pq} \bullet (\mathbf{R}_1^T(\mathbf{C}_{\leq 1} \odot \mathbf{B}) + \ell \cdot (\mathbf{X} \odot (\mathbb{1} - \mathbf{X}) \odot (\mathbb{1} - 2\mathbf{X})))) \\
&= (\mathbf{I}_{pq} \bullet (\mathbf{R}_1^T(\mathbf{C}_{\leq 1} \odot (\mathbf{C} - \mathbf{R}_3)) + \ell \cdot (\mathbf{X} \odot (\mathbb{1} - \mathbf{X}) \odot (\mathbb{1} - 2\mathbf{X}))))
\end{aligned}
$$

Since this holds for any (p,q), we reach the Jacobian $\mathbf{J}_{\mathbf{a}}^{abd}$ (5):

$$
\begin{aligned}
\mathbf{J}_{\mathbf{a}}^{abd} &= \partial \mathbf{J}^{abd}/\partial \mathbf{X} \\
&= \mathbf{R}_1^T((\mathbf{R}_1\mathbf{X})_{\leq 1} \odot (\mathbf{R}_1\mathbf{X} - \mathbf{R}_3)) + \ell \cdot (\mathbf{X} \odot (\mathbb{1} - \mathbf{X}) \odot (\mathbb{1} - 2\mathbf{X}))
\end{aligned}
$$

References

1. Baral, C., Gelfond, M., Rushton, N.: Probabilistic reasoning with answer sets. Theory Pract. Logic Program. (TPLP) **9**(1), 57–144 (2009)
2. Bordes, A., Usunier, N., Garcia-Duran, A., Weston, J., Yakhnenko, O.: Translating embeddings for modeling multi-relational data. In: Burges, C., Bottou, L., Welling, M., Ghahramani, Z., Weinberger, K. (eds.) Advances in Neural Information Processing Systems, vol. 26, pp. 2787–2795 (2013)
3. Chakraborty, S., Fremont, D.J., Meel, K.S., Seshia, S.A., Vardi, M.Y.: Distribution-aware sampling and weighted model counting for sat. In: Proceedings of the Twenty-Eighth AAAI Conference on Artificial Intelligence. AAAI 2014, pp. 1722–1730. AAAI Press (2014). http://dl.acm.org/citation.cfm?id=2892753.2892792
4. Cohen, W.W., Yang, F., Mazaitis, K.: TensorLog: deep learning meets probabilistic DBs. CoRR abs/1707.05390 (2017). http://arxiv.org/abs/1707.05390
5. Denecker, M., Kakas, A.: Abduction in logic programming. In: Kakas, A.C., Sadri, F. (eds.) Computational Logic: Logic Programming and Beyond. LNCS (LNAI), vol. 2407, pp. 402–436. Springer, Heidelberg (2002). https://doi.org/10.1007/3-540-45628-7_16
6. Eiter, T., Gottlob, G., Leone, N.: Abduction from logic programs: semantics and complexity. Theoret. Comput. Sci. **189**(1–2), 129–177 (1997)
7. Eiter, T., Ianni, G., Krennwallner, T.: Answer set programming: a primer. In: Tessaris, S., Franconi, E., Eiter, T., Gutierrez, C., Handschuh, S., Rousset, M.-C., Schmidt, R.A. (eds.) Reasoning Web 2009. LNCS, vol. 5689, pp. 40–110. Springer, Heidelberg (2009). https://doi.org/10.1007/978-3-642-03754-2_2
8. Flach, P., Kakas, A. (eds.): Abduction and Induction - Essays on Their Relation and Integration. Springer, Dordrecht (2000). https://doi.org/10.1007/978-94-017-0606-3
9. Gelfond, M., Lifshcitz, V.: The stable model semantics for logic programming, pp. 1070–1080 (1988)
10. Gottlob, G., Pichler, R., Wei, F.: Tractable database design and datalog abduction through bounded treewidth. Inf. Syst. **35**(3), 278–298 (2010)
11. Grefenstette, E.: Towards a formal distributional semantics: simulating logical calculi with tensors. In: Proceedings of the Second Joint Conference on Lexical and Computational Semantics, pp. 1–10 (2013). http://www.aclweb.org/anthology/S13-1001
12. Heule, M., Järvisalo, M., Suda, M. (eds.): Proceedings of SAT Competition 2018: Solver and Benchmark Descriptions, Department of Computer Science Series of Publications B, vol. B-2018-1. Department of Computer Science, University of Helsinki (2018)
13. Hobbs, J.R., Stickel, M.E., Appelt, D.E., Martin, P.: Interpretation as abduction. Artif. Intell. **63**(1–2), 69–142 (1993)
14. Inoue, K., Sato, T., Ishihata, M., Kameya, Y., Nabeshima, H.: Evaluating abductive hypotheses using an EM algorithm on BDDs. In: Proceedings of the 21st International Joint Conference on Artificial Intelligence (IJCAI 2009), pp. 810–815 (2009)
15. Kakas, A.C., Kowalski, R., Toni, F.: Abductive logic programming. J. Logic Comput. **2**(6), 719–770 (1992)
16. Kate, R., Mooney, R.: Probabilistic abduction using Markov logic networks. In: The IJCAI-09 Workshop on Plan, Activity, and Intent Recognition (PAIR 2009), pp. 22–28 (2009)

17. Kazemi, S.M., Poole, D.: RELNN: a deep neural model for relational learning. In: Proceedings of the Thirty-Second AAAI Conference on Artificial Intelligence, (AAAI 2018), pp. 6367–6375 (2018)
18. Manhaeve, R., Dumancic, S., Kimmig, A., Demeester, T., Raedt, L.D.: Deep-ProbLog: neural probabilistic logic programming. CoRR (2018). http://arxiv.org/abs/1805.10872
19. Marek, W., Subrahmanian, V.S.: The relationship between stable, supported, default and autoepistemic semantics for general logic programs. Theoret. Comput. Sci. **103**(2), 365–386 (1992)
20. Nickles, M.: Differentiable SAT/ASP. In: Proceedings of the 5th International Workshop on Probabilistic Logic Programming, PLP 2018, pp. 62–74 (2018)
21. Poole, D.: Probabilistic Horn abduction and Bayesian networks. Artif. Intell. **64**(1), 81–129 (1993)
22. De Raedt, L., Kimmig, A.: Probabilistic (logic) programming concepts. Mach. Learn. **100**(1), 5–47 (2015). https://doi.org/10.1007/s10994-015-5494-z
23. Rocktäschel, T., Riedel, S.: End-to-end differentiable proving. In: Guyon, I., et al. (eds.) Advances in Neural Information Processing Systems, vol. 30, pp. 3788–3800. Curran Associates, Inc., Long Beach (2017)
24. Roth, D.: Integer linear programming inference for conditional random fields. In: Proceedings of the International Conference on Machine Learning (ICML 2005), pp. 737–744 (2005)
25. Roth, D., Yih, W.T.: Global inference for entity and relation identification via a linear programming formulation. In: Introduction to Statistical Relational Learning, January 2007
26. Sakama, C., Nguyen, H., Sato, T., Inoue, K.: Partial evaluation of logic programs in vector spaces. In: Proceedings of the 11th Workshop on Answer Set Programming and Other Computing Paradigms (ASPOCP 2018) (2018). 10.29007/9d61
27. Sato, T.: A statistical learning method for logic programs with distribution semantics. In: Proceedings of the 12th International Conference on Logic Programming (ICLP 1995), pp. 715–729 (1995)
28. Sato, T., Kameya, Y.: Statistical abduction with tabulation. In: Kakas, A.C., Sadri, F. (eds.) Computational Logic: Logic Programming and Beyond. LNCS (LNAI), vol. 2408, pp. 567–587. Springer, Heidelberg (2002). https://doi.org/10.1007/3-540-45632-5_22
29. Sato, T.: Embedding Tarskian semantics in vector spaces. In: AAAI-17 Workshop on Symbolic Inference and Optimization (SymInfOpt 2017) (2017)
30. Sato, T., Inoue, K., Sakama, C.: Abducing relations in continuous spaces. In: Proceedings of the 27th International Joint Conference on Artificial Intelligence (IJCAI-ECAI 2018), pp. 1956–1962 (2018)
31. Selsam, D., Lamm, M., Bünz, B., Liang, P., de Moura, L., Dill, D.L.: Learning a SAT solver from single-bit supervision. In: International Conference on Learning Representations (ICLR 2019) (2019). https://openreview.net/forum?id=HJMC_iA5tm
32. Tamaddoni-Nezhad, A., Chaleil, R., Kakas, A., Muggleton, S.: Application of abductive ILP to learning metabolic network inhibition from temporal data. Mach. Learn. **64**, 209–230 (2006)
33. Widdows, D., Cohen, T.: Reasoning with vectors: a continuous model for fast robust inference. Logic J. IGPL/Interest Group Pure Appl. Log. **23**(2), 141–173 (2015)

Author Index

Printed in the United States
By Bookmasters